THE FIRST HELICOPTER BOYS

THE FIRST HELICOPTER BOYS

THE EARLY DAYS OF HELICOPTER OPERATIONS
THE MALAYAN EMERGENCY, 1947–1960

DAVID TAYLOR

THE FIRST HELICOPTER BOYS
The Early Days of Helicopter Operations - The Malayan Emergency, 1947–1960

First published in Great Britain in 2019 by
Air World
An imprint of
Pen & Sword Books Ltd
Yorkshire – Philadelphia

Copyright © David Taylor, 2019

ISBN 978 1 52675 413 4

The right of David Taylor to be identified as Author of this work has been asserted by him in accordance with the Copyright, Designs and Patents Act 1988.

A CIP catalogue record for this book is available from the British Library.

All rights reserved. No part of this book may be reproduced or transmitted in any form or by any means, electronic or mechanical including photocopying, recording or by any information storage and retrieval system, without permission from the Publisher in writing.

Typeset by Aura Technology and Software Services, India

Printed and bound in England by TJ International Ltd, Padstow, Cornwall

Pen & Sword Books Limited incorporates the imprints of Atlas, Archaeology, Aviation, Discovery, Family History, Fiction, History, Maritime, Military, Military Classics, Politics, Select, Transport, True Crime, Air World, Frontline Publishing, Leo Cooper, Remember When, Seaforth Publishing, The Praetorian Press, Wharncliffe Local History, Wharncliffe Transport, Wharncliffe True Crime and White Owl.

For a complete list of Pen & Sword titles please contact

PEN & SWORD BOOKS LIMITED
47 Church Street, Barnsley, South Yorkshire, S70 2AS, England
E-mail: enquiries@pen-and-sword.co.uk
Website: www.pen-and-sword.co.uk

Or
PEN AND SWORD BOOKS
1950 Lawrence Rd, Havertown, PA 19083, USA
E-mail: Uspen-and-sword@casematepublishers.com
Website: www.penandswordbooks.com

Contents

Author's notes		vii
Prologue		xii
Chapter 1	Flying in the Dark	1
Chapter 2	So, What is a Helicopter Like to Fly?	21
Chapter 3	Improvement and Advancements	33
Chapter 4	Air Transport and Psychological Warfare	48
Chapter 5	Tales from the Horse's Mouth – Pilots	51
Chapter 6	Tales from the Horse's Mouth – Crewmen	95
Chapter 7	Tales from the Horse's Mouth – Other Personnel	116
Chapter 8	Crewroom, Reunions and Lift-Off Chat	132
Chapter 9	Brief Notes on Past Members	140
Chapter 10	More Pilot Tales from the Horse's Mouth	148
Chapter 11	Bits and Pieces	179
Chapter 12	Jungle Forts and Airstrips	212
Chapter 13	Malaya: Circa 1948-60	259
Chapter 14	Goodbye Emergency, Hello Confrontation	269
Appendix		284
Notes		313
Index		314

Author's notes

Although there have been many books written about operations during the Indonesian Confrontation – and the enormous contribution made by the helicopter squadrons to the successful outcome of those hostilities – I realised there was nothing of a similar nature concerning the Malayan Emergency, which ended in 1960.

A major difference between these two 'limited conflicts' was that by the time of the Confrontation, 1962, helicopter numbers had increased dramatically, the aircraft now being flown not only by pilots with experience gained during the Emergency, but also a new breed of specialist helicopter pilot, transferring straight from *ab initio* training into the world of rotary wing, thus having the benefit of intense and extended training in all aspects of rotary wing flying, arriving in theatre with many hours under their belts, and a sound knowledge of the techniques they would be required to employ.

'The Emergency' on the other hand, occurred during the formative years of RAF and NAS helicopter operations, the very early days in fact, when equipment and knowledge were much more basic. Operational procedures were still under development, and even though the aircraft flew on frontline service, the pilots were basically still under training; or perhaps they could have been described as 'test pilots at war'! This is the story that needed to be told, so I decided to plug the gap, to bring to note the priceless contribution made by the original 'guinea pig' pilots of 110, 155, 194, 848 NAS, and the Casualty Evacuation Flight during the Malayan Emergency, and quietly cement their rightful place in helicopter history.

During the eighties Cyril Turner (an ex 194 Squadron CO) and Alec Watson (Casualty Evacuation Flight, and 194 Sqn), working together, collected and collated a list of any names recalled of personnel who had served during the period when the events depicted in these pages took place. Then, on 27 October 1986, fourteen of them met for an informal get-together in the George & Dragon, a Princes Risborough pub – must

THE FIRST HELICOPTER BOYS

So long ago, few remaining. Back row: Bob Gafney, Pat Lumb, Ces Holmes, Peter Petowski, 'Jacko' Jacques, Dave Williamson, Ted Shuvalski. Front row: Des Hodges, John Dowling, 'Nobby' Clarke, Alec Watson, Frank Bishton, Cy Turner, Ken Hawkins.

have been an exceedingly friendly pub too, for the room, reunion dinner, along with B & B, was offered for just £20 per person! Ah, but those were the days!

In 1990, with around 125 names on the growing list (which now counted amongst its ranks members of the Naval Air Service 848 Sqn Association), and enthusiasm for the project mounting, it was decided to put the group on a more formal footing; so it was that the Helicopter Operations (Malaya Emergency) Association was formed. Over the next twenty-three years, during their annual reunions, members spent many a happy hour together recalling those days of the Emergency (1948-60), when RAF and NAS operations were slowly being formulated. These were not just once-a-year type friendships, but the lifelong, camaraderie of the service type friendships, those of people who had experienced something new and different together. They were – those that remain, still are – continually in touch, by letter, phone, meetings, and later, email.

Many of the stories, and much information derived from these contacts, or taken from the Association newsletter *Lift-Off*, therefore truly come 'from the horse's mouth' so to speak, being written by the air and ground crews who for many years formed our group. What follows is a nostalgic

AUTHOR'S NOTES

insight into those times, with tales that are usually confined to the annual reunion, the bar at the local branch of the RAFA or ACA, or various Naval wardrooms.

Many of the pilots were ex-WWII, who, given the amount of surplus aircrew at the cessation of hostilities, volunteered to switch to flying helicopters rather than the alternative of demotion in rank and the possibility of 'flying a desk', or even worse. (One of our pilots who had, until recently, been flying Mosquitos in combat, suddenly found himself employed for a time stripping wheels and tyres off military vehicles, and corporals could be spotted wandering around sporting the AFM, or even DFM!) The wartime mentality that existed between air and ground crews prevailed, both on the squadrons, and now in the Association. Everyone was on first name terms; rank and formality came into the mix only when absolutely necessary, just as had been the way in Malaya. The pilots flew aircraft kept airworthy by a ground crew who ensured the aircrew were as safe as possible when airborne in 'their' aircraft. What worked well during the Second World War – that comradely cement provided by service life – worked just as well in Malaya. We were a cheerful, friendly group.

Due to falling membership as age took its toll – many members taking that final flight, so to speak – the Association is no longer extant, but *Lift-Off* does survive, and is available, via email, to anyone whose name is on file. If you have an interest in any ex RAF or NAS Far East helicopter operations, including Confrontation, please contact dt@deltatango.net

THE BALLAD OF ONE FIVE FIVE

Come one, come all, where'er you may be
Sit down a while and listen to me
The truth I will tell of the world's greatest skive
On a Whirlybird squadron numbered One Five Five

There was Claydon and Geddes, and a boss they called Ron,
And Browning and Puddy, but now Puddy has gone.
Best bunch of guys you ever could meet
We sweated together in tropical heat.

Old Wal' you know was in charge of the store.
Finding spares for our choppers, his biggest chore
For the kites they were ragged, all tattered and torn
And we worked like the devil to keep them airborne.

The aircraft themselves once totalled fourteen
The pilots and crewmen wore jungle green.
As they flew overhead, our hats we would doff
Thinking, there goes another, to be written off.

The first we lost went into a stream
Some parts of that one have yet to be seen.
From then on we lost them, 'bout every two weeks
On beaches, in clearings, even the creeks.

The end of the story is sad to relate,
They gave us Sycamore's 'fore it's too late.
And once these aircraft began to arrive
It was the end of our squadron, the bold One Five Five.

Thanks are due to squadron members 'RAB' and 'Terry', who penned the original words, which I have taken the liberty of amending slightly.

*

THE 194 SQUADRON LAMENT

Thanks for the memory, of twitching Westland flights
O'er Korbu's cloudy heights
Of Ulus, Pengulus, and steamy jungle nights
Kinrara or bust

Thanks for the memory, of flogging through The Gap
While the crewman finds the map
Of Monsoons, flies, quick DIs, and night-stops at Legap
Kinrara or bust

Thanks for the memory, of Inters in the rain
Vibrations on the brain
Our only hope of time off is jankers, so it's plain
Kinrara for us

There's a Swan-Hog down to Tengah
And a comm to Jason Bay
For NCOs there's the Kinta
Or if your blood is blue, head for Kota Bahru

So thanks for the memory, of clearings down below
Where only fools would go
The hole's too small, trees too tall, but who the hell's to know
There are termites in the tail-cone, and the revs are far too low
Kinrara, it's bust

Prologue

In the late 1920s the Malayan Communist Party was formed, their objective being to establish a communist controlled republic in Malaya.

When a Japanese invasion of Malaya seemed imminent in 1941, a network of subversive agents was needed to operate behind enemy lines if the country was occupied. Ironically, the only organisation capable of carrying out this work was the Communist Party, who formed the mainspring of the resistance. After the war the Malayan Communist Party revived its aim of establishing a communist state. It fomented labour disputes and infiltrated public organisations.

By the beginning of 1948 the Communists realized that their efforts were little more than an irritant, so embarked on a programme of intimidation, demonstrations, murder and sabotage. Having openly committed themselves to armed resistance they set themselves a three-stage programme. Firstly to cause terror and economic chaos in rural areas. Secondly to 'liberate' selected rural areas. Thirdly to 'liberate' urban areas and declare a communist republic. They estimated that each stage would take six months. They failed, but it took the government and security forces twelve years to bring the emergency to a successful conclusion.

Throughout this prolonged period the RAF had three main tasks: support of ground forces; transportation, including air supply and the positioning of airborne and parachute forces; and, finally, reconnaissance. By 1954 the threat of armed revolution had more or less been broken.

*

During 1955 federal elections were held to hasten transition from colonial rule to independence. This was achieved on 31 August 1957. The United Kingdom, Australia and New Zealand agreed to continue to provide assistance during the final phase of the emergency.

British plans to bring a greater degree of independence to the remaining British territories in South East Asia included the incorporation of British

PROLOGUE

North Borneo and Singapore Island into a Greater Malaysia. This aroused fierce opposition from Indonesia which saw its dreams of total domination of Borneo slipping away.

In 1962 elements in Borneo, strongly supported by Indonesia, objected to the proposed Federation, and rebellion broke out on 8 December 1962. Although the initial revolt was crushed early in 1963 an increasing number of raids began to take place from across the Indonesian border.

On 16 September 1963 Greater Malaysia came into existence with the full support of Britain, Singapore and the North Borneo States of Sarawak and Sabah. The arrangement was approved by the United Nations. Indonesia immediately broke off diplomatic relations with Malaysia.

Guerrilla incursions continued, many involving regular Indonesian forces. These were initially confined to Borneo, but later there were attacks on the Malayan mainland and Indonesian paratroops were dropped north of Singapore. Since war had not been declared the armed forces were unable to pursue enemy troops or intruding aircraft across the Indonesian border. Hostilities continued until August 1966 when a peace treaty was signed between Malaya and Indonesia.

The experience the RAF had gained in Burma and Malaya stood it in good stead. Air Vice-Marshal C.N. Foxley-Norris stated, 'The Borneo campaign was a classic example of the lesson that the side which uses air power most effectively to defeat the jungle will also defeat the enemy.'

These campaigns had seen the helicopter introduced into service, almost directly into front-line operations, and from that point on there was no looking back, for rotary wing technology advanced to keep pace with the rest of aviation: head design, composite/titanium blade technology, computer control, head-up displays, so on and so forth. All now even allow for advanced aerobatics: loop, rolls and such, all of which were impossible in the times of which we are about to read.

The country involved was then known as Malaya, only becoming Malaysia in 1963.

Chapter 1

Flying in the Dark

As Old As They Are New

Although Leonardo de Vinci, George Caley, and such pioneers had dabbled with the basics of rotary flight in the seventeen & eighteen hundreds, lack of any practical form of propulsion put a brake on things. It was the likes of Igor Sikorsky that finally cracked the problem in the late 1930s, the Russians always being ahead in helicopter design technology, although Sikorsky later flew the coop, becoming an American citizen.

*

Looking back is no bad thing, despite what happened to Lot's lot in that biblical tale, for those who do look back and survey the past may be vouchsafed some preparation as to what is expected in the future. Not a lot of good to the aged, then, but to look back in the latter stages of life is to switch

Early morning mist and cloud in the valleys.

the nostalgia button to 'On'. Doing so, particularly in the case of those who served in Malaya, immediately conjures up visions of youth, limestone cliffs, mountains, endless miles of thick, verdant jungle and, particularly, rather basic forms of rotary winged aircraft, i.e. early helicopters.

As one of our pilots stated years later in the foreword to my autobiography *A Suitcase Full Of Dreams*, 'David Taylor served with me when I was flying helicopters in Malaya during the early days of RAF rotary wing support operations. Exciting times, especially so in that the flying took place on the front line of a long-forgotten campaign – the Malayan Emergency, 1948-60. By today's standards, the tactics, the flying techniques, and the machines themselves were all rather primitive, so life was always interesting, frequently difficult, and occasionally alarming.'

*

Inter-service rivalry as to who orders what equipment, from wherever, and for whom, has existed since long before the Royal Flying Corps and the Royal Naval Air Service were amalgamated in 1918 to form the Royal Air Force, leaving the Royal Navy as a separate entity. This often created a situation which found one service bidding against the other for the limited resources available, failing to take account of the country's needs as a whole

1948 Hoverfly Royal Mail for Balmoral.

FLYING IN THE DARK

1947-48 Hoverfly.

rather than just their part in things. And as far as recognizing a possible use for the helicopter in future operations went, the Royal Navy were often way ahead of the Royal Air Force. In fact the Navy had actually placed an order with Sikorsky for 240 of their R4Bs during the Second World War, but with the end to hostilities this was cancelled.

To be strictly accurate, RAF involvement with rotary wing flying had begun as far back as 1934, when a small number of Avro-built Cierva C30A autogiros, known as the Rota – rotary winged right enough but requiring forward speed to turn the rotor, therefore incapable of hovering – entered service with the School of Army Co-operation at Old Sarum. Later, during the war, these aircraft were employed on radar calibration duties around the coast of Britain. The RAF's first true helicopters – nine Sikorsky R-4Bs, known in the Service as the Hoverfly Mk1, and part of that original Royal Navy order – were shipped over from America on Lend-Lease terms and used to form a helicopter training school at RAF Andover early in 1945.

Small numbers of these Sikorsky R-4Bs – or Hoverfly Mk1 – and the improved Sikorsky R-6, or Hoverfly Mk II, served on trials work with the Airborne Forces Experimental Establishment at RAF Beaulieu, 657 Air Observation Post Squadron at RAF Andover, and RAF Middle Wallop, until 1950. In addition, the King's Flight operated a Hoverfly I for a brief period, delivering urgent mail from Dyce to Balmoral, where it operated from the cricket pitch.

THE FIRST HELICOPTER BOYS

1947 RAF trials flight crew.

Hoverfly approaching Balamoral.

FLYING IN THE DARK

Though useful experience was gained during these Hoverfly operations, the aircraft's capabilities were very limited and, owing to an acute US dollar shortage post war, difficulties were experienced in obtaining sufficient spares to keep the American-built machines operational. This led to their withdrawal from service in 1950 for return to the States. So, although it could be said the RAF had been conducting trials with various marks of the Sikorsky Hoverfly, along with other diverse types, since the mid-forties, the units involved were considered to be no more than test and demonstration teams, with little thought being given to actual purchase, or the forming of a squadron. Thus by the end of the 1940s, at least from an RAF point of view, the helicopter was still relatively new and untried as a piece of military equipment. A result of this dithering by the Air Staff was that the RAF found itself at the back of the queue when they finally did decide to place an order with Westland for the limited supplies of the S51 Dragonfly – the only type currently available that appeared able to fulfil at least some of the requirements – for all production models were already on order for the Royal Navy. A result of all this was that the RAF – once an Air Staff Requirement was forthcoming – found itself 'cap in hand' seeking help from their lordships at the Admiralty. It seemed like now *was* the time, Air Staff finally being pushed into action, that Requirement request having been brought about by the currently developing situation in Malaya.

The Malayan Emergency was one of the major post-Second World War conflicts. The CTs – to which communist terrorists were commonly referred – called themselves the Malayan Races Liberation Army (MRLA). Their stated aim was to win over the local population and overthrow the government. A result of this serious threat to democracy was that thousands of British and Commonwealth troops were sent to Malaya to put down the uprising completely.

It was early March 1949 when the Chiefs of Staff were informed that operations in Malaya were being hampered by the length of time needed to evacuate casualties, having to recover them over long distances through difficult terrain: around two-thirds of the country consisted of dense, mountainous jungle, almost down to the beaches, barely accessible in places. The availability of helicopters would therefore make a huge difference in the event of a patrol finding themselves in such a position. An aerial casevac would ensure operations could continue without delay, rather than troops having to withdraw from an operation to escort casualties out of the jungle down a long and possibly difficult track. Not only might this be detrimental to the condition of the casualty, but the patrol would also be obliged to break off possible contact with the enemy.

Helicopters would also assist greatly in the 'troop morale' side of things. What the presence of the helicopter meant to the men on the ground was summed up by a letter to 194 Squadron, penned by one army commanding officer: 'What soldiers in the jungle appreciate is the fact that should anything go wrong, they can rely on someone descending from the skies to pick them up.'

As a result, three Dragonflys were urgently requested, so as to form a casualty evacuation trials unit; a possibility that had been suggested the previous year but, in the absence of an Air Staff Requirement being issued, nothing had been done about it. The Admiralty had already ordered the Dragonfly from Westland in large enough numbers to fill the company's order book. But, after taking delivery of the first six – taking into account that Air Staff Requirement, and no doubt some arm-twisting from on high – they reluctantly agreed to release three aircraft for trials with the RAF.

There was still much to be learned from flying these aircraft in the tropical heat and humidity of the Far East, as opposed to the English climate where preliminary testing had been carried out. In this new environment, performance was found to be considerably reduced: new aircraft; a new type of flying; along with fairly inexperienced rotary wing pilots. (The Navy suddenly found themselves unable to make good on their offer of some preliminary training,

Test flight at Seletar for new-build Dragonfly.

FLYING IN THE DARK

for, upon arrival of the first two RAF pilots sent to Gosport, they discovered the Navy's first, and at the time only, Dragonfly, to be a tangled mess of twisted blades and shattered Perspex, lying on its side. Oops! Clearly, someone else was also struggling to come to terms with the then, as yet unaccustomed, and somewhat mysterious, facets of rotary flight!)

These were not only a new type of aircraft being introduced into service, it was an entirely new concept of flight. Definitely pioneering work, with pilots really pushing the limits. Everything about it was different, mostly having to be learned in the field, and on Operational Service!

The following tongue-in-cheek, though eminently memorable – as was the intent – article in *Training Memoranda* (*Tee Emm*) explained as such:

Don't Get Helicopped!

Helicopters are now being used in the service – not many at present, but more are coming along – and we think you should know something about them. We don't mean know how to drive them – there are special Training Flights for that – but know how not to get 'copped' by them, when you are in the role of an innocent but curious bystander. For they are not quite such simple things as they look, and when on the ground can be very dangerous to people in the vicinity who are not aware of their funny little ways. So here's some gen about them, which may prevent you helicopping it unawares.

First, note the main rotor, that is the big propeller affair on top. This rotates in a horizontal plane about the vertical axis of the aircraft, but the height of the blade tips above the ground varies depending on the revs, and also of course on the slope of the ground on which the aircraft is standing. The average height is about five to six feet – and that is also, unfortunately, about the height of most men. You should, therefore, at once get rid of any assumption that because the rotor is *above* the aircraft it is also above *you*. There is no future in approaching a helicopter within the radius of the main rotor, when the engine is running, **even if the rotor is not in motion**. (There's even less future, of course, in doing it when the rotor *is* in motion.) For though the helicopter rotor may be at rest when the engine is running, it can be set going in a second when the pilot engages the clutch, and the pilot has not got a 360° range of vision.

Next, note the tail rotor, that is the small propeller on the starboard side of the tail. This rotates vertically and is in line with the fore and aft axis of the aircraft. The tips of this, too, are about five feet from the ground, or nicely at chest height; and this also can be at rest when the engine is running, but liable to be started up any minute by the pilot who can't see behind him. Moreover, being smaller it is not so easily seen (but just as easily felt), and, in addition, it is situated in what would normally be a safe area with more conventional aircraft.

To sum up, therefore, treat helicopters with respect, and don't think they can be approached in the same way as a Lancaster or even a Moth – however anxious you may be to get up close and see how the darn thing works.

Tee Emm **Vol 5 No. 2 May 1946**

*

There was good reason for calling the Malayan war against communism an 'Emergency'. In 1948, Malaya's economy was still in a critical state following the depredations of the Second World War, and security, via the London insurance market, was vital to the country's recovery. If the uprising had officially been declared a 'state of insurrection', this would have automatically entailed a reassessment of insurance policies, leading to the imposition of higher premiums for war risks, which most companies could ill afford. If, on the other hand, the violence and unrest was simply declared to be a 'state of emergency', then the insurance issue could be neatly side-stepped, premiums would remain the same as in peace time, and everyone could concentrate on ousting the bad guys and getting the country back on its feet, communist insurrection or not. And so for twelve long years everyone resolutely stuck to this euphemism, even if the figures told a different story. By July 1960, when the conflict was officially declared at an end, some 1,865 members of the security forces had been killed in enemy action and 2,473 civilians murdered, not to mention the nearly 7,000 Communists who met their end in the conflict.

*

PUSHING THE ENVELOPE

Although the Far East Air Force Casualty Evacuation Flight was officially formed at Kuala Lumpur on 1 May 1950, it was to be two years before their aircraft were actually based there.

The first RAF helicopters to arrive, three crated Dragonfly HC2s, came from the UK by sea, to be assembled and test flown by 390 MU at RAF

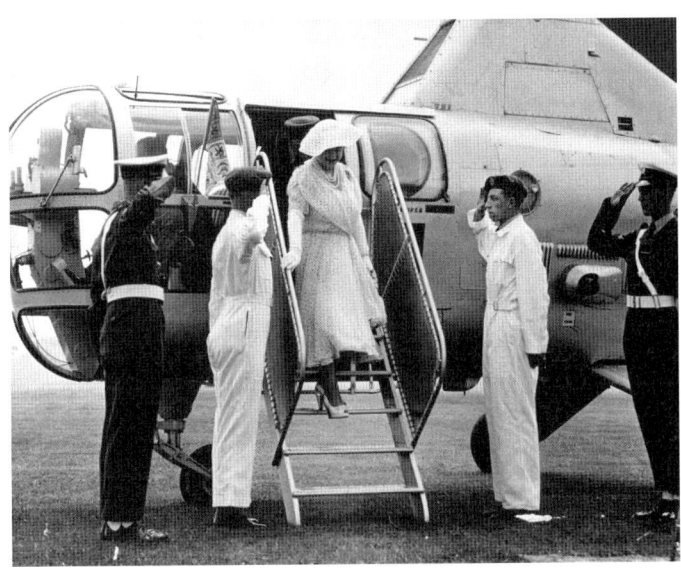

1950's Dragonfly, fit for the Queen Mother.

Seletar during April and May of 1950. Once declared airworthy, and signed off, they and their groundcrews relocated to RAF Changi.

At first the Flight comprised three Westland Dragonfly Mk II helicopters, three pilots, and supporting ground crew, and was the forerunner of No 194, the first RAF squadron to be equipped solely with helicopters. The CO was Flight Lieutenant K. Fry, the other pilots being Flight Lieutenants J.R. Dowling, A.J. Clarke, and Flying Officer A.J. Lee.

There is a little confusion here already, for the Squadron Operational Record book entry compiled for 1/5/50 reads:

> *The Casualty Evacuation Flight was formed at Kuala Lumpur on the first of May 1950 under the original title of Casualty Air Evacuation Unit, with a strength of three officers and thirteen airmen. Three NCOs of ASDP Air Ministry were attached to the unit for the initial period of three months to uncrate the aircraft and to train the servicing personnel.*
>
> *The officers appointed were:*
>
> > *Flight Lieutenant K Fry*
> > *Flying Officer A J Lee*
> > *Flying Officer G Meywick*
>
> *and two Dragonfly HC MkII.* [No mention of Dowling, or Clarke!]
> *The unit remained at Seletar, attached, until 22nd May 1950.*
> *The helicopters flown on 22nd April were the first to be flown in the Colony.*
> *The Flight moved to RAF Changi on the 22nd May, leaving Dragonfly WF311 behind as Command Reserve, and trials commenced to determine Take-Off performance at varying loads.*

This entry was compiled by Flight Lieutenant K. Fry, the CO, so you'd think he would know!

Another significant entry from the ORB around this time:

> *13/6/50 Air Commodore Briscoe CBE became the first medical officer to fly in the pannier. 5/7/50 An internally stowed stretcher carrier was air tested satisfactorily and demonstrated to various Air Force and Army officers for comment. It was decided this locally designed and manufactured carrier was an improvement on the Westland/Sikorsky external pannier, and*

FLYING IN THE DARK

approval was given for the building of a special lightweight stretcher for use with it.

During July, F/Off Meywick left the unit to become officer i/c Detachment Labuan, his place taken by Flight Lieutenant JR Dowling DFC, ex-UK.

Ah ha! so now we know!

*

The Dragonfly had eventually been accepted by an unwilling RAF as the 'experts' believed that reduction in performance in the Far East – compared to that obtained during an English summer, in which the initial trials had been conducted – would be minimal. Ground crews were trained by Westland, as were four pilots, each of whom received a fifteen-hour familiarization course before being sent to the Far East. This then was the basis of the Far East Casualty Evacuation Flight, which then managed to operate in the Malayan environment for sixteen months before losing an aircraft. This happened on 24 October 1951 when Dragonfly WF308, flown by Flight Lieutenant Fry, fell back into a jungle clearing as it was climbing out with a Gurkha casualty in the basket-stretcher. The machine was completely wrecked but pilot and casualty were only slightly injured and were airlifted out the next day by another helicopter. WF308 was never recovered and it was quite impossible to determine the cause of the accident.

All Dragonflys had been reserved for an Admiralty order which was expected to take two years to fill, and FEAF had asked for more, the requirement in Malaya by now far beyond the task of the two remaining aircraft. The Admiralty agreed to release two more in October, and the new Mk4s, with metal blades and power-assisted controls, were received late 1952 and early 1953. In their last month of operation as a Flight they suffered their first casualties. WZ845, one of the new aircraft, flown by Flying Officer Walters, crashed with two passengers on board (Major Barker, SAS, and Mr Toulon, Deputy Police Chief). In-flight rotor failure at 3,000 ft. It disintegrated as it fell, killing passengers and crew.

All Dragonflys were now grounded until the rotor heads had been tested by Magnaflux crack detectors, a long process which at first had to be repeated after every hundred hours of flying. When two more were found to be cracked, flying time was reduced to fifty hours. Only when rotor heads arrived with the spider arm threads milled instead of cut, was this waste of valuable flying time eliminated.

THE FIRST HELICOPTER BOYS

Dragonfly engine changes were not infrequent.

All Whirlwinds had been ordered for the naval programme too, and even if NAS 848 Squadron *was* diverted to FEAF, there was no possibility of meeting demands for the RAF. In answer to a request by Sir Gerald Templer for a helicopter with a tactical ability, the Admiralty had sent out 848 with their ten American-built S55s, stripped of all sonar equipment.

By contrast, the Navy's aircrew were all operationally trained and had even carried out some training flights while en route to Singapore. Their aircraft were fully serviceable, and all they needed was in-theatre familiarization flights.

Performance trials showed that the S55s could carry five armed troops and operate from the same small clearings used by the Dragonfly. Although their cruising speed was about the same, sixty knots, they could carry up to three stretcher cases and two walking wounded. The winch hoist had a cargo hook and could carry netted loads up to 800 lbs. They pioneered tactical troop deployments in which they were led to the scene by a Dragonfly; they then rapidly deplaned their troops while the Dragonfly remained at the hover, an armed airman in the doorway to give covering fire. This was the first known use of the pathfinder helicopter.

Under the command of Lieutenant Commander Jim Suthers, they arrived at NAS Sembawang on 8 January 1953. (Much later (1969) Simbang became the only NAS station to be commanded by a Royal Marine officer).

Sembawang, a few miles from Singapore, was to provide helicopter facilities for the Far East Fleet. All their new machines, and those for repair, were received there.

FLYING IN THE DARK

848 Squadron over local scenery.

848 Engine change in clearing

Originally intended as a bomber station for the RAF, the airfield had been carved out of a rubber plantation in 1937. It was transferred to the Admiralty two years later – on paper anyway – and plans were made to convert it into a major naval aircraft repair yard to support the projected Far East Fleet with its four aircraft carriers.

At this stage, the Whirlwind was an aircraft whose performance under tropical conditions had never been investigated. Full operational trials were carried out with all aircraft being flown to the limits. To improve performance, they were stripped of all items considered non-essential for their task.

*

The very large operational area extended from the Thai border in the north to the extreme southern area of Johore. The whole of Malaya could be covered, and each aircraft carried a junior NCO airframe or engine fitter, with servicing kits and spares travelling the same way. Aviation fuel was pre-positioned or air-dropped by Valetta. High humidity and temperatures, plus the fact they had to fly troops from sea level to areas over 4,000 ft, made necessary the development of special techniques for lifting out of jungle clearings, many of which were only 240 ft long, 150 ft wide and surrounded by trees rising up to 200 ft.

By 22 May 1950 the Casualty Evacuation Flight was ready to begin operational trials. On 14 June a British soldier was flown from Segamat to Changi, thus inaugurating RAF helicopter operations a few weeks ahead of the first American helicopter sortie in Korea. Quite impressive really. And on 28 June a Malay constable with gunshot wounds was lifted by helicopter directly to a military hospital at Johore Bahru, probably becoming the first person to have their life saved by an RAF helicopter. But it turns out the RAF weren't the first, as further research was to reveal.

THE VERY FIRST HELICOPTER RESCUE

In the Second World War the US Air Commandos were an irreverent, unruly band of mavericks who cared little for the spit and polish of military life, but fought courageously. They operated independently of the rest of the military chain of command, and felt free to introduce new ideas to warfare. Among these was this new gadget called a helicopter. It was a Sikorsky experimental machine known as an YR-4B, and was on trial, based in India.

The Air Commandos' chance to test the new machine came when Tech Sergeant Ed Hladovcak (commonly known as 'Murphy', for as someone said, 'who in hell knows how to say Hladovcak') crashed in an L-1 Vigilant liaison plane along with a trio of His Majesty's soldiers, one suffering from malaria, two with bullet wounds, miles behind Japanese lines in Burma.

FLYING IN THE DARK

An L-5 Sentinel pinpointed their location but could not land. The YR-4B was 500 miles away in India.

'Murphy' and the three Brits crawled, thrashed, and climbed until they were deep inside the jungle, half a mile from their wrecked plane. Here they hunkered down, watching as Japanese soldiers scoured the wreckage of the L-1, secured the crash site, and fanned out. As the day progressed and the heat became insufferable, the voices of patrolling Japanese came closer, their uniform leggings occasionally visible through the undergrowth.

That afternoon, another of the 1st Air Commando Group's L-5 Sentinel liaison planes flew overhead and dropped a note. It read: 'Move up mountain. Japanese nearby.'

On 21 April 1944, Air Commando boss Cochran sent radio instructions for 2nd Lieutenant Carter Harman to proceed with a helicopter to Taro, 600 miles away in northern Burma. The YR-4B's usual range was 100 miles, so Harman prepared the helicopter for the marathon journey, throwing four jerry cans of extra fuel in the unused co-pilot's seat. 'It was April 25 before I reached Taro,' said Harman. 'I had been stopping to refuel from the jerry cans.'

Meantime, a message had been received from the Chindit airstrip, codenamed Aberdeen, carved out of the jungle behind Japanese lines. Just four words: 'Send the eggbeater immediately.'

That meant proceeding from Taro to Aberdeen, 125 miles to the south, beyond the limited range of the YR-4B. But Aberdeen-based L-5s were pinpointing Hladovcak's location, and the plan was to use the YR-4B and Harman for the pick-up. It was an ad hoc solution, the kind of improvisation at which the Air Commandos excelled.

Next day, the three British soldiers were reported to be much worse, their wounds becoming infected. The heat refused to subside, and there were insects everywhere, especially mosquitoes which were known to carry a virulent strain of malaria.

Said Harman: 'I worried about the often unreliable 200 hp Warner piston engine that powered my YR-4B. I wondered if I could get to the clearing where the men were waiting. I would lift them to the riverbank, where liaison planes could take over. Since I could only carry one man at a time, I would make four round trips. Helicopters were still new and we were still learning that they did not like hot weather. They didn't like Japanese soldiers, either, being exceedingly vulnerable to any kind of gunfire.'

'I flew from Aberdeen to the sandbar where I rendezvoused with an L-5 Sentinel, which in turn led me to the clearing where Hladovcak and the three British were struggling to stay alive. I did not see any Japanese troops, but was told they were all around. I wondered if the engine and helicopter would hold together trying to pull off a job that was more rigorous than anything for which the YR-4B had been designed.'

Harman was later told that Hladovcak 'went crazy' when he saw the 'eggbeater' arriving, having of course never seen a helicopter before. Harman was pushing the YR-4B to the limit when he landed in the clearing in a swirl of flying dust and pieces of greenery. Murphy loaded the most seriously injured British soldier aboard. The YR-4B strained, vibrated, and took off, making it to the sand bar where a liaison plane flew the British soldier to safety.

Said Harman: 'I hauled out a second British soldier, still searching the jungle canopy for Japanese troops, reaching the riverbank, when everything went wrong. The Warner engine seized. There was a clunking sound and lots of vapor around the engine. It had overheated and wasn't going to restart. I was going to have to spend the night on the sand bar. I didn't see how our luck could hold out much longer, and I wondered if this was the night the Japanese would overrun Hladovcak and the remaining British soldier.

'It was a long, lonely night, and come morning there was low cloud cover, but nothing to prevent flying, if only the engine would start.' It did. Harman was able to pick up the third British soldier and get him to safety, leaving Edward 'Murphy' Hladovcak alone in the jungle.

Murphy held out. Harman was able to go in again, but as the YR-4B approached the lone Hladovcak, soldiers broke out of the treeline about 1,000 feet from him. 'Too late,' thought Harman. 'After all this work, it's too late!' Hladovcak was shouting out loud about Japanese troops bearing down on him. 'But I got there first,' said Harman. 'Hladovcak climbed on board. I put the aircraft into a hover. Now the troops swarmed directly beneath us and for a moment the YR-4B threatened to seize again. The helicopter sank back towards the jungle. Then, I was able to get full power, and we climbed away.'

Harman took Murphy all the way back to Aberdeen, where they were told the troops had in fact been Chindit irregulars, intent on rescuing Murphy. There were Japanese nearby but Harman never actually saw them. 'When I bounded off the ground with Murphy on board, we were escaping from our own guys.'

This first helicopter rescue was the beginning for rotary-wing aviation.

That helicopter performed yet another rescue, one that sometimes is erroneously cited as history's first helicopter rescue. On 26 Jan 1945,

FLYING IN THE DARK

Captain Frank Peterson flew an R-4 to evacuate a wounded weather observer, Private Howard Ross, from a 4,700-foot mountain ridge in the Naga Hills of Burma. Peterson flew with a co-pilot, 1st Lieutenant Irvin Steiner. That was a very early helicopter success, but it came eight months after Harman flew the first such mission, paving the way for the helicopter missions of today.

*

At Changi there was still much to be learnt, both by air and ground crews, though it quickly became obvious that although the helicopter was an ideal aircraft for the type of warfare currently being performed across the Straits over in mainland Malaya, the climatic conditions certainly were not.

In 1950s Malaya, apart from areas under cultivation, the terrain was either primary or secondary jungle. Primary jungle had trees of 200 feet plus; secondary was dense, almost impenetrable jungle. A foot patrol might average 1,000 yards a day in secondary, three miles a day in primary.

The almost continuous monsoons are north-east in winter and south-west in summer. Winds are local and variable at treetop height, and there is no wind at all at the bottom of deep clearings where pilots had to take off after a rescue or delivery operation.

The Dragonfly, with its limited instrumentation – weight needed to be kept to a minimum – did not have Instrument Flight Rules capability, could not fly at night, and needed to avoid the heavy rain showers which so frequently erupted without warning in Malaya. Heavy rain could damage the wood and canvas rotors fitted to the early models, although later the RAF received the Dragonfly HC Mk2, with all-metal rotors. The curved Perspex surfaces of the Dragonfly cockpit, allowing for no wipers, were very bad for visibility in rain.

Another danger was when making a steep descent. The downward air flow from the rotor balanced out the upward flow from the descent, reducing mass flow through the rotor. This resulted in a faster rate of descent for a given engine power, with the chance of a heavy landing, and reduced stability.

Using 100 octane fuel, contained in four-gallon disposable cans known as 'Flimsies', meant that refuelling needed to be arranged in advance, occasionally via air drop, and much first-line servicing equipment had to travel with the aircraft.

THE FIRST HELICOPTER BOYS

As they carried only VHF radio, the pilots were unable to talk to ground patrols, so needed to rely on the Army's AOP flight Austers (actually 656 Squadron RAF back then, but with Army pilots), who had good communications via their AOP/MF net throughout Malaya, whether the aircraft were airborne or not. It was because of this lack of communication that, until 1953, when casevac helicopters were still virtually irreplaceable, all operations were, whenever possible, accompanied by a fixed wing aircraft, usually an Auster.

It was found that, under local conditions, the Dragonfly could not hover outside ground effect with more than thirty minutes fuel and a payload of 200 lbs.

To many problems the helicopter provided an ideal solution, but jungle warfare against terrorists posed difficulties, to which answers were not to be found in the older military text-books.

*

Most contacts with the CTs took place in the dense, steamy jungle which formed around three-quarters of this country's land mass, of which the enemy had extensive experience, having lived and fought there, in support of the Allies, through the Second World War.

By the middle of 1951 the Malayan Scouts under Colonel Calvert were operating along the jungle fringes in small commando-type groups. They were the most likely to meet the enemy in large numbers, and looking after them became a major responsibility for the Flight.

The troops soon came to know that should they be wounded, injured, or fall sick, a radio call could bring help in a short time and, because a fifteen-minute helicopter flight was equivalent to a three-day march through the jungle, a hospital, with intensive care, was never far away. In the first two years of the emergency, casualties had to be carried on stretchers to the nearest airstrip, where they could be evacuated by Auster and, later, the Prestwick Pioneer.

A typical casevac mission would be initiated by a radio call giving details of the condition of the casualty and location of the nearest existing clearing. The patrol leader would be responsible for ensuring the clearing met with the minimum standards required to enable a helicopter to either land or hover sufficiently close to the ground to permit the casualty to be put on board. In some cases the unit would need to make a new clearing, using plastic explosive to fell massive trees. Once a request was approved by Air

Headquarters, the pilot and crewman would be briefed and the helicopter dispatched.

Flying over jungle is sometimes compared with flying over a vast green sea. In conditions of poor visibility – often mist between hill and mountain obscured tree tops in the valleys – it could be a difficult task to locate a clearing precisely. Once the patrol heard the helicopter it would 'put up smoke', guiding the helicopter to the exact location. The pilot and crewman (forerunner of today's loadmaster) – if indeed the helicopter's limited payload allowed one to be carried – would be looking out for smoke coming up through the trees.

With visual and possibly radio contact established and the LZ identified, the challenge was to make a descent into the clearing. During the approach a careful lookout would be kept for any tree-stumps, branches or undergrowth that might be too close to the underside or tail rotor when landing, and, just as important, any obstructions to the subsequent take-off.

Once the helicopter had landed, or established a hover close to the ground, the crewman, if carried, would supervise loading the casualty who, within a few minutes, would be safely on his way to hospital. Except in dire emergency the engine was never shut down in a clearing – in fact a FEAF Standing Order forbade it – for failure to restart would not only jeopardize the casualty's rescue, but could result in the helicopter being stranded in a remote clearing now too small to permit a recovery party being flown in.

Because the Casevac Flight proved so successful, additional helicopters were based in Malaya and the scope of their operations extended to include troop-lifting, supply drops and other tasks which could not be carried out by fixed-wing aircraft.

In Feb 1953 the Far East Casualty Evacuation Flight was re-formed at Kuala Lumpur, now becoming 194 Squadron, the RAF's first truly operational helicopter unit,[1] still equipped with Dragonfly helicopters, now the Mk 4. At the same time 848 Squadron Royal Naval Air Service, equipped with the American-built Sikorsky S55, arrived. No. 155 Squadron RAF was re-formed at RAF Kuala Lumpur in September 1954 with Westland Whirlwind Mk 4, and by July 1956 No. 194 Squadron had completely re-equipped with the Bristol Sycamore, the first completely British designed and built helicopter.

By December 1956 No. 848 NAS Squadron, having done a magnificent job, was withdrawn from Malaya.

THE FIRST HELICOPTER BOYS

New arrival at KL. First Sycamore being inspected.

Chapter 2

So, What is a Helicopter Like to Fly?

The dominant fact about the helicopter is that lift is provided by the rotation of its main rotor/s. In a fixed-wing aircraft, lift is, of course, generated by the forward movement of the wings. But the creation of lift by revolution of the rotor (or rotary wing) makes the helicopter independent of forward movement. 'The rotors are, in fact, a form of rotating wing,' said Flight Lieutenant Ken Fry, CO of the RAF's first operational helicopter unit.

The basic controls of a helicopter, and the methods by which they control the aircraft, are quite different from the controls of a fixed-wing machine. There are no ailerons, no elevators, no flaps, and no air-brakes on a helicopter, nor is there a rudder. The aircraft's forward movement is controlled not by the throttle but by the cyclic stick. This, situated in the same position as would be the control column in a fixed-wing aircraft, also controls backward and sideways movement. To move ahead, the pilot pushes the cyclic stick forward. This increases the angle of attack of the main rotor, causing the rotor to tilt forward slightly. The rotor is on a fixed driveshaft though the individual blades are free to move as dictated by the stick, via an ingenious device created by Sikorsky. Push the stick forward and the blades in the rear quadrant of the disc have increased angle of attack, the forward ones less, thus the drive shaft causes the fuselage to tilt forward and the aircraft moves ahead. To move backwards, the cyclic stick is pulled back, thereby reversing the procedure. Sideways movement of the stick will take the aircraft left or right.

Movement of the collective pitch and throttle causes the helicopter to rise and descend. The throttle, usually built into the end of the collective pitch lever, is twisted back and forth rather like the throttle of a motor-cycle. When the pilot lifts or lowers the collective pitch lever, he changes the angle of attack of the main rotor, thus increasing or decreasing lift according to whether he wishes to climb or descend. Keeping the critical rotor revs in the narrow 'black' window is achieved by interplay between the twist-grip throttle, the collective lever, and the cyclic stick, a bit like rubbing your tummy and patting your head at the same time.

The rudder pedals, situated in the usual place, turn the aircraft left or right by changing the angle of attack of the tail rotor blades, which revolve in the vertical plane, thus moving the tail of the aircraft left or right.

The Westland Whirlwind Mk2, or HAR4, was big and bulky, powered by the nine cylinder Pratt and Witney Wasp radial engine which produced 600 hp. It was cumbersome and clumsy but punched below its weight and the crews who flew it loved it. It had power-operated flying controls, but only a single system, so loss of hydraulics could have dire consequences, the pilot requiring the strength of a gorilla to fly the aircraft for more than a few minutes in manual.

By contrast, the MK10, or HAR10, as used during the Confrontation, was sleek, streamlined and powered by the Bristol Siddeley Gnome Turboshaft engine, a third of the weight of the Wasp and producing 1400 hp. The critical rotor rpm was maintained by a fuel computer, easing the load of the pilot. It also had the luxury of dual hydraulic systems, so in the event of loss of primary hydraulics, the secondary system took over ensuring a safe return to terra firma. It could fly faster, further, carry a greater load and was easier to fly (although both required the same consummate skill to get in and out of those tiny clearings in the trees).

The cockpit of the Westland-Sikorsky S51 Dragonfly is far simpler than the cockpit of a fixed-wing aircraft. Basic instrumentation only was fitted, early helicopters not being equipped for blind flying. Differences in instrumentation are mainly associated with the rotor, such as rotor rpm (which is critical), and transmission gearbox temperature.

Helicopters are capable of taking off from wherever the aircraft is standing, without the need to taxi (although at airfields they are usually required by Air Traffic Control to do so, either on the ground or at the hover). While increasing engine power, via the twist-grip throttle, the pilot pulls up on the collective lever, increasing the angle of attack of the rotor blades, at the same time maintaining rotor rpm. As the aircraft leaves the ground the pilot adjusts the collective pitch to hold height. Now the aircraft tends to swing left or right because of the wind, or torque caused by the rotation of the main rotors, so the pilot holds his position steady by moving the tail rotor with the rudder pedals. After pausing for a moment on the ground cushion, the pilot pushes his stick forward, gains speed and climbs away.

Once in the air, the pilot immediately notices that the aircraft is able to swing back and forth like a pendulum. The helicopter can perform an

SO, WHAT IS A HELICOPTER LIKE TO FLY?

amazing variety of highly unusual manoeuvres. It can be flown backwards, banked up to ninety degrees – providing the speed is high enough, and can be braked in the air. He does the latter by pulling back the cyclic stick while at the same time reducing power to prevent a climb; he then applies power to prevent further loss of height, which brings the helicopter to a standstill. The helicopter can revolve continuously around a fixed position on the ground by simple application of rudder. She can fly sideways: from the hover, the pilot moves the stick to the left, making the aircraft tilt left, and drag thus caused to the tail rotor swings the nose left; then the application of right rudder will hold the helicopter straight. The helicopter can also hover, remaining perfectly stationary above a given spot on the ground.

When a helicopter lands, it merely hovers over the landing point and then gets progressively lower until it sinks to the ground. Coming in to land, the pilot reduces power by decreasing collective pitch, and approaches into wind. As he nears the ground, he reduces speed and adjusts power to maintain a constant rate of descent. The aircraft encounters a 'ground cushion' of air pressure, caused by the impact of rotor downdraught against the ground as the helicopter gets lower. The pilot holds height at around ten feet and decreases forward speed to zero. He then reduces power until the wheels touch down, at which moment he reduces power further to stay firmly put.

S51 Dragonfly in clearing.

The S51 Dragonfly requires a landing area of between two and two-and-a-half times its overall length, though smaller aircraft need less space.

Once on the ground, the helicopter pilot can taxi backwards and forwards by using the same control movements as in the air. Taxying is virtually flying on the ground, but without using sufficient power actually to lift off and become airborne. The pilot brakes by pulling back on the stick, or by applying his non-differential wheel brakes.

How easy is flying a helicopter compared to fixed-wing flying? Experienced fixed-wing pilots have to start from scratch when they first fly a helicopter, just as they do when they first tackle any other new aircraft type. But an average fixed-wing pilot solos a helicopter after four to eight hours dual, some solo after two or three hours. It is said to be rather like formation flying, or any other new manoeuvre. Suddenly something clicks, and it just comes. But, once he has mastered the basic principles, the helicopter pilot can never relax in quite the same way as a fixed-wing pilot sometimes can. Flying a helicopter demands continual concentration and constant coordination. Moreover, the servo-assisted controls require real manual effort to move them. In addition, the Dragonfly cannot be trimmed to fly hands-off, and pilot reaction in an emergency must be far quicker. But with its slower speed and the closer view it gives of the countryside, the helicopter is probably more fun to fly. There is little doubt that the average fixed-wing pilot can master a helicopter just as easily as he can convert to any other new type of aircraft, provided he keeps his wits constantly about him and is prepared to fly the aircraft all the time.

BLADE TRACKING

As with any rotating mass – in the helicopter's case, the rotor – any out-of-balance will soon make itself known in the form of vibration. Therefore the main source for vibration in helicopters is likely to be from the main rotor – described by the pilot as low frequency (usually referred to as a 'one per', i.e. one per rotation), the cause being one blade out of plane in the rotor disc. The cure for this is to track and adjust the blades via small trim tabs.

The time chosen for tracking was early morning, when the air was still. Pilot and ground-crew would assemble, pilot on board. Ground-crew would then mark the blade tips with different colour chalks. Once all this was done as many bods as were available would climb into the cabin, so as to stabilise

SO, WHAT IS A HELICOPTER LIKE TO FLY?

the aircraft, then the engine was started. With full power, engine and rotor rpm synchronised, and a 'thumbs-up' from the pilot, the designated mechanic would prepare the tracking flag: a 36" x 8" light-coloured canvas strip with brass eyelets top and bottom, mounted on top of a long pole via two arms and bungees. The flag section of the pole was on a swivel, controlled by the mechanic. The whole contraption had been carefully positioned (before start-up) at the edge of the rotor disc, then laid down.

On the given signal from the pilot the pole would be carefully raised, flag parallel to the aircraft fuselage. Then the mechanic would slowly swivel an arm towards the disc until the blade tips just clipped the flag – a steady hand, strong nerve, good judgement and eyesight required. Once he had visible markings on the flag it would be moved clear and laid down again. The engine would be shut down and rotor braked to a standstill. Now it was a matter of checking which blade, or blades, were out of track and adjusting that blades' trim tab. The above procedure was then repeated until all blades were tracking satisfactorily. As can be seen – H & S eat your heart out – the system was fraught with danger, but these were the learning days of helicopter operations, when everything was experimental and often held a degree of uncertainty.

Whirlwind blade tracking.

Dragonfly blade tracking.

Sycamore wheel change, Brian Purvis at the hover!

SO, WHAT IS A HELICOPTER LIKE TO FLY?

Should a blade change be required in-field, the tracking flag would be constructed on site, using bamboo etc. Similar rules often applied should a main gearbox change become necessary, a jury-rigged frame being constructed on site, which is where local knowledge and labour came in handy.

These days, of course, tracking is 'all done by mirrors', or should that be lasers!

Another phase of servicing that was fraught with danger, and not infrequently practised back then, was changing a wheel while the aircraft was held in the hover, often while non-squadron personnel looked on with wide-eyed disbelief. I don't suppose 'elf & safety would have approved, but it did the job with a minimum of delay.

Flight Lieutenant Paul Gray

Paul served in Malaya with 194 Squadron from 1958 until the Sycamores were grounded with blade problems mid '59. 194 Sqn were then amalgamated with 155 Sqn to become 110, still flying the Whirlwind 4. As the Sycamores gradually returned to service, so the Whirlwinds were returned to the UK for conversion to Mk10 standard. On his return to the UK in March 1961, Paul attended RAF Staff College, after which he returned to Malaya as CO of 66 Sqn Belvederes. He was a group captain by the end of his service:

> *For some seemingly unknown reason the captain of a dual control helicopter usually sits on the right, as opposed to the left hand seat of a fixed wing. This is possibly to do with the fact that as that was the position the first trainee sat when under training, it was decided to leave him in that familiar seat on completion. That is the way one theory goes, but ask any helicopter pilot and most will either not have a suitable answer, or will come up with some entirely different, and possibly unlikely, explanation! This being the case, I always had a lot of respect for the instructor, for with the collective control positioned in the centre – on most machines – they had to be able to fly from either side, capable of handling the controls with either hand. Could have been confusing at times.*

THE FIRST HELICOPTER BOYS

Flight Lieutenant Jim McCorkle

Flight Lieutenant Jim McCorkle in cockpit.

After training in the USA, then delivering various aircraft across the Atlantic, Jim flew bombers in Europe and the Middle East during the Second World War, plus Dakotas 'over the hump' in Burma. Post-war he participated in the Berlin Airlift, converting to helicopters in their early days. With over 50,000 hours in his log, Jim had a host of stories to tell. His book, *Time Just Flew*, tells more:

Posted to the Far East I was first attached to 194 Squadron, based in Kuala Lumpur, as the Squadron Training Officer. My job was to train pilots new to the Sycamore in the jungle theatre. Navigation over the dense jungle, and map-reading to avoid getting lost, were important skills to develop. So too was how to control the helicopter when descending into tight jungle clearings, and out of them, with little margin for error. Complete knowledge of one's aircraft and its components was essential. How far could be flown with a given amount of fuel? How much load could be carried with safety, and within limits? How does one judge ground-speed, wind drift, and actual track by outside references?

Many of these lessons could be learned accumulatively by flying in the Dry Season, when forward visibility was good. During the Monsoon Season it was a different matter. Coping with reduced visibility. With low cloud covering high ground many of the geographic features which aided navigation would now be obscured. All these factors had to be taken into consideration, took time to absorb. In addition, pilots had to be trained to cope with emergencies, such as engine failure. There aren't many open spaces in the jungle, so pilots had to learn to track along rivers, where small islands may offer an emergency landing ground.

SO, WHAT IS A HELICOPTER LIKE TO FLY?

Radio communication was also a problem in Malaya. Jungle forts – manned by Malayan Police Field Force personnel – offered either a short runway, where Pioneer aircraft could land, or a helicopter landing pad. These forts were also equipped with refuelling facilities – fuel having to be parachuted in with the rest of their supplies.

If a helicopter engine fails in flight there is only one sure consequence: you are going to descend rather quickly, so maintaining a safe altitude above ground is advisory. In the event of engine failure it is essential the pilot immediately lowers the collective lever at once, or the effect of drag immediately starts to reduce main rotor RPM, and if this is allowed to continue, the rotor becomes totally ineffective, and the helicopter will rapidly accelerate downward, completely out of control.

In powered flight, the main rotor accelerates air downward; this can be seen as the helicopter rises to a hover, after take-off. In flight, if the engine fails and the pilot immediately lowers the collective lever, the pitch angle of each main rotor blade is rapidly reduced, and drag decreased. Because the helicopter has now started a descent, this produces an upward flow of air through the main rotor, a free-wheel unit in the engine assembly coming into play, allowing rotor RPM to rapidly increase. When close to the ground this can be used to greatly reduce the high rate of descent. If the landing area is clear and flat, a safe zero-forward speed can be achieved for touchdown. If the ground is not clear at the point of landing, at least a zero rate of descent can be achieved, with the chance of personal survival greatly increased.

Part of my job was to ensure that every pilot was checked-out on fully auto-rotational landings each month. This involved flying above the base airstrip at altitudes of 1,000 feet, switching off the engine, an entry into auto-rotation, descend to just above ground-level over a selected, flat area, and a nose up-flare to kill the forward speed. This, combined with a smooth upward pull on the collective lever, would arrest the rate of descent completely. Levelling the fuselage with a forward push on the Cyclic would result in a gentle, level landing, similar to a touchdown from a low hover.

It was essential that these emergency landings were practised regularly.

194 Squadron 1952/54 at RAF Kuala Lumpur.

194 Squadron Aircrew, Sycamore days 1956.

SO, WHAT IS A HELICOPTER LIKE TO FLY?

110 Squadron Butterworth 1959. Author top row, far right.

110 Squadron Aircrew 1959. Top row: Mike Bailey, Tom Bennett, Tom Browning, Don Geddes. Seated: Taff Walker, Ken Claydon, George Puddy, Frank Barnes (CO), P/O Hurley, Bill Stevens, Paul Gray, Nobby Clarke.

THE FIRST HELICOPTER BOYS

Above: Aircrew and crewmen on Ops. Flight Lieutenants Tom Browning, George Puddy, Squadron Leader Frank Barnes, Flight Lieutenant Deke Bradley, kneeling- Sam Saunders, Merv Scopes, Dave Taylor, Fred McDonald.

Left: Aircrew practising roping from a Sycamore. And I thought the idea was that aircrew remained with their aircraft!

Chapter 3

Improvement and Advancements

At the end of the 1940s the helicopter was still relatively new and untried as a piece of military equipment but it quickly proved its worth in RAF service in 1950-59 during the Malayan Emergency.

The campaign against communist terrorists in Malaya, which began in 1949, brought with it an urgent need for a means of evacuating wounded soldiers from the jungle. To meet this requirement a Casualty Evacuation Flight equipped with three Westland Dragonfly HR2 helicopters formed at RAF Changi, Singapore, in April 1950.

RAF Casevac Flight. Dragonfly makes a practice landing in a typical clearing.

Dragonfly descending into a fairly open clearing.

The Dragonfly – a Westland-built version of the American Sikorsky S51 but powered by the British designed Alvis Leonides engine – was a small and very basic helicopter with just enough room for three passengers to squeeze in behind the pilot. The RAF used the Dragonfly in Malaya because it was the best helicopter out of the limited few available at the time – but it was far from ideal for the job. Underpowered, it could lift vertically from a jungle clearing, but with fuel enough for just thirty minutes flying; and it lacked Instrument Flight Rules (IFR) capability.

In addition the Dragonfly's centre of gravity had to be adjusted for all big weight changes in the cabin by moving 17½ lb lead weights around. The curved Perspex surface of its windscreen gave good visibility as long as it was not raining, but in Malaya it was like a greenhouse for the hardworking pilot hunched over his manual controls.

Despite the aircraft's limitations, Dragonflys of the Casualty Evacuation Flight – now commanded by one of the RAF's outstanding helicopter pioneers, Flight Lieutenant John Dowling[2] – soon proved their worth, the first operational sortie being flown on 14 June 1950.

IMPROVEMENT AND ADVANCEMENTS

THE PROOF OF THE PUDDING

The tropical heat and humidity of the thick, verdant jungle through which his patrol was stealthily advancing was debilitating and draining, easily leading to a loss of concentration. Suddenly it wasn't, for the relative quiet was shattered by the unexpected, dreaded sound of alien rifle fire.

Crack! crack! crack! The tables had turned. But although the patrol had stumbled into an ambush, they quickly regained the initiative, accurate return fire soon managing to drive off the terrorists. But those initial three bullets had smashed savagely into the chest of Private Tim Moreton. This was the eighth day of this troop's patrol; following up on reports, they were scouring the green hell of the Malayan jungle in search of these very terrorists.

The second bullet punctured Moreton's left lung, leaving him gasping for breath, and coughing up blood. The third bullet ripped into his right arm, shattering bone. From this point Moreton has got only a couple of days to live, unless he can get immediate, skilled medical care. But the nearest hospital is more than a week's trek away, so Moreton's patrol commander acts quickly. He got on the radio and transmitted to the patrol's base. 'Send helicopter' was the message, along with the coordinates of their current position.

A little while later a low-flying AOP Auster came in sight. Immediately, a smoke-bomb emitted a thick white plume which curled up into the air, through the trees, indicating the patrol's position. Over the radio, the Auster pilot is soon in contact with the patrol commander. 'Make for an LZ two hundred yards north-east,' he directs.

Three agonizing hours later, having battled against the jungle every inch of the way, while also remaining wary of another possible ambush, the ten-man patrol burst into a clearing which the Auster had taken only minutes to reach. Once there, as directed by another Auster pilot's instructions, and several hours intensive work, the patrol had cleared a suitable LZ with their machetes.

Then they heard it: the distinct sound of a helicopter's rotor blades beating the air. Glancing up, Moreton sees the life-saving RAF helicopter hovering 300ft above the clearing.

THE FIRST HELICOPTER BOYS

From the pilot's point of view the LZ looks to be little more than the length of the aircraft he was flying, the trees all around rising to 200 feet or more above the ground. But he controlled it well, slowly allowing it to descend over the centre of the clearing, keeping the rotor well clear of swaying branches which could damage its blades. He held it ten feet above the ground on a cushion of air, downdraft flattening the undergrowth into a huge bowl. He then allowed it to continue its slow, downward path until, gently, the wheels kissed the ground.

Moreton feels himself lifted and laid carefully in a basket-type stretcher inside the helicopter.[3] Through the green Perspex roof he watches the rotors turning rapidly above him. Then, on the application of power, they turn faster and faster until, as if magically, the helicopter rises. A momentary hover on the ground cushion – pilot assessing the situation – before it climbs above the tree-tops, the nose lowers, then helicopter and its casualty fly off towards base. In a little over an hour Moreton is lying in hospital, awaiting an operation. His life has been saved by this magical beast.

More than 4,700 personnel were rescued from the Malayan jungle in this way by NAS and RAF helicopters. Without such life-saving intervention, many of them would probably have died.

It soon became clear that flying the Dragonfly, adjusting its centre of gravity and supervising the loading of a casualty was really a two-man job. When picking up a casualty, the pilot had so much to do that one of the soldiers usually lent a hand by holding the cyclic pitch and throttle control while the aircraft was standing on the ground.

Initially another pilot was carried in the back to do what he could to ease the load – even though there was only one set of controls – and at the same time familiarise himself with the terrain. Of greater importance perhaps was the need for refuelling, coupled with the need to diagnose and rectify each fault as it developed. For all these tasks, a qualified aircraft technician was needed, and the second pilot was initially replaced by a senior NCO aircraft fitter. Later, as experience was gained, these were superseded by a volunteer, corporal airframe or engine fitter to act as another pair of eyes and hands for the pilot, and also to carry out running repairs. Despite the

IMPROVEMENT AND ADVANCEMENTS

initial lack of financial incentive, there were plenty of volunteers. These junior NCOs were in effect the RAF's first helicopter crewmen, but it was to be late 1965 before the job became officially recognised as an aircrew category, backed up by rank, and a brevet.

*

When an Army patrol asked for a pickup, an Auster spotter aircraft usually flew out to locate their position and find a suitable landing site for the Dragonfly. If none was available, explosives and power saws would be dropped for troops to prepare one, while the Dragonfly moved to a forward landing ground and awaited call-up.

By the end of 1950 the Dragonfly had lifted twenty casualties. It soon became common practice for the crewman to spray the surrounding jungle with Sten gun fire to keep down the heads of any lurking bandits before the aircraft landed.

In 1951 terrorists who had ambushed an Army vehicle were pursued and successfully engaged by a Dragonfly carrying a soldier with a Bren gun. Thereafter it became common practice to arm the Dragonfly with movable Bren guns when the occasion demanded. The helicopter gunship had arrived, well over a decade before the Americans used it in Vietnam.

Not too sure on the dates of the above reports, but the first such written report in the Squadron F540, or ORB (Operational Record Book), offers the following: *April 1952, WF311 Flight Lieutenant Lee.... strafed a bandit's clearing using a bren gun. The first reported instance of the operational use of an 'armed' helicopter by British forces.*

The trouble with written records is that you can't ask them questions, and the ORBs are completed by a designated officer, some more meticulous than others as to what is, or is not, reported.

An example of the importance of the helicopter was demonstrated in 1952 when a complete patrol of seventeen men of the Cameroonian Highlanders, plus a captured terrorist, were lifted from a small jungle clearing by a single Dragonfly making multiple sorties. The soldiers, all exhausted and sick after twenty-nine days in jungle swamp, would have been a further thirteen or so days from help by foot and conventional ground transport.

*

On 1 February 1953 the Casualty Evacuation Flight, then based at Sembawang naval airfield, Singapore, was expanded to become the RAF's first helicopter squadron: No 194. Up to that time the flight had evacuated

265 casualties – with just one fatal crash – and established a whole range of techniques for using helicopters in jungle warfare. The Dragonfly also helped evacuate aborigines to secure villages where they could be protected from terrorist attacks. These really were pioneering times, both air and ground crews being pushed to their limits.

If ground forces suffered a casualty they would call Army Headquarters to advise of the nature and location of the casualty, either an existing LZ or one constructed by clearing trees and bush where the casualty was resting. An LZ needed to be at least eighty by fifty metres, with surrounding undergrowth cleared to avoid damaging the tail rotor.

Other duties for the helicopters included carrying voice broadcasting equipment (later known as Skyshout), to appeal to terrorists to surrender, and spray gear to destroy their crops. Another important task was lifting captured terrorists out of the jungle and getting them to intelligence experts for interrogation in a matter of minutes compared with the five days it would take on foot. Helicopters also brought dead – sometimes long dead! – bandits out of the jungle for identification.

If an infantry patrol which had to call up a helicopter for a casualty evacuation (casevac) also had a dead terrorist on their hands, they might ask for the aircraft to take the body as well, but weight considerations often prevented this. There were ways of compromising however. A Dragonfly pilot picking up a wounded Gurkha was puzzled to see a sack put in the aircraft with the casualty. After taking off he found it contained a severed head.

In 1953 a squadron (848) of Royal Navy Sikorsky S55 Whirlwinds arrived in Malaya for troop-carrying tasks, and these aircraft were often led to their objective by a Dragonfly, which then hovered in the vicinity with a soldier giving covering Bren gun fire. By the end of 1954 the Dragonfly had completed nearly 6,000 sorties, during which they had evacuated 675 casualties and lifted more than 4,000 passengers and 84,000lbs of freight.

*

It was 1954 when 194 Sqn began to re-equip with the Bristol Sycamore HR14, although the last Dragonflys were not retired until June 1956 – what was left of them, that is! The stylish-looking Sycamore, which was the first British-designed helicopter to go into production, had a better performance and serviceability rate than the Dragonfly. In addition its cabin was bigger, and it handled more positively.

Another great improvement over the Dragonfly was that the Sycamore's centre of gravity could be altered by redistributing a water mix between

IMPROVEMENT AND ADVANCEMENTS

an under-cockpit-floor tank and a tank located in the tail rotor pylon via pipes and an electric pump, rather than by moving weights about the cabin; but like all early helicopters it had manual controls which kept the pilot's hands, feet, and powers of concentration, fully occupied all the time. There were also problems with the Sycamore's wooden rotors swelling in tropical conditions.

The Sycamore was generally fitted with a folding bench seat for three people in the rear, behind the pilot plus one other in the front. Alternatively, two stretchers could be carried across the cabin by replacing the doors with a Perspex blister, or just leaving the door off altogether. Like the Dragonfly, the Sycamore was generally tasked with casualty evacuation. It also undertook a variety of other tasks, including VIP transport – it had after all been designed with the role of aerial taxi, or executive transport in mind – and 'sky-shouting' tape-recorded messages to terrorists. Because of the problems with the larger Whirlwind helicopter, the Sycamore often had to be pressed into use for cargo-carrying tasks too. The Sycamore had never been intended for this work, having been designed as a civil-executive type machine, and air taxi, so, on occasion, specific tasks had to be allocated to squadron's lightest pilot so as to allow the largest possible payload to be carried.

*

Great things were expected of the Westland Whirlwind HAR4s of No 155 Squadron, formed at Kuala Lumpur for troop-carrying tasks on 1 September 1954. The Whirlwind was a licence-built version of the Sikorsky S55, a classic design with the engine in the aircraft's nose mounted backwards at a 45 degree angle, so as to drive the rotor via an angled shaft and mechanical clutch.

Refuelling was carried out from sealed four-gallon flimsies, positioned in advance at the site. A quick stab to the can's seal – using the commando-style knife which was part of the crewman's kit issue – and a flick of the wrist saw the seal removed; then another quick stab in the opposite corner of the can, for air release, heft it up, and pour. We used a standard, chamois-lined funnel, modified so it clipped onto the upper of the two spring-loaded flap-covered steps which allowed access to the cockpit on the starboard (pilot's) side. The fuel filler was located below and to the side of this step. The empty cans were then – exercising extreme care – thrown aside, clear of the rotor disc (which was still turning), but we would make sure they were well clear, preferably covered over, before giving the pilot the OK for take-

THE FIRST HELICOPTER BOYS

Above: 155 Squadron depart on ops – look out for that pioneer!

Left: Gurkhas lend a hand refuelling a Whirlwind.

IMPROVEMENT AND ADVANCEMENTS

off, otherwise there was the possibility of them being blown out and up, and then drawn down into the disc and damaging the blades.

The Whirlwind cockpit, with side-by-side seating, was above and behind the engine and directly beneath the rotor, while the cabin was below and close to the ground, giving easy access through the large sliding door.

The engine's position basically resolved the centre-of-gravity problems experienced with the Dragonfly by placing most of the load directly beneath the rotor head. It also gave good accessibility for servicing, making life easier for ground crews.

The Whirlwind was a large aircraft, the pilot being seated 7 to 8 feet above the ground. This therefore was a height the crewmen needed to negotiate when boarding with the rotor turning. To do it correctly took a set sequence: left foot on the fixed, protruding step, 2-3 ft off the ground, and by use of fixed handgrips, pull yourself up; there were then two spring-loaded kick-flap steps (which closed after use) for right and left feet, and you would now have your right foot neatly poised ready to step over the sill and into the cockpit, always bearing in mind that the rotor was turning only a foot or so above your head, so there was an urgent need to duck as you entered via the sliding side window! – then the left foot, and you were in. Except during heavy rain, these side windows usually remained open during flight.

Servicing in the field.

THE FIRST HELICOPTER BOYS

Above: Gearbox change in the field.

Left: Pete Dace climbing aboard. Note clearance to rotor; if it was turning the next phase was, head down and fold yourself up!

IMPROVEMENT AND ADVANCEMENTS

Behind the seat, at shoulder level, was a small alcove, handy for Sten gun stowage. At the rear of this alcove was the hydraulic tank filler: difficult to reach if the tank needed topping up in flight, i.e. in the case of a hydraulic leak, as crewman Al Payne once found out!

The Whirlwind's cabin measured 10ft long by 5ft wide by 6ft high, and a winch could be mounted above the door.

A squadron of Royal Navy Sikorsky S55s, supplied by America under the Mutual Aid Defence Pact (Lend Lease) for use in the anti-submarine role, had proved highly successful in troop-carrying work in Malaya, the US Marines having pioneered the use of the S55 as an assault transport in Korea. There was pressure to replace these naval S55s in Malaya because they were dependent on spares supplied from America (paid for in US dollars), and the Americans were making political noises about equipment supplied for use with the NATO alliance being diverted to fight a colonial – albeit anti-Communist – war.

Unfortunately the Westland-built Whirlwind in its tropicalized Mk 4 form was considerably heavier than the US built version because of various British modifications, such as self-sealing fuel tanks and the use of thicker skinning. There were also major faults with the redesigned fuel system, which often prevented use of the last forty gallons carried in the rear tanks.

To cope with Malayan conditions, Whirlwinds often had to be flown continuously at full power, and the overworked Pratt & Whitney Wasp engines developed endless faults, including power deficiencies, magneto faults, oil starvation, and starter trouble. It was said the engines were overhauled Harvard units anyway (probably to do with that US dollar shortage). There was also an acute shortage of spares, and the rotor blades deteriorated in the negative climatic conditions. Theoretically the Whirlwind should have been able to carry eight troops, but in Malayan conditions this was often reduced to one. When the Whirlwind performed more or less as intended however, it was invaluable: it made a significant contribution to the successful conclusion of the Malayan Campaign.

The main tasks of the Whirlwind were to supply the jungle forts, take small parties of troops to forward areas, and fly sick and wounded people to hospital. The usual tactic was to use them to deploy troops to where they could attack terrorist gangs located by jungle patrols or air reconnaissance, and to cut off retreating bandits by dropping patrols astride the paths behind them.

The Whirlwind carried a variety of loads, including tracker dogs, spare parts for tractors and bulldozers, used to construct runways at the jungle forts), even geese for use as watchdogs at these forts, and cats, to ward off rats.

THE FIRST HELICOPTER BOYS

Tractor in helicopter sized parts.

The aircraft also carried out crop-spraying sorties to destroy paddy and tapioca cultivations which the terrorists hid in deep jungle. No. 848 Sqn NAS also pioneered and developed techniques for dropping SAS parachutists over the jungle. The Whirlwinds were capable of reaching any point in Malaya from their base at Kuala Lumpur by using fuel pre-positioned by air drop from Valetta transports. For maintenance in remote locations, each aircraft usually carried a junior NCO airframe or engine fitter with servicing kit and spares.

Despite its shortcomings, the Whirlwind did much to convince many influential military men of the potential of troop-carrying helicopters – even if the RAF was at the time more interested in spending its share of the defence budget on V-bombers and supersonic fighters.

*

The Dragonfly, Sycamore and Whirlwind pilots who pioneered the RAF's support helicopter expertise during the twelve-year war against the terrorists displayed airmanship of the highest order. With temperatures up to 100°F and 100 per cent humidity, high ranges of hills, rain forests with trees growing above 200 feet, and frequent thunderstorms causing excessive turbulence, Malaya was far from being ideal helicopter country.

Taking off and landing vertically in tiny clearings surrounded by high trees could produce an unpleasant aerodynamic phenomenon known as a vortex ring, which increased the rate of descent no matter how much power was applied.

IMPROVEMENT AND ADVANCEMENTS

155 Sqn at work – Westland photo.

Even though we were engaged in a war zone we rarely saw it as such. We were reminded of it only by the fact that when flying we were armed, albeit lightly. The enemy had no anti-aircraft weapons, and rifle fire was only a worry when flying low. No, any danger to us came mainly from our own machines, for these were the very early days of helicopter warfare, and it was a learning period for both air and ground crews.

Between 1954 and 1958, 194 Squadron flew 34,000 Sycamore sorties, and 155 Squadron flew 45,000 Whirlwind sorties. By 1958 the security forces had been so successful the terrorists were now contained in a small area of the country, the state of emergency running down. Consequently the Sycamores of 194 Sqn were mainly engaged in a flying doctor service around the Malayan villages and visiting isolated police posts.

After four years of operations the squadron was having so many serviceability problems with its Sycamores that often only one or two were available for use each day. After two fatal crashes within three months in which all perished – XJ319 and XF267 – caused by wooden blade disintegration, the Sycamores were grounded in April 1959, and remained so for nearly a year until successful modifications by Farnborough had been made to the rotors (the substitution of UHU as opposed to Araldite was the tongue-in-cheek suggestion of one waggish pilot!)

*

THE FIRST HELICOPTER BOYS

In August 1959, 194 and 155 Squadrons merged to form 110 Squadron, based at RAAF Butterworth, north Malaya. Operating at first with Whirlwinds only, then with Sycamores when they were again cleared for service, 110 Squadron flew 8,000 operational sorties before the Malayan Emergency officially ended on 31 July 1960.

In the final stages of the campaign, operations were concentrated in a small area near the Thai border, 110 Sqn being mainly engaged on the resupply of forward positions, flying fresh troops in, and lifting the sick and wounded out.

During ten years of operations in Malaya, all types of RAF helicopter lifted 110,000 troops, 19,000 other passengers and 25,000,000 lbs of cargo. Just over a year after the end of the emergency, the RAF received new turbine-powered helicopters (the Whirlwind Mk10) better able to cope with Malayan conditions. They were to be used with good effect in a new jungle war against Indonesian infiltrators in Malaysia – as Malaya had now become – and Borneo.

The Malaysian government were later to issue a medal (Pingat Jasa Malaysia, or Malaysian Service Medal) for service during the Emergency, but only for those serving after Malaya became Malaysia, post-independence, 31 August 1957. This unfairly precluded those who had served in the early years, from 1948, during which the majority had fought and died!

110 Squadron Sycamores at RAAF Butterworth North Malaya.

IMPROVEMENT AND ADVANCEMENTS

110 Squadron aircraft on ops, now in Rescue yellow; troops out, fuel in.

Chapter 4

Air Transport and Psychological Warfare

Crop Spraying Operations

Most tasks performed by helicopters during the Malayan campaign were in the transport role: troop-carrying, passengers, casualties, freight, reconnaissance and liaison flights, and a rare instance of an armed helicopter being used as a gunship. But there was one unique aspect of the offensive in which they did participate, introduced after the terrorists withdrew into deep jungle areas from late 1952 onwards. This was the spraying of terrorist cultivation plots with toxic liquid. Disruption of the terrorists' established methods of food supply ensured that crop production became the most important factor to affect their ability to survive. They were thus compelled to deploy numbers of their forces to remote jungle areas to produce the food necessary for their survival. These cultivations were small and screened by jungle, but visible from the air. Aborigines, frequently pressed into service as additional labour on these plots, also provided an intelligence screen, making it almost impossible to approach on foot undetected. Ground troops were occasionally employed to destroy cultivations discovered in secondary jungle during the course of routine operations, but it was quickly realized this was an uneconomic use of manpower, and that aerial attack offered the best means of destroying these plots. With high explosive and fire bombs proving ineffective in this role, a scheme for the use of chemical sprays was proposed.

Sodium arsenite was used with effect, but the danger this afforded to the lives of the indigenous population made it politically unacceptable. ICI suggested Fernoxone, but the toxic spray that eventually proved most effective was a mixture of trioxene and diesolene. This formed a non-poisonous herbicide that killed all types of vegetation and rendered the ground unusable for a period.

Search and location of cultivations was carried out by 656 Squadron Austers, an increasing commitment for these aircraft once the terrorist cultivation programme began in 1952.

Once a number of cultivations had been located, a spraying operation was mounted, using both light and medium helicopters. The first of these was Operation Cyclone 1, on 31 August 1953 in the Kluang and Labis area of Johore. Many cultivations fairly close together had been located in the Mar Okil Forest Reserve. Marked by Austers, they were strafed by DH Hornets of 33 Squadron to eliminate any possible ground resistance. Two 848 Squadron S55s, and an S51 helicopter were then flown into the area and, operating in pairs for safety, managed to deal with twenty plots on the first day. As remaining cultivations were more scattered, the daily achievement was reduced. But with the two S55s spraying for a day and a half, and the S51 a further two days, some thirty cultivations had been dealt with, plus one terrorist killed during associated ground operations. A lesson learnt from the operation was that Auster reconnaissance was an essential part of the crop spraying force, it being difficult to spot cultivations from a helicopter once it had descended to operational height for the task in hand.

Operation Cyclone 2 was carried out shortly after the first, and by the end of 1953, eighty-eight cultivations had been destroyed from the air by S51 and S55 helicopters.

A total of five crop spraying operations had been carried out by February 1954 before a temporary reduction in available helicopters brought operations to an end for some months. They recommenced before the end of 1954, then lack of sufficient aircraft both for spraying and reconnaissance brought operations to a close for the remainder of the campaign.

Crop spraying operations helped render terrorist camps in deep jungle untenable, effectively forcing their inhabitants to reconnect with the civil population to obtain essential supplies, thus increasing the security forces' chances of contacting them. However, even more effective than aerial spraying of cultivation plots in persuading the terrorists to leave their jungle hideouts were the arts of psychological warfare, which provided a further example of the employment of the air transport support forces, both medium and short range aircraft, in a quasi-offensive role.

*

Leaflet Drops and Loudhailing Operations

At the start of the Emergency the technique of loudhailing from the air had not been developed, thus the role of the Air Force in psychological warfare was limited to the dropping of leaflets. These were despatched from supply-drop aircraft and occasionally by bombers at the conclusion to an air strike. As on supply drops, 55 Air Despatch Company, RASC, provided personnel on leaflet dropping sorties.

With loads of up to 800,000 leaflets, it was found that a good distribution was achieved over an area 1,000 yards square by despatching 5,000 leaflets at a time at the end of a static line. If accurate drops of a limited quantity into small pinpoint targets were required, a 656 Squadron Auster was employed.

The technique of broadcasting recorded messages from aircraft was not introduced into the campaign until October 1952. General Templer, Director of Operations, borrowed a US Army Dakota for experimental purposes. As a result, two Valettas were fitted with broadcast equipment, beginning operations in 1953. But they were too noisy, and Valettas were replaced by Dakotas in December 1953. The Dakota, although obsolete in the RAF, was more suited to loudhailing than the Valetta, engine noise not being as intrusive. A lower cruising speed also enabled broadcast time on each sortie to be increased.

In January 1954 an Auster was equipped for loudhailing missions over small targets on the fringes of the jungle, or adjacent to roads, where accuracy was important, and the use of Dakota or Valetta was uneconomical. In the following month a further loudhailing Auster was added to C Flight of 267 Squadron, but when the remaining Valetta crashed on the slopes of Mount Ophir, north-west of Johore, in February 1954, the flight was left with just one Dakota and two Austers. In March 1954 a second Dakota was acquired, and with the arrival of a third Dakota in January 1955, 267 Squadron Voice (or Sky-shout) Flight attained its maximum complement. This flight usually operated from Kuala Lumpur, but in January 1959, 267 Squadron, now renumbered 209, was detached to Bayan Lepas, Penang, to carry out loudhailing in support of ground force operations in Northern Perak and Kedah. The cessation of anti-terrorist operations in Johore at the end of 1958 and the concentration of ground force activity in the mountainous regions of Northern Malaya resulted in the disestablishment of the Auster element, the loudhailing equipment carried by these aircraft rendering them suitable for broadcasting operations only over relatively flat terrain at low altitudes. In addition, for reasons of safety, they could not venture too far from lines of communication. The Voice Flight continued to operate from Penang until the end of the Emergency, its two remaining Dakotas transferring from 209 to 52 Squadron in November 1959.

Chapter 5

Tales from the Horse's Mouth
Pilots

Master Pilot McMasters, 155 squadron. In flight photo taken by Al Payne.

THE FIRST HELICOPTER BOYS

Squadron Leader (Cy) Cyril R. Turner AFC

Cy Turner at one of our reunions.

On completion of the RAF Staff College course at the beginning of 1955 I was hoping for a posting to Canberras. Instead I was told that I was to take over 194 Squadron at Kuala Lumpur, Malaya, flying helicopters.

I spent two and a half months on the helicopter conversion course at South Cerney flying the Westland Dragonfly, and in spite of my earlier reaction, this really did prove to be the beginning of a very happy relationship.

The Air Ministry had arranged for me to take my family with me, but on arrival I was ordered to report to the AOC. I was torn off a strip for bringing my family since, although the trouble in Malaya had been labelled an Emergency, for convenience of the business community, it was in fact a full blooded war against a ruthless and determined enemy – the Communist Terrorists (CTs).

Four operational squadrons were based at Kuala Lumpur. One was equipped with the Scottish Aviation Pioneer STOL Aircraft, both the single and twin engined version, plus one Dakota 'Voice Aircraft' which had a loud hailer for broadcasting propaganda messages over areas where the CTs were known to be hiding. The second squadron was the Royal Navy's 848, equipped with American Sikorsky S55 helicopters, mainly for ground troop deployment. Thirdly, RAF 155 Squadron had Westland Whirlwinds (a Westland version of the S55 built under licence), also operating in a troop-lift role.

My Squadron, RAF, 194, was equipped with Bristol Sycamore and Westland Dragonfly helicopters. The latter were being phased out, to be replaced by the Sycamore. When I took over, there were ten Sycamores and four Dragonflys on

TALES FROM THE HORSE'S MOUTH – PILOTS

strength. Most of the airmen were National Service, and I have nothing but praise for their first class attitude and reaction to the pressures put upon them.

The squadron's operational directive covered: tactical movement of troops, including reinforcement of outposts; tactical reconnaissance; casualty evacuation; search and rescue.

Although we were involved in all these roles, casevac was the squadron's primary activity. We were however called upon more and more frequently to carry troops and cargo. The Sycamore was never designed for such a role, since at most it was only possible to carry two fully-equipped troops compared to the eight an RN Whirlwind could take. This presented problems when concentrated deployment of troops was necessary to carry out surprise operations.

On one occasion it was necessary to deploy 100 fully equipped men as a matter of urgency. Unfortunately all the Whirlwinds had been grounded that day and I was called on to undertake the task. My own serviceability was low and I had to pressurise my ground staff to produce as many serviceable aircraft as possible within twenty-four hours. They worked through the night, and around dawn I was able to take five Sycamores on the operation, leaving one for casevac standby.

The SAS were assembled at the advanced landing zone (LZ) and we shuttled 100 fully equipped men into and out of the deep jungle where they went successfully into action against the CTs. This action was completed in less than three-and-a-half hours flying time: a record I feel for helicopters not designed for troop-carrying.

Because of the need for swift casualty evacuation, one aircraft and pilot was always standing by on immediate readiness from dawn to dusk and at weekends. The service was important to troops on the ground for two reasons: it saved them from having to escort casualties down a long and possibly difficult track out of the jungle, after which they would lose contact with the enemy in what might have been a tactically advantageous operation; secondly, and of immense importance, a high level of morale was maintained because *troops knew that if they had the misfortune to become a casualty they would always be helicoptered out of the jungle and get to hospital in a relatively short time. This was illustrated when a patrol of the Malayan Regiment was ambushed and suffered eight casualties. A helicopter happened to be in the area and the pilot made four sorties to lift out the casualties in around thirty-five minutes.*

One of the not-so-pleasant tasks was the uplift of bodies of dead CTs, required for intelligence purposes – particularly when they had been dead for a few days. This was less gruesome than the Paras' macabre practice of decapitation, and flying out the heads only!

A considerable burden was placed on the pilots. Weight limitations and the need for maximum fuel loads made carrying a navigator impossible. Navigation over the jungle to find a hastily cut clearing was rather like flying over the sea, since primary jungle forms a canopy of unbroken green foliage with no specific landmarks to check position. Pilots had to maintain visual contact flight, and after a relatively short time they got to know the operational area well. In addition, because of the swift deterioration in weather conditions, pilots had to develop the ability to identify symptoms, particularly when flying among so-called hills of up to 6,000 ft. It would be all too easy to get trapped in a valley with the sudden blocking of both ends by swiftly-lowering clouds full of destructive turbulence and very heavy rain. This was often accompanied by an unpleasant thunderstorm.

The role of the crewman was all-important. Operations were often long, and frequent refuelling necessary. The stay in the operational area might last several days, and the crewman would be required to carry out servicing in all trades, often with no support facilities. For instance, the rotor-head on the S55 had thirty-one grease nipples, all of which required attention every five hours flight time, without fail. He also provided invaluable guidance in negotiating the descent into, and climb out of, clearings, and in helping ground troops to load casualties on stretchers.

Both pilot and crewman were armed and carried survival packs. These were invaluable, as was proved when the engine

TALES FROM THE HORSE'S MOUTH – PILOTS

of my Dragonfly lost power over primary jungle and I crashed. Although injured, I eventually escaped out of the jungle, but had to spend two months in hospital.

The Bristol Sycamore HR14 was better adapted for the casevac and troop lift roles, although it had not been designed for these. The centre of gravity could be adjusted by an electrical pump – such a boon when hovering in a clearing taking on a casualty. In the Dragonfly the pilot had physically to lift and place weights on a post above the flight instrument panel. This was hit-and-miss, and a difficult manoeuvre when hovering in a clearing.

While the Dragonfly was narrow, the Sycamore was wide – easily facilitating the accommodation of a stretcher or two fully equipped soldiers. In addition, the crewman could sit next to the pilot as a lookout, instead of sitting behind him as in a Dragonfly. However the low sweep of the rotor blades and unguarded tail rotor was always a matter of concern when passengers were carried, or when there were uncleared tree stumps in a tight jungle clearing.

There were three types of landing zone: Permanent bases which ground troops established, and from which they carried out offensive patrols. They would normally prepare a helicopter landing pad, and some of these left much to be desired. The foundation was prepared on a slight rise with a strip bamboo mat battened down on it. This mat was not serviced and in time the bamboos became non-resilient and cracked easily. With the onset of the rains the foundation became undermined, making landing quite hazardous. In one case the wheel of a Sycamore jammed in the mat and it rolled over when the pilot tried to lift off. Where practicable I preferred to hover rather than set the helicopter down.

The second type of LZ was the fort. Eleven forts, used as bases for offensive operations in deep jungle, were manned mainly by the Malay Police Field Force. They offered support and protection for the locals. Most set up a shop, and some had a school. All had helicopter landing pads.

The third type of LZ was the unprepared (emergency) clearing. An inexperienced unit would have little idea of the number of trees to chop down to enable a helicopter to

Dragonfly at Kumin. Flight Lieutenant Pinner's crash after engine failure.

carry out a controlled approach into a 'hole in the jungle'. They might leave huge stumps at the base of the trees felled, making it impossible to put the helicopter down. They might not have cleared the area of fallen branches, undergrowth etc, which would tend to dissipate the ground cushion so essential to effect a clean lift-off. On a number of occasions pilots had to turn down a clearing and pass on instructions through their base as to what was needed.

Apart from my accident (see page 64), and despite all the problems, this was an enjoyable and rewarding tour of duty.

Flight Lieutenant Bill Stevens

Cy (Squadron Leader Cyril Turner, the incoming CO) came down to the squadron on Saturday morning, having just arrived the previous day. I was about to carry out an air test on a Sycamore and he asked if he could come along.

We took off from the dispersal and moved over to the grass strip alongside the runway. The test schedule called for a full power vertical, we made about 60ft when the clutch failed –

the engine noise was unbelievable – but we were soon back at our take-off point without any damage, apart from a wrecked engine.

'Does this often happen?' asked Cy.

Well it did when the Wing Co Flying (Wing Commander Williams) had a similar failure as he was crossing the Pahang River on the approach to an LZ – a dunking, but fortunately no damage to the pilot or crewman.

That must have stuck in his mind, for years later, when ruminating by letter, he touched upon it again; 'Names crop up and one's memory is stirred to recall some interesting times. One cannot forget the very fine spirit which existed within the squadrons, 194 and 110 in my case, and the great support given by the crewmen. They must have thought they were pushing their luck on some sorties, eg Wing Commander Williams ditching in the Pahang River following clutch failure while making an approach to an LZ. One of the early Sycamore incidents.

Flight Lieutenant Jim McCorkle

I had the good fortune to be Training Officer on three squadrons of helicopters in Malaya, starting in 1957 with 194 Squadron. Then I was posted to CFS staff, South Cerney. Next posting was 110 Sqn, Butterworth. Then came CFS staff, Ternhill, where I was an examining officer, and a flight commander. When 103 Sqn reformed with the Whirlwind Mk.10, I was posted back to Singapore, based at Seletar. During my tour there, I was promoted to a newly formed position known as Wing VTOL Leader. My task was to fly with every helicopter instructor to standardise the training methods, and to fly with every chopper pilot in the Far East theatre to award Transport Command ratings. I also had to teach them night and instrument flying. Instrument rating checks were carried out according to experience. This included flying with army pilots based at Kluang, flying the Scout – small turbine-engined army jobs. This kept me rather busy. I also went on operations in Sabah, Borneo, and Labuan, Malaysia. I believe this job gave me the highest flight time of any helicopter pilot in the Far East; I even had to check out the lads in Hong Kong. I flew almost 2,000 helicopter hours in the Far East, and was informed I was to be promoted to squadron leader. I was posted to Air Ministry, London – a desk job – so I resigned my commission, and had that turned down twice before they finally gave in. I returned to UK then emigrated in April 1965 to a job in Canada, flying commercial helicopters. Most work was oil industry related: offshore Canada, India (Bombay), Singapore, and Indonesia. I ceased flying commercially at age 72, because the company could not, or would not, pay the very high insurance rate that came with my age bracket. Total hours, on a great number of different choppers, was a little under 15,000. It was a great life, and I enjoyed meeting every one of the men I flew with.

Flight Lieutenant Brian 'Jacko' Jacques

According to my log book, on 14 November 1952 I was detailed to go and look for a Vampire pilot who had parachuted into the Jungle near Mawai, South Johore. I set off from Changi in VZ 960 (fabric rotor blades and no servo control on the ex-RN Mk 1) with Pilot Officer Floyd, another Vampire pilot, as observer. We searched the area and eventually spotted a parachute in the tree tops. No sign of the pilot. As we were flying at tree-top height it had been arranged that a Valetta flying above us would be our radio link to HQ. I tried to call the Valetta to request them to relay a message, but although we could see it flying over us, we received no reply. To try and attract the Valetta's attention I asked my passenger to fire a Verey flare. This he did, and to my horror, the helicopter immediately developed a violent 'one per'. With difficulty I managed to maintain control and made a forced landing at Mawai, several miles away. On inspecting the rotor I saw a gaping hole in the fabric of one blade. When I questioned Pilot Officer Floyd he admitted that, being a fixed wing pilot, he had fired the Verey upwards. I've heard of shooting oneself in the foot, but never your rotor blades! However, a rescue helicopter was despatched from base, and Sergeant Moss patched the blade

TALES FROM THE HORSE'S MOUTH – PILOTS

with fabric and dope. We then flew back to Changi with next to no vibration. The missing Vampire pilot walked out of the jungle several days later. Pilot Officer Floyd was returned to base in the rescue helicopter – never to be heard of again!

Next – and I don't think Squadron Leader 'Jock' Henderson would have minded me telling this story – a classic example of 'Do as I say':

When he arrived at Kuala Lumpur, having just come out from UK to take over 194 Sqn, he got all the pilots together for a pep talk. He particularly stressed that some Casevac Flight pilots were in the habit of going into clearings that were less than fifty yards in diameter, and that this was to cease.

A few days later 'Johnny' Bell-Walker, Squadron Engineering Officer, came into the squadron office to report that somebody had damaged the rotor tips of one of the helicopters – obviously when going into a clearing that was too small. Jock was furious and immediately sent for the F700 – only to find he was the last person to fly the aircraft!

One day, flying from Kuantan to KL with a brigadier somewhere near Temerloh, he leaned over my shoulder and said, 'Land by that track down there.' Thinking this was of some military importance, I duly obeyed. Telling me to wait a minute, the brigadier got out, walked across to a pineapple field, cut one off and climbed back on board. 'OK,' he said, 'Carry on.' Having got safely airborne again we continued our flight, the brigadier regularly feeding me chunks of fresh pineapple. You couldn't do that with a fixed wing aircraft!

It was the Saturday of Whitsun, 1952. I was on detachment at Kuantan, supporting the 1st/10th Gurkhas, and had been sent to the airfield – literally no more than a field – to pick up a bod from the incoming 'civvy' Beaver and take him back to the Gurkha camp. While waiting for the Beaver, which was late, I met the local police commander who introduced me to the chief accountant from the local bank as 'an excellent fellow who is always most obliging when one wanted a loan or overdraft' and who was waiting for the Beaver to take him on to Kota Bahru for the Whitsun holiday. The thought struck me that for such a short holiday he seemed to have a considerable amount of baggage. However, eventually the Beaver arrived and the police officer and I helped him with it while he boarded the aircraft, then met our respective passengers and we went our separate ways.

On Tuesday, the holiday over, the bank manager arrived at his bank to find it had been completely cleaned out of cash. It was now obvious what had been in the chief accountant's luggage. Frantic messages were sent to Kota Bahru but the bird had flown – over the border and into Siam. History does not record what happened to the police officer, but I earned many a pint by telling that story.

Sergeant Joe Ward

People do all things for a crust, some are farmers, some are fishermen, some are fliers – I became a flyer. I had my first command on 1 May 1943, my last on 30 April 1983.

Rattle your abacus and it works out I was a pilot for forty years. I started on the ubiquitous Tiger Moth, followed by Stearman, Vultee Valiant, Harvard, Oxford, Anson, Catalina, Mosquito, Meteor and finally the Canberra PR3. I had several incidents in the air but got them all back safely. I then forgot all the above and switched to helicopters. I have flown ten different types of helicopter and crashed four times. When a helicopter hits the ground out of control it tends to break into a lot of small pieces – that is not the time to be there. One learns to become 'fleet of foot', and few could have beaten me over the first fifty yards getting away from a prang.

Sergeant Joe Ward

TALES FROM THE HORSE'S MOUTH – PILOTS

In 1955 I was posted to 194 Sqn, and converted to the Sycamore. A very enjoyable tour, though I spent most of my time up at Ipoh, apart from a month in Hong Kong on riot control. Tourex in December 1957, I had flown 820 hours, carried out 250 ops and lifted 121 casualties. To me it was just a job. OK, hairy at times, but still a job. However, people in high places thought otherwise. I was gazetted in August and the following year received a letter stating I had to front up at Buckingham Palace where Her Majesty the Queen was graciously pleased to award me the DFM.

A Nice, Quiet Cup of Tea

I carried many senior officers, both army and air force, during my tour with 194 but my favourite was Brigadier Alexander: a fine officer and a perfect gentleman. I took him to high-powered meetings, into holes in the jungle, to hospitals where he visited the wounded and to the Cameron Highlands for strawberries and cream. Usually he was on his own but sometimes Colonel Lee of the SAS accompanied him.

Once, he had the chopper booked for the day – with an early start. As he arrived I gave him a smart salute and held the door open as he climbed in. This time there were just the two of us, and as we set course for the first location I asked him about the day's programme. 'We've a fair bit to do,' he said, 'Maybe we won't get it all finished.' It looked like being another long day.

As we made our first landing in the grass at the edge of the jungle, a soldier suddenly appeared from amongst the trees and threw up a salute as the brigadier stepped out of the chopper. Then, with a 'Would you follow me, sir,' he was off. We scampered after him and eventually came to a clearing where about half a dozen men were bivouacked. Tea was brewing and the brigadier and I were each given a large metal cup – the container that fits under a water bottle – full of marvellously hot, steaming tea; a good pint of it and very welcome after our flight. I enjoyed a quiet fag while the brigadier chatted to the lads.

After about ten minutes we were on our way again; this time only a few more miles along the fringe of the jungle. After we had landed we went through the same routine of salute, tea, chat, fag and off again. On our third landing the brigadier says, 'The boys are so good to us, did you know that each of them puts a pinch of his tea ration into the pot for us? It would be very bad manners to refuse, wouldn't it – create quite the wrong impression, eh?' What could I do but agree with him? Three landings, three pints of tea, no worries so far – but how many more to go?

Number four landing and another pint, followed by landing number five. The brigadier was the first to weaken; after returning the welcoming salute he asked where he could relieve himself. No such problems for me though. No sooner had the engine died than with a well-practised movement, the door was open, my zip down and the starboard wheel got the lot. As they say, us helicopter pilots are not just pretty faces, you know. But my relief was short-lived; we were only just beginning.

Landing number six followed, along with its accompanying pint; the same for number seven. By landing number eight my kidneys had gone into overdrive and the starboard wheel was positively glistening. Landings nine, ten and eleven and the brigadier was still returning the salute before asking where he could...

We didn't bother with lunch – there just wasn't any room left after eleven pints of hot, steaming tea. On the way to our twelfth visit the brigadier asked, 'How long to the next landing?' The pressure was building remorselessly and the kidneys had moved into hyperdrive. After leaving site number twelve the brigadier said, 'There's one more to go, do you reckon we can make it?' Although I said Yes, we nearly didn't. By the time we came into land the brigadier had already got his zipper down. This was no time for niceties. As I threw the helicopter at the ground the passenger door was immediately flung open. As he jumped out the brigadier aimed at the port wheel with his left hand and returned the waiting soldier's salute with his right. The soldier's face was a picture. His eyes flashed from the brigadier's epaulettes, as if to confirm that it was a brigadier that he was saluting – though there was nothing in regulations to deal with a situation like this – and then down to

TALES FROM THE HORSE'S MOUTH – PILOTS

the brigadier's left hand. What he saw raised a smile; despite all that brass, deep down the brigadier was more or less the same as the rest of us.

It was an effort, but we just had to down that thirteenth pint before finally heading for home – chortling all the way as we recalled the dangers of dropping in for just a quiet cup of tea.

Squadron Leader Cyril R Turner AFC

A MATTER OF SURVIVAL

This is an account of how the crew and casevac survived after a crash in the jungle of central Malaya on 3 March 1956 when the engine of their helicopter cut soon after an SAS casualty had been uplifted from a jungle clearing. The characters in this epic affair were:

Dragonfly Helicopter XB255
Pilot: Squadron Leader Cyril R. Turner AFC, Officer Commanding 194 Squadron
Crewman: Corporal Pat Lumb, 194 Squadron
Casualty: Trooper Fred Watkins, Special Air Service.

Squadron Leader Turner's crash site. Note the tree through the cockpit area.

THE FIRST HELICOPTER BOYS

Wing Commander Williams at Turner's crash site.

This is the pilot's story:

As CO of 194 Squadron RAF, this eventful day, 3 March 1956, started, as my routine day usually did: a briefing of the squadron pilots, check on aircraft serviceability, servicing and other relevant problems, then a reluctant withdrawal to my office to survey an ever mounting 'in-tray', and the very empty 'Laugh and tear up' tray.

I was shaken out of my reverie when the phone rang. It requested my immediate presence at Flying Wing Operations Room. Here I was advised that a Valetta supply-drop transport aircraft was feared to have crashed in the mountainous area of central Malaya and that I was to fly up forthwith with an allocation of search aircraft to take charge of and coordinate the search.

Having organized the aircraft etc, I shot up to my married quarter to collect my jungle survival gear and pack an overnight bag, telling my wife if I did not get back that evening, when we were due to attend a dinner party, she was to go on without me.

TALES FROM THE HORSE'S MOUTH – PILOTS

I took off in Westland Dragonfly XB255 with crewman Corporal Pat Lumb. We headed for Ipoh, where we had a squadron detachment. From here we then flew on to Fort Brooke, where I established my base and set up the search programme.

Rather quicker than anyone could have anticipated, pilot Flight Sergeant Ted Shuvalski found the aircraft wreckage near the top of a mountain. Ted flew me to the area, and a close, low level inspection confirmed that, as far as was concerned, it was most unlikely anyone could possibly have survived – the wreckage being strewn over a wide area.

It is pertinent at this juncture to divert a little and mention that at a previous and similar crash, two bodies were found some distance from the crash area, an indication they must have survived the initial crash, but had subsequently perished. Later, 22 SAS CO, a major whose name I regret escapes me, had made it clear that if there was a similar crash he and his Doc would definitely parachute in, just in case there was a chance of survivors.

Since the cloud, the weather generally, and the terrain at the crash site were, in my opinion, quite unsuitable for a para-drop, I advised Ipoh to ground any attempt for a para-drop and I would return forthwith to give a full briefing of the situation.

And this is when it all started!

Just as I was about to take off for Ipoh, the fort commander rushed out and said there was a casevac to be picked up from the SAS base known as Paddy's Ladang.

When a casevac call is received, all else is dropped, and an immediate pickup organized. I changed my plan, and with crewman Pat Lumb, took off for Paddy's Ladang, an SAS base set deep in primary jungle. Finding it was one thing, landing something else entirely.

Even holding steady just a couple of feet above the ground it proved difficult to get the casualty aboard due to the restricted area offered by the clearing, but between the SAS and crewman Lumb, they eventually managed to secure the stretcher, Trooper Watkins' feet protruding on a specially fitted fuselage box.

It was obvious we had a very sick lad on our hands. Not a victim of CT (communist terrorist) action, Trooper Watkins was actually suffering from a serious bout of malaria. He was delirious, with a high temperature, so it was a relief to all when I carefully manoeuvred the aircraft, lifted out of the clearing, and set course for Ipoh. The worst was over, or so I thought.

After about five minutes the aircraft began to lose power, so, as a precautionary measure, I headed for a nearby river, the main line of communication in the jungle. Then, at about five hundred feet, the engine cut completely.

Trying not to panic the two lads behind, I instructed them as casually as possible to hold tight. The helicopter was descending in auto-rotation, and I aimed for the brighter green foliage of some bamboo – the softer option. But to my horror a much higher tree loomed up out of nowhere, between the aircraft and the bamboo.

Since we were now descending at a fairly fast rate, I had no option but to 'flare' the aircraft to alight on top of this tree. It literally, and magically, 'skewered' the aircraft, the main trunk breaking through between my legs, tearing through my right arm and hammering my chest and head – after which, needless to say, as far as I was concerned, came oblivion. And that should have been it. But no. No one was killed on impact, and the aircraft didn't catch fire.

The first to regain his faculties was crewman Pat Lumb. His injuries were, in his words, 'a broken arm, bruising and cuts'. I was hanging upside down, still strapped in. They rushed over and got me down, breaking my fall as best they could, carrying me to the river bank. I became aware that the water around my feet was red, and to my horror I saw blood gushing out of my right arm. I flapped hanging flesh back into place and put pressure on the brachial artery. At this point I remember seeing Pat and Fred rummaging around in the wreckage, which was lying almost inverted just off the river bank.

The sequence of events subsequently are not really clear in my memory – the fact that this happened some fifty years ago, a clear recollection is not possible. However, I do remember telling Fred Watkins, since he knew the area and was an accustomed jungle fighter, to take control. The location in which we crashed was termed a 'black' area; in other words, well covered by the communist terrorists.

TALES FROM THE HORSE'S MOUTH – PILOTS

Now Watkins assumed command. He was anxious to get underway before he again became delirious. The first priorities were to retrieve any onboard weapons. The CTs would almost certainly have seen or heard the crash and would in all likelihood be heading our way. Watkins knew we had to get away from the crash site as soon as possible. They quickly dressed my arm with the shell dressing that all SAS personnel carry, though unfortunately the morphine that comes with it had been lost. Watkins then loaded Lumb's rifle – which Pat had never had cause to use before – and we were ready.

Watkins recalls thinking, 'We had to get away before I got too ill to do anything. The plan was to follow the river along until it got deeper, then build a bamboo raft, sail downstream and hope for the best.'

I do recall moving off, following the flow of the river, which we hoped would, more or less, lead us close to Paddy's Ladang, the SAS base. Fred had tucked the butt of his rifle under my left armpit, tugging me along, with his parang in his other hand, hacking through the undergrowth. Pat, following up behind, had our survival pack on his back. The river was fast flowing and very rough, and since we were being forced precariously close to the edge, Fred decided to hack inland. The haze in my memory deepens here. I seem to remember Fred vomiting when he tripped, and I think I tried to scoop the vomit from his mouth to stop him choking. As he recovered we continued to hack our way through this tortuous jungle until I seem to remember a clearing. There I saw what I could only think was a family of aborigines, looking utterly astonished. I can dimly recall Fred giving them curt instructions in Malay – how fortunate it was he had a grasp of the language. By this time I was becoming progressively weaker – I had lost a fair amount of blood, the pain in my chest increased markedly every time I took a deep breath, and my head, which had been thumped by that tree, experienced the 'mother and father' of all headaches.

From this point on my memory becomes very unclear, but I do seem to recall two of the abos moving off down river, the rest leading us through the jungle. I can remember wading through a marshy area, which enabled a number of leeches to take up accommodation on the lower part of my anatomy, to accompany the other numerous insects already established.

As we came to a small rise I can recall hearing crashing in the adjacent jungle causing us to lie prone in fear. Then, to our enormous relief, out popped our SAS friends. I think they came through on two sides, and they were armed to the teeth. We were then carried back to Paddy's Ladang where, by coincidence, the troop there were on the radio, therefore able to raise the alarm of the crash and casualties. They were indeed pleased to see the survival ration pack which I seem to remember Pat was very reluctant to give up! I also seem to recall one of the SAS lads gleefully giving me a jag of morphine because of my condition. In a short time, out of the blue came a helicopter, piloted by Ted Shuvalski. He flew us to Ipoh, and there, by another coincidence, was a Valetta transport aircraft.

In spite of the weather, which I seem to recall was rather grim, the pilot decided to take off and return us to Kuala Lumpur, and from there by ambulance to Kinrara Military Hospital.

In the above account I have referred, on occasions, to 'coincidences' if they can be called such, and feel it relevant to enumerate them, viz: I had been fortunate to pancake the helicopter so that it was literally skewered and perfectly balanced on the top of the tree, instead of crashing through in which case it is very doubtful that any of us would have survived. We crashed by a river, which is the only line of communication in dense jungle. I ascertained later, when I wanted to reward the aborigines who helped us, they could not be traced, and were probably under the control of the communist terrorists.

Fred Watkins ability to instruct the aborigines in Malay. The speed with which the SAS party were able to pick us up. The close proximity of Ted Shuvalski and his helicopter. The presence of the transport aircraft at Ipoh to fly us back to Kuala Lumpur without delay. The coincidences do not end there, for there were more at Kuala Lumpur. My wife, who had been misinformed about the seriousness of my condition, decided, as instructed, to go to the dinner party – but for the first time the car would not start. By the time she was able to get someone to sort the problem, she was told that the Valetta aircraft bringing me in was about to land. So she changed plans and went down to the airstrip to see the aircraft in. She was under the impression I would be jumping out of the aircraft, slightly bruised maybe. She was shocked to see me lifted out on a stretcher, blood spattered and barely conscious.

Group Captain Peter Broad, station commander Kuala Lumpur, happened to rub shoulders with a Colonel Gareh, commandant of Kinrara Hospital, at a cocktail party, and mentioned my crash that day and subsequent removal to his hospital, whereupon the colonel muttered that he'd better get down there before his 'butchers' got hold of me!

Colonel Gareh happened to be a plastic surgeon. He was correct about the possible action of the duty surgeons who were in fact preparing to take off my arm below the elbow. The colonel stopped this activity and decided to attempt a flesh and skin graft since, because of the time lapse, I was told the torn flesh had gone rotten. When I came to, next day, with the offending arm all plastered up, the colonel told me that being a tropical climate there was only a 50/50 chance of success of such a graft, and if the worst happened he would probably have to take the arm off closer to the shoulder.

So many 'coincidences', or were they? I wonder. My money was on the 'Old Boy Upstairs' taking a hand in the affair, as I had requested once we were going down.

The graft was a partial success, though I had to have a further graft at Halton Hospital on my return to the UK.

I had already decided to retire from the RAF under the terms of a then White Paper calling for such voluntary retirements, and the trauma of the whole affair had a marked effect on my wife, since we had such a young family.

My retirement was dated from the time I left the hospital, who did a very good job, although I finished up with a twenty per cent disability.

As I look back, I am certain I owe my life to Pat Lumb, and particularly to Fred Watkins, who contributed so much to secure our survival in spite of the fact that he was a very sick lad. I therefore recommended they be considered for some recognition. Fred received the Queen's Commendation.

THE FIRST HELICOPTER BOYS

Flight Lieutenant Ball Walker, probably pilot who flew the salvage crew (Jack Feely and Jeff Wicks) in to the wreckage of XB253 which crashed during take-off from a clearing on 7 November 1953. Pilot Flight Sergeant Manson unhurt. A/c remains were rediscovered mid 2000 by a group of Malaysian Air Historians.

Another view of XB253 crash, minus personnel.

TALES FROM THE HORSE'S MOUTH – PILOTS

We all three more or less recovered, but as far as I am aware, the repair to Pat's broken arm was not a complete success, and I recall him telling me that memories of the whole episode still haunt him.

Almost thirty-seven years later, we three met again, on 7 November 1992, the first reunion of the newly formed Combined Helicopter Operations (Malaya) Association. And what a reunion that was.

Sergeant Joe Ward

It was in 1954 when, as member of 58 Squadron flying PR Canberras, I read two books in the crewroom. One was Spencer Chapman's *The Jungle is Neutral* and the other, *Unbroken*, the maritime exploits of the submarine written by its captain, Lieutenant Commander Mars.

Fast-forward to 1956, Malaya, 194 Squadron, and me detached to Ipoh.

My task this morning is to transport two senior police officers to a kampong in the jungle south-east of Ipoh. The village penghulu's son is in trouble: he has been consorting with the CTs. While he is being admonished I have a long chat with the penghulu and discover it was he who led Spencer Chapman through the Japanese lines to the west coast, and on to the island of Pankgor. On the west coast of Pankgor is a beautiful beach known as Emerald Bay. It was into this bay that Lieutenant Commander Mars brought his submarine, unbroken, and rescued Spencer Chapman.

Ain't it a small world!

Night Attack

Apart from the toll of wounds received in battle, the jungle itself (and its inhabitants) added their own bizarre quota of casualties to the long list. Private Frank Burdett was one such casualty.

In February 1959, a platoon of New Zealanders serving with the combined forces were airlifted by helicopter to a small aboriginal settlement deep in the central highlands of Malaya. Their task was to seek out and capture, or kill, a band of Communist Terrorists known to be operating in that remote area. They were also to attempt severing an enemy courier line running north-south between cells. Watched by the friendly Temiar tribespeople (to whom helicopters were now a familiar sight), the soldiers assembled, strapped on heavy backpacks, and slowly filed into the jungle, following a trail that wound steadily upwards into the Cameron Highlands.

Ever alert for booby-traps or signs of human passage, the Kiwis finally penetrated into suspect territory. In the eerie semi-twilight of the jungle floor they were soon saturated with sweat. Their green uniforms already showed evidence of the unfriendly embrace of creepers and vines, armed with hooks and thorns seemingly designed to rip clothing and skin indiscriminately. In this strange environment one's estimation of distance travelled could be misleading. Each forward step has to be won the hard way, progress often measured in feet per hour. Late in the afternoon of their second day's march, the platoon leader was relieved when they finally stumbled into a small clearing created by a rock slide from a limestone crag jutting above them. This might give him the opportunity to ascertain their present position with reasonable accuracy. After a wary search, blinking in the bright sunlight, the men shucked off their backpacks and turned to check each other out for leeches, or cuts which could turn septic in a remarkably short space of time. First-aid and personal hygiene attended to, they enjoyed a brief snack and rested their weary muscles. Climbing up to an exposed ridge on the shoulder of the crag their leader was able to take several compass bearings on some distant but prominent peaks, thus fixing their position with greater accuracy. Setting up his transceiver, radio operator Private Burdett established contact with base camp. He relayed a progress report, including grid references of their present position. Ending his transmission with a cheerful 'All's well here, will transmit again at 08.00 hours,' Burdett signed off and packed his equipment. Little did he know then how much that next transmission would mean to him, and that he would not be operating the set for the morning broadcast. The next time he would enter that small clearing would be in a dramatic fight against time in an attempt to save his life.

'Come on lads, we can still cover some more territory before we make camp for the night,' said the group leader as the troops filed into a leafy twilight.

Night falls with amazing abruptness in the tropics, but the seasoned troopers were well prepared before darkness enshrouded them. A fire was out of the question since it could give away their presence, so a cold meal was consumed. Flimsy shelters were built and sentries posted. It wasn't long before bone-weary soldiers turned in for some well-earned rest.

Inside his one-man basha (a shelter made of ferns and small branches) Private Burdett stirred uneasily, drowsily becoming aware of a presence beside his bed shaking the flimsy structure.

'What the blazes do you want?' he sleepily inquired, thinking it was probably his turn for guard duty.

The answer was a deep electrifying growl that set his hair on end. Fully awake now and aware of a pungent animal odour, he stretched out his arm to reach for his rifle but screamed out in agony as his shoulder was seized in a bone-crushing grip. Moments later, the luckless radio operator felt himself being dragged bodily through the collapsing walls of his shelter. He screamed again, in mortal fear, until a blow from a massive paw silenced his hysteria.

For a few moments, panic and uncertainty reigned in the camp. The rest of the soldiers, fearing an enemy attack was in progress, were reaching for their weapons in the stygian darkness, bumbling about as they gathered their wits. Suddenly one of the Kiwis turned on a powerful flashlight, sweeping its beam around in a wide arc, revealing a scene that chilled their hearts. Transfixed in the bright light was an immense tiger, tail twitching fitfully, its eyes balefully aglitter, reflecting like two enormous emeralds. Dangling from its powerful jaws, like a rag doll, hung the blood-soaked body of one of their comrades. An ominous growl emanated from the huge beast's throat as it slowly backed away, still retaining its prey. For a few brief seconds no one moved or spoke. It was impossible to shoot without endangering each other, or the life of Private Burdett, if indeed he was still alive.

A rapid burst of automatic fire directly into the tree canopy had the desired effect. Startled by the gun flashes and the sudden noise, the striped monster dropped its limp victim and with two enormous bounds disappeared into darkness.

Carefully the unconscious soldier was laid onto an unrolled poncho and examined in the light of several flashlights. Immediately apparent to all were the deep gashes across his face and abdomen, as well as the badly chewed-up shoulder, still bleeding copiously. Curtly the troop commander issued orders as he applied field dressings to the worst wounds, and applied first-aid to the best of his ability. 'Some of you backtrack down the trail to the clearing we rested in today and start felling trees. We have to make that clearing big enough for a helicopter to land, and prepare a pad for it to set down on. Also, have some smoke signals ready to assist the pilot in finding us.'

He nominated those who were to go, reminding them to blaze the trail for those who were to follow up, carrying their injured buddy.

'Cut branches and lash several ponchos together to make a stretcher. We'll take turns at carrying him back to the clearing.'

Turning to a corporal he knew was qualified to operate the radio, he quoted the message that was to be relayed at 0800 hours. This included the map reference of the proposed helicopter LZ. Silently he gave thanks for the undoubted accuracy of that location.

Next day he would be similarly grateful.

Flight Lieutenant Jim McCorkle

An Interrupted Family Outing

> *Next morning, at home in Petaling Jaya, my wife Bunnie and I decided to take our children for a swim at the RAF base. It was meant to be a lazy day's outing, picnic lunch thrown in. Having arrived at the pool and secured a snug picnic area in the shade, I told my wife I'd pop round to 194 Squadron to see if any mail had come in.*
>
> *'Don't be long,' Bunnie said, as she busily undressed the baby.*
>
> *'Won't be a jiffy,' I replied, knowing the offices were just a few minutes' stroll from where we sat.*
>
> *As I checked the mail slots in the pilots' crew room, the corporal on duty informed me that both standby pilots had been called out on emergency flights to the south of KL, and would be away for most of the day. No sooner were the words out of his mouth when the squawk box connected to the Operations Room erupted into life.*
>
> *'Are there any other serviceable helicopters available?' queried the Duty Ops officer.*
>
> *The corporal nodded yes to me, holding up a notice board that revealed all I needed to know. Depressing the talk button on the intercom, I replied, 'Affirmative, Sycamore XG529 is serviceable, and has 65 gallons of fuel in the main tank.'*
>
> *Recognizing my voice the Duty Controller muttered a 'thanks be to God' and rapidly filled me in on the casualty evacuation flight so urgently needed.*
>
> *'Can you nominate a pilot we can call in to do this?'*
>
> *Without hesitation I replied, 'Yes, I'll do it myself.'*
>
> *'Good,' said the Ops Officer, 'Dr Ross will be with you in a minute.'*

TALES FROM THE HORSE'S MOUTH – PILOTS

He passed me the map references I'd need, and with a heartfelt 'Good luck', signed off.

Scanning the large map of Malaya pasted on the crew room wall, I quickly pinpointed the location of the new LZ and transferred it to a spare map, which I stuffed into my pocket. Since my flight suit was home being laundered I chose to fly dressed as I was; shorts, a striped blue and white tee-shirt, and open-toed sandals. An outfit totally unsuited for jungle trekking, should the need arise! I shrugged, grabbed my helmet and raced out to the dispersal. During a rapid but thorough pre-flight, I confirmed the main tank to be full, 65 gallons, the reserve tank, empty. Two minutes later the rotors were turning, the medical officer ducking his way into the cockpit. He was still fastening his seat belt as the wheels left the ground.

It was a beautiful morning for flying, clear blue skies, small puffs of white cumulus cloud casting shadows on the ground, light winds, excellent visibility. We sped across the sprawling outskirts of KL as Flight Lieutenant Iain Ross finished strapping himself in. Mountains to the northeast seemed to have been etched against the horizon. Using the airborne frequency, I informed Operational Control that, to save valuable time, I intended to fly a direct course to my objective. This was a significant departure from the usual technique of following well-established routes such as rivers, roads, railway lines, or clearly delineated valleys, where map-reading was much easier and there were numerous landing spots in case of emergency or inclement weather.

Having obtained their official blessing, I climbed to 5,000 feet and made a bee-line for the Cameron Highlands. Away to the west I could see the mangrove swamps that marked the shoreline, the reflected glitter of sunshine on the Straits of Malacca. Soon the suburbs disappeared behind, to be replaced by the rising ground of Malaya's mountainous region. I made the first position report overhead Fraser's Hill.

My course now took us over virgin jungle, where tenacious creepers and assorted vines festooned all but the sheerest limestone crags, jutting out like fangs beneath us. Viewed from the air, at close quarters, the jungle canopy presents an almost unbroken vista of greyish greenery, not unlike thousands of cauliflower heads carelessly tossed together. Occasionally sunlight glinted off rivers which wound their lazy way to the sea. To me, each river, each mountain peak, represented familiar landmarks to which I could update our rate of progress, reporting our position to Ops Centre. I was constantly computing: distance travelled, fuel consumed, distance still to cover, and the all-important timing. Almost two hours after departing KL we swept over huge tea plantations of the Boh Valley, almost 7,000 feet above sea level. Here, during days long gone, sultans, princes, and tourists came to play golf, log fires in their snug holiday cabins warding off the chilly night air.

The Alvis Leonides engine consumes about 25 gallons per hour in the cruise. Since take-off we had used around fifty of our sixty-five gallons, the remaining fifteen gallons enough to keep us airborne thirty-six minutes. Glancing at the map I decided to divert to Fort Brooke to replenish our dwindling fuel supply. Notifying Operations, I started a slow descent into a natural amphitheatre created by the conjoining of three separate valleys, steep heavily-wooded slopes on all sides. Fort Brooke sits on a rounded knoll around which loops a fast-flowing river. It is one of the few jungle outposts that, due to topography, didn't have an airstrip. But it did have two helicopter landing pads.

As we touched down on the upper pad, Inspector Jock Currie (CO of the Fort) ducked under the whirling blades to greet me with his usual cheerful grin. I quickly filled him in on the nature of our mission, and requested extra-fast refuelling. His face fell as he related news that had me going over my calculations with renewed urgency. Apparently a recent air-drop of fuel had gone awry. Some chutes candled, the resulting heavy impact rupturing the drums. Ruefully, Jock admitted, 'We don't have a drop of aviation fuel.'

Perusing my map once more, again estimating distance, time, and fuel requirements, if the grid reference of the clearing was accurate (all too often they were not), if I could locate it without delay, if it was large enough to permit safe entry, and exit (very often they weren't), I estimated I could do the pick-up and then fly to Fort Chabai some thirty miles to the north – if we didn't have a head wind, and if the fuel gauge was accurate. A lot of ifs on which to stake human lives! Asking Jock to inform base of my intentions, I restored rotor RPM to operational, and without further delay, lifted off.

Using minimum power where possible, I snuck the helicopter over several rises to finally enter the valley of the Sungei Perolak, zooming over the bamboo longhouse where the Kiwi troops had assembled. In mere minutes we covered miles the troops had so patiently trodden, and a welcoming sight greeted my anxious gaze: a plume of white smoke rising vertically from the trees ahead. Spiralling almost straight up, it indicated an almost non-existent wind condition. This would allow me to choose the easiest approach for a descent into the new clearing, which proved to be uncomfortably small. However, my lightweight condition allowed a controlled, slow descent, alighting gently on the jungle floor. Iain Ross was out of the cabin almost before the landing was complete, and made his way to the waiting soldiers. Moments later, he returned to inform me the troops carrying the injured man had not yet arrived and were not expected for at least twenty minutes.

Yet another dilemma! To leave the engine idling for that length of time would use the fuel needed to reach Fort Chabai, but a FEAF standing order forbade the shutting down of helicopter engines in suspect territory. This was especially important in clearings not large enough to accept more than one chopper. Another consideration was the fact that the Alvis Leonides engine was notoriously temperamental, difficult to restart after a brief shutdown in warm climates.

The New Zealanders looked up in surprise as the engine became silent, rotor blades drooping to a standstill. Their eyes opened even wider when I stepped out of the cockpit, dressed in natty sports attire!

Doc Ross was escorted out of the clearing towards the patient.

From start up in Kuala Lumpur to shut down in the clearing, the engine had been running two hours and twelve minutes. Calculating 25 gallons per hour, we had consumed approximately 55 gallons, leaving an estimated 10 gallons. Fort Chabai lay thirty miles north. At 85mph cruising speed, say 21 minutes. That ten gallons should keep us airborne an estimated 24 minutes. 'You're cutting things a bit fine, Jim boy!' I silently told myself.

Eventually the exhausted stretcher crew stumbled into sight, Doc Ross already administering to the young soldier. The patient was transferred to the rear cabin, the plasma bottle strung up, and Doc Ross rotated his seat to face the rear and continued to monitor Burnett's vital signs.

'He's really in a bad way. Needs proper treatment as soon as possible,' he said.

Gravely acknowledging this, I started the drill for boosting the engine. Mentally I crossed my fingers and, with a muted prayer, switched on. It was sweet music to my ears when that powerful engine burst into lusty life at the first attempt! Moments later we were rising out of the trees and on our way north. To proceed in a direct line would mean climbing over high ground, already capped with domes of towering cumulus, guaranteed to create turbulence that would distress my passengers, as well as increasing fuel consumption. I therefore chose to head slightly east, down the valley, before continuing on the northerly heading. My eyes kept flicking from trees ahead to the fuel gauge, now just above the red 'zero' line. Dangerously low.

The endless carpet of trees seemed to trundle past at a snail's pace, the minute hand of my watch seeming to whiz around like the second hand. Time flew, we crawled across the verdant landscape. Butterflies started a fandango in my stomach as the fuel gauge sank ever lower.

Suppose my calculations were wrong! I thrust the unwelcome thought from my head and concentrated on flying as smoothly as humanly possible. As low as we were – just above the treetops, on the lee side of the mountains – we were out of radio contact. Transmissions would go unheard, except by any high-flying airliner. Like a particle whirling in its own galaxy, we were alone, dependent on fate, and my decisions. Occasionally we would overfly tiny gravel bars in a loop of the winding river, the temptation to set down almost overpowering.

'That soldier will die if we delay getting him to hospital,' I found myself muttering. An inner voice would then counter with, 'We'll all die if you don't set down before the engine runs out of fuel.'

Tension in the cockpit mounted. Even Doc Ross fell silent. I found myself leaning forward, as if to urge greater speed.

Some eighteen long minutes after lifting out of that little clearing, a welcome sight came into view. A huge red scar stood out clearly on a green slope directly ahead: a prominent landmark formed by a long-ago landslide. It was used by all aircrew flying into Chabai. 'Pioneer' pilots habitually turned onto a westerly heading over this gash, let down into a narrow valley for a short distance before committing themselves to a ninety-degree right turn into another cleft. From which there was no turning back. The airstrip at Chabai would then be in view, a narrow cul-de-sac that ended in a steep incline. One way in, one way out. Today, the westerly turn into the valley was a great lift to my spirits. My navigation had been perfect. But the fuel gauge needle seemed to be hanging against the stops. For one heart-stopping moment the engine spluttered. It then resumed its even-tempered purr, my knuckles whitening on the controls. Below, a raging white torrent foamed madly between huge rounded boulders. Hardly the best place to suffer an engine failure.

The right-angled turn and welcome sight of the grassy runway slid into view. Avoiding any abrupt movement of the controls, or change in attitude which could cause the remaining fuel to surge away from the immersed fuel pump, I gently wheeled the Sycamore onto the ground in a running landing. We taxied clear of the active strip into a holding pen, leaving the runway clear for any other arrivals. A numbing cramp in the fingers of my right hand made me aware just how tightly I had been grasping the cyclic control during the last few minutes.

Switching off all systems, and waiting for the rotor blades to cease turning, I turned to Iain Ross and gave him a big relieved smile. The police inspector in charge of the fort then approached and was duly informed of our needs. I asked for the main tank to be filled to capacity, and requested an accurate check of just how much fuel it required to achieve this. As this was fulfilled, Iain Ross and I stretched our legs, walking around a little to unwind. We were treated to a much-needed drink of fresh, cold mountain water. It tasted like nectar.

The patient was carefully monitored; he seemed to be holding up remarkably well, considering his plight. Final calculations with the tank brim full, revealed we had used 64 of our 65 gallons. The remaining gallon would have kept us in the air approximately two minutes, or three miles! That was cutting things much too fine. In aviation, the saying is, the only time you have too much fuel is when you're on fire!

The remainder of the flight to Tai Ping Military Hospital was completed in record time, again taking a bee-line course. Now with good radio contact, we found the hospital staff to be awaiting our arrival at the helipad, the patient being quickly wheeled into an operating room without delay. Doc Ross remained in attendance. With the helicopter again refuelled, I departed along regular routes for the return flight to Kuala Lumpur, leaving private Burdett in capable hands.

Some six and a half hours after I had left my wife and family, I rejoined them at the swimming pool, to be greeted by my very irate wife: 'And just where the hell have you been all this time?'

She forgave me when I told her the story of Private Burdett's ordeal.

I'm pleased to say that although he was badly scarred, Frank Burdett survived and was repatriated to New Zealand.

Many years later I was emailing another Kiwi soldier I'd met on flight duty. He asked what areas of Malaya I had been working. I replied that my flying duties took me all over that peninsula, with many operations in the north, close to the Thai border. I told him I brought out another Kiwi soldier who had been viciously mauled by a tiger (I'd discovered this same tiger had killed five aborigines of the Temiar tribe). Rather excitedly he exclaimed, 'I was talking to him a couple of days ago on email! His name is Frank Burdett!'

I asked my new friend if he would contact Private Burdett and give him my email address, explaining I was the pilot who had flown him out that Sunday morning. Eventually Frank and I established contact and, after all those years, we now exchange daily messages.

TALES FROM THE HORSE'S MOUTH – PILOTS

Jim McCorkle's *An Interrupted Family Outing* story was subsequently taken up by the NZ Malaya Vets Association in their magazine *Selamat*, where it was introduced as 'A story of the nerve-wracking casevac flight of 1 NZ Regt soldier Pte Frank Burdett, who was seriously injured in a tiger attack in 1959':

> 'Jim McCorkle, the story continued, defied the odds on this flight, taking a gamble he would not normally take because a Kiwi soldier lay injured, his chances of life hanging on a swift transfer to hospital. You know what they say about pilots: "There's old pilots and bold pilots but there's no old and bold pilots." Jim wasn't bold but he did bet his life, Frank's, and that of Doctor Iain Ross on his technical knowledge and flying skills. Frank's casevac was unusual foremost because a tiger caused his injuries, but also for the calculated risks Jim took, and his choice of flying clothing.'

Outstanding Inter-service Cooperation

At about 1700 hrs on 21 March 1955, Lieutenant Commander Miller was flying WV198, 'K', of 848 Squadron, from Kluang to Sembawang when he experienced a complete engine failure. He managed to make a forced landing on uneven ground in a swamp near Layang Layang at VP 437 663 (Johore grid). After landing, the helicopter toppled over, damaging the main rotors, gearbox and starboard undercarriage. Within half an hour the helicopter was spotted by a Valetta and a Canberra and a party of Gurkhas sent out to them.

Unfortunately they did not get there until the next day and, after an anxious night out in an area frequented by terrorists, Miller and his co-pilot Lieutenant Price were evacuated after four Gurkhas, Lieutenant Lloyd and Lieutenant Commander E. Wilson had been flown in by WV 195, 'G'.

A survey party was sent into the jungle from NAS Sembawang, and they decided that salvage by road and track was feasible, but that to do this a bridge would have to be built to span a stream, and a 200-yard road of timber would have to be built across a marsh. To accomplish the task, men of the RE Gurkha Regiment were called in from Kluang. The operation was a formidable one, but in spite of the hazards it was completed in four days. But to bring the helicopter out of the swamp with only negligible (further) damage, seven officers, approximately 100 troops and 25 vehicles were employed. The helicopter was eventually winched and pulled out of the swamp, brought across the bridge constructed by troops, and hauled many miles. The whole operation was a great success, but the efficiency with which it was carried out was to a large extent due to the fine work performed by the Gurkhas, who were of an average age of 18, all young trainees. When the helicopter went back into service it had the Gurkha's RE Regimental Badge painted on its side.

Flight Lieutenant Jim McCorkle

At the Squadron base in Kuala Lumpur one Sunday morning, I was in the office as standby-pilot ready to undertake any mission that might be called. Looking out of the window I noticed a man dressed in civilian clothes walking around the Sycamore I had just prepared for flight. I walked out, approached the stranger and, in a clear voice, advised him that he was trespassing in a restricted area. Kuala Lumpur was a Civil/Military airfield, the Military section being clearly delineated. The well-dressed stranger came close, and in a quiet voice apologised. 'I suppose I should have come over to your office before looking at the helicopter.' As he spoke he produced identification which revealed he was an Air Vice Marshal in the Royal Australian Air Force. His name was Hancock. 'I have just been posted in as the new Officer Commanding,' he advised.

We walked back to the office where I had to be close to the telephone, and sat together as he told me more about himself. Apparently he had never flown helicopters, although his experience was quite varied as to types of aircraft flown. I informed him that I was the Squadron Training Officer, and sort of jokingly said, 'Well sir, if you want to convert to helicopters, which are the largest part of your new command, I can convert you to type.'

He was very pleasant to chat with, easy and relaxed. I took to him immediately, and thought I'd soon be seeing him again. That turned out to be correct, because the new boss was soon travelling around, getting to know his men and the general set-up of our command structure. It wasn't long before I was told that the boss wanted to learn to fly the Sycamore, and I was formally introduced by my squadron commander.

In the air, as my student, there was no sign of the difference in rank between us. He was a good student who quickly cottoned on to everything I pointed out. This helped me relax, ignore the rank gap, and we became friends.

At this time, there was a rerun of an old British sitcom programme on television called 'Ancock's 'alf 'our. It starred comedian Tony Hancock...who always dropped his 'aitches when speaking. One morning I was sitting in the half-crowded crew room waiting for my illustrious student to arrive, when one of the pilots who had just returned from a two-week leave asked me if he could take the Sycamore up for a refresher flight, pointing to my machine. 'No,' I said, 'You can't 'ave it. It's reserved for 'Ancock's 'alf 'our!'

Little did I realise that behind me the men were now standing at attention and had gone quiet. There was a little puff of warm air at my right ear, and an Australian-accented voice whispered, ''Ancock...is 'ere!'

There was a loud roar of laughter, enjoyed also by the new CO. It turned out he had a good sense of humour. The training trip went well and I sent the air vice marshal solo that day. I flew him on numerous occasions when he had to go somewhere in a hurry, and we always put the dual controls in so that he could keep his hand in. When he was posted back to Australia, everyone commented on the fact that he had been a good boss, well-liked by all.

A number of years later I was serving my third tour in Malaysia, based at RAAF Butterworth near Penang. I was now Training Officer for 110 Squadron. One day, I was informed I would have a VIP trip the following morning. I prepared as usual and, brasses polished, waited beside Group Captain Case, the CO. He was a burly Australian, with a sort of pugnacious attitude. He told me the VIP was his boss, and he was looking forward to bending his ear during the flight. It was to the military hospital at Taiping, an easy forty-five minute flight along well-recognized routes.

A transport aircraft drew up and shut down its engines. Doors opened, stairs were put in place, and the VIP descended.

He was dressed in the uniform of the Marshal of the Royal Australian Air Force, but he was none other than my former pupil! When it came to introductions, Mister Hancock stepped out of line and came up to me with his hand outstretched. 'Mac! What are you doing here?'

He was as surprised to see me as I was to see him, in his reflected glory as the Number One in the RAAF! I jokingly remarked that we did not have dual controls in the Sycamore in which we were to fly, but they could be fitted. His attitude confirmed he liked the idea. 'Ten minutes only sir, and we will be ready.'

Group Captain Case was not amused at losing his chance to bend Hancock's ear, but what could he say? That evening, my wife and I were delighted to be seated at the VIP table, and enjoyed a fabulous meal.

*

Master Pilot Alan Stanley Clarke

by
Flight Lieutenant Tom Browning

During the Second World War Nobby flew the Lancaster, amongst other aircraft, moving on to Air Sea Rescue later. Then came Malaya.

Outwardly, a quiet man who spent much of his time in the crew-room making crossbows, he was an expert in their use. He'd probably had more success with one than the rest of us would have had with our Smith & Wesson .38s had we ended up in the Ulu – which, of course, is just what happened to Nobby and Sycamore XL 822.

I remember waiting in what seemed a long line of Sycamores at Grik (but was probably only three or four), at the start of a troop-lift of some

Tom Browning at a reunion.

Kiwi soldiers. We were going to a big clearing and reckoned the max load for the Sycamore was three.

Nobby was first to go and I watched him lift off. Or rather attempt to. You could see the Sycamore straining to get off the ground. Eventually it gave up and one soldier and his kit got out. Or was it just his kit – my memory is a bit hazy here. Anyway, the Sycamore eventually staggered off and the troop lift got underway, but with much reduced load. The Sycamore had a useful payload of 540 lbs which equated to three soldiers at the then accepted figure of 180 lbs per man. A later check showed that our Kiwis averaged 180 lbs *stripped*, plus similar weights for their kit which they tossed so effortlessly into the cabin!

Nobby, whose navigation was calculated by the number of cigarettes it took to smoke between sectors, must have been on overdrive that day. He had a wonderful fund of stories amongst which his account of his 'sightseeing' flight in the barrage balloon assigned to his charge early in his career (I read it as a schoolboy in *Tee Emm* so I know it's true). Having ditched an Anson in the North Sea, the crew spent a wretched night, their dinghy tied to the miraculously floating Anson, only to discover that by the dawn's early light they were a couple of hundred yards off Southend – or was it Clacton, or even Blackpool? – pier, and could have waded ashore at any time. His stories were always a wonder and delight to hear!

*

Lieutenant Commander Breese, 848 NAS

> 848 Squadron, the Royal Navy's first operational helicopter unit, was formed at the end of October 1952. In just over two months it became land-based in Malaya for operations over the jungle.
>
> I was appointed to the squadron on its formation and stayed with it until December 1953. During that time we flew over 3,500 hours, lifted well over 10,000 troops into and out of the jungle and evacuated 275 casualties. We also carried out miscellaneous tasks which included supply dropping, reconnaissance and target-marking. The squadron was equipped with ten Sikorsky S55 helicopters (Whirlwind), a large range of spares and comprehensive ground equipment, supplied by the United States under the Mutual Aid programme.

THE FIRST HELICOPTER BOYS

We sailed from Portsmouth in HMS Perseus *on 12 December 1952, and on 8 January 1953, when near Changi point, flew off the aircraft to the Royal Naval Air Station at Sembawang on Singapore Island.*

We soon had our first incident: one of the aircraft forced landing in a clearing on the federation side of the Johore Straits because its tail-rotor control had become jammed.

With one aircraft detached to maintain guard, the rest proceeded to Sembawang. Here the squadron AEO was embarked in a winch aircraft and was soon being winched down into the clearing where the S55 had landed. The trouble was soon located and rectified, and within two hours the helicopter arrived at Sembawang.

Now began a period of intensive training for the task ahead. It appeared likely that our most exacting flying would be into and out of jungle clearings, so it was decided to concentrate training on work of this kind. First, a circle 50ft in diameter was marked on the airfield, into which vertical descents from 200ft were made. Next, a similar area was cleared in some 80ft rubber trees on the edge of the airfield and, lightly laden, the aircraft were taken into that. With familiarity came increasing confidence, both in the helicopters and ourselves, and in a short time we were taking in maximum loads.

Our thoughts now turned to the final test: descents into the 200ft deep primary jungle. As none was available on Singapore Island, the army, who had a jungle training school in Johore, readily agreed to cut a clearing there. This was soon ready, and daily flights were made across the Straits and into the clearing.

On 21 January, three aircraft were detached to RAF Kuala Lumpur to carry out trials, including aircraft performance, methods and equipment for the emplaning and deplaning of troops, supply dropping, use of the external sling, and winching of casualties. Later, in conjunction with the RAF, methods of vegetation-spraying were evolved.

Towards the end of January we were given our first operational task, a casualty evacuation. On 2 February, trials now complete, we gave a demonstration of our capabilities to representatives of the army and police. From then on work increased, and by the end of March it had become a flood.

TALES FROM THE HORSE'S MOUTH – PILOTS

Troops deplaning from WV194, 848 squadron RN Whirlwind during training.

The aircraft were behaving magnificently, and it became obvious that if we intended to work the aircraft to capacity – as jobs in hand demanded we should – we would require additional pilots, to which approval was forthcoming.

We still had only three helicopters based at KL, three others, and four reserves based at Sembawang. Now, with the pattern of operations becoming clear, showing a need to concentrate all six operational machines at KL, this was accordingly effected. With no hangar space available, the aircraft were out in all weathers. In spite of this, serviceability remained high. It invariably rained overnight, and one got into the habit of ruising the collective-pitch lever before starting to drain the water from the rotor blades. Then, after priming, two to four seconds on the starter were enough to get the engine running. This easy starting saved us what would have become endless battery trouble for, as trolley accumulators were available only at KL and Sembawang, ninety per cent of all starts had to be made on the aircraft batteries. Reliability, lightness of control, and good manoeuvrability, made the S55 suitable for operation in Malaya. Though experiencing the usual stability deficiencies of helicopters, one could nevertheless be quite relaxed when at the controls. The performance, taking into account the high temperature and humidity experienced in Malaya, tallied with the estimated performance given in the makers' handbook. The fact that the fuel tanks are under the cabin floor, thus allowing the filler caps to be at a convenient level, proved to be a great advantage, as fuelling was invariably from fifty-gallon drums, via a four-gallon tin and special chamois filter. One great disadvantage however is that there is only ten inches of clearance under the rear of the fuselage, discounting the boom. Without detriment to their anti-ground-resonance properties, we increased the pressure in the main oleos, thus improving this ground clearance a little, at the same time lifting the tail rotor a trifle higher.

Except when looking across the cockpit, downward and forward view in the S55 is extremely good, so it was necessary to carry an observer as a lookout only for the more difficult clearings. The fact that an observer up front meant one less soldier in the cabin had to be faced. When troop-lifting, only the leading aircraft carried an observer. Having navigated to and identified the clearing, he would, if necessary, deplane with the troops to supervise work on improving the clearing. If that was not necessary, he deplaned at the end of the first sortie, employed himself in lining up the troops for emplaning and supervising the refuelling. On a big lift, when relief pilots were available, he would additionally run the pilots' roster. Refuelling usually took place every second or third sortie, and as it took only about four minutes, reliefs had to be on the ball to avoid delay.

Although at first, one bit of jungle looks the same as any other, pilots soon learned to note small features and, having once been to a clearing, could invariably find it again without the aid of an observer, nor reference to the one-inch map.

For casevacs an observer was always carried. Such operations were invariably from hastily cut clearings, so the observer, apart from his value as navigator, proved invaluable as a lookout for his side of the aircraft, and the tail rotor. If winching was necessary, he tipped up his seat and climbed down into the hold to operate the winch control from there.

Casevacs were the most satisfying of all operations, for here the helicopter was essential. Frequently a ten-minute lift saved a gravely injured man five days of being carried through

TALES FROM THE HORSE'S MOUTH – PILOTS

Casevac Litter.

the jungle – probably the difference between life and death. On the other hand, troop lifts were the most interesting of operations, as one could carry in the troops, then follow their progress from a distance. Troop lifts were always a mad rush, split-second timing needed to get the men into the clearing as quickly as possible. Sortie after sortie would be flown, until eventually one lost count.

For one of the most interesting troop lifts in which I took part, I was detached to attend briefing for an op to be mounted the following day. The intel, as I remember, went something like this: An Auster pilot had reported spotting CT cultivation in deep jungle and it seemed probable there was a camp in the vicinity. The object of the operation was to attack the camp, if found, and destroy the crops. The troops would be lifted to a position some distance from the cultivation. From this position they would make a reconnaissance, then attack the camp at dawn the following day. The Auster pilot had also reported a small natural clearing on the bend of a river a suitable distance from the cultivation. Owing to the height at which the reconnaissance had been carried out, he could not be sure

THE FIRST HELICOPTER BOYS

the clearing was entirely suitable, as tall trees overhung either side. Our instructions were to put the troops into the clearing as quickly as possible, or, if the clearing was not suitable, to place them as near as possible. Hoping for the best, but fearing

848 Squadron trooplift.

155 squadron en route to a Trooplift.

TALES FROM THE HORSE'S MOUTH – PILOTS

Trooplift underway.

No 1 Australian Regiment. An early morning troop lift from Grik, north Malaya. Troops awaiting lift to begin; crewmen gathered around a/c nose whilst pilots and army officers discuss tactics. Photo courtesy of Royal Australian Army photographer.

the worst, we decided to take three aircraft, two of which were fitted with winches, and position them at the emplaning point that afternoon, as fog was expected to cover the area first thing in the morning.

With ground crews and equipment and our overnight bags aboard, we were airborne from KL soon after lunch. Arriving at our destination, we prepared the helicopters for the following day's programme. Then, with the troops available, we exercised them in the emplaning and deplaning drill. By now it was dusk, so we dispersed to our quarters: for some an attap (palm leaf) hut, others a tent. After dinner that night we were able to discuss the coming operation with the pilot who had made the reconnaissance, along with the company commander of the troops being lifted in.

Next morning at take-off time, sure enough the fog was there. Our fighter escort of DH Hornets, with whom we were in touch, reported the whole area to be covered by low cloud. They had enough fuel to enable them to stay on patrol another hour. Soon the cloud had lifted sufficiently for us to get airborne. Flying at 200ft above the jungle, in line astern, we soon reached the clearing, and our worst fears were realized. It may have been OK for a casevac, but was definitely unsuitable for a troop lift. Nearby, however, was a patch of secondary jungle with trees only 75ft high, so we decided to winch the troops into that. After our talk with the spotter pilot the previous evening we'd anticipated the need to winch the men while hovering outside the ground cushion, so had accordingly reduced the number of troops carried in the winch aircraft for the first sortie. Sending the third aircraft back to the emplaning point, we hovered in turn over the selected spot and, one at a time, down through the trees went the troops. At times they disappeared from the view of the winch operator, but he carried on lowering, and fortunately no one got hung up.

As soon as the first troops were in the clearing, the Hornets were dismissed; we'd heard them on the radio, but had never seen them. Now began a race back to the emplaning point, then back to the embryo clearing, where the first troops in had already made an impression on the jungle with their parangs. By the next sortie the clearing was large enough to go in and

TALES FROM THE HORSE'S MOUTH – PILOTS

hover at about 18ft, thus allowing the troops to drop from the end of a scrambling rope.

We could now increase our load and, with the assistance of the third aircraft, the lift proceeded apace. Back at base we disembarked the observers, who had now completed their job in the air, allowing yet another soldier to be carried into the clearing by each aircraft. At the clearing we found sufficient ground cleared for the helicopters to touch down, so from then on the troops deplaned in the normal manner. By mid-afternoon the lift was complete, and we were enjoying a quick lunch, while the aircraft were being refuelled and greased ready for the flight back to KL.

For us ended a most interesting operation. For the troops, it had only just begun. They could be certain of staying in the jungle five to ten days. Then, if they were urgently required for another operation, they might be lifted out. If not, they would have to walk, so great is the demand for the services of the helicopters.

Presentation to Flight Lieutenant Burke after completing 1,000 hours on the Whirlwind. Crewman Len Raven.

THE FIRST HELICOPTER BOYS

Above left: Flight Lieutenant Tom Bennett. The tiger was, of course, a cardboard cutout.

Above right: Master Pilot Carl Stubbs.

Left: Squadron Leader Ron Penning, the boss.

Chapter 6

Tales from the Horse's Mouth
Crewmen

Above: Crewman's View.

Right. Crewmen – It's raining, so what!

THE FIRST HELICOPTER BOYS

Sergeant Bob Bowman

Flight Lieutenant 'Chips' Fry and myself had been at Grik for a day or two following the casevac of a member of the Royal Marine Commando unit based there. Things were fairly active in the north at that time and it was decided to keep our helicopter on stand-by in the area. After a few days, as there had been no call for our services, it was planned to return to Changi the next day. With everything ready for departure there was quite a bit of the final day remaining and nothing else for us to do.

The troop sergeant major, realising we were a little bored, invited us to accompany an escort party on a trip to the river a few miles away where they were to meet and return with an incoming patrol. We were assured there was no danger as the immediate area had been declared 'white' and that it would be a wonderful opportunity to view the countryside from the ground. I was advised not to encumber myself with my Sten gun, but was loaned an automatic pistol just in case. It occurred to me that this was a safety precaution which presented less danger to my travelling companions in the event of any trouble. On the strength of the assurance of complete safety we accepted the invitation, set off in a convoy of three vehicles: Chips Fry was in the leading truck – a passenger vehicle to accommodate the incoming patrol; the other two, which carried the escort, were small open pick-ups, each carrying eight people. I was in the rear of the last vehicle with seven marines, one of whom was armed with a Bren gun.

After clearing the village we turned on to a track just wide enough for the vehicles to get through; the ground rose steeply on either side and was covered with thick jungle growth. It was very uneven, with not many straights, and as we approached one sharp bend a burst of small arms fire caused me no little surprise. We had run into an ambush. The Bren gunner's reaction was instant, but unfortunately his weapon wasn't up to it; it jammed after one round. A close second in reaction time was the driver. His incredibly rapid acceleration round the bend caused the marine sitting next to me to fall out of the truck.

TALES FROM THE HORSE'S MOUTH – CREWMEN

Immediately we had rounded the bend the vehicle was stopped and the sergeant in charge ordered everyone back to the ambush position – I naturally assumed that didn't include me. At the same time my neighbour who had made the involuntary exit was making a rapid return to the truck, minus his rifle. He didn't appear to have any serious injury so he was turned about and sent to recover his rifle which, fortunately, was still where it had fallen. The ambushers had made a rapid getaway, and only spent cartridge cases were to be found. They had however managed to get a few rounds on target: the marine sitting opposite and one forward of me had been hit in the shoulder, and a bullet hole had appeared in the side of the truck between me and my left-hand neighbour, with evidence of some hits found on the engine. The wounded marine was taken to the leading vehicle where he received treatment.

As soon as things calmed down we went on our way to the river, picked up the patrol and returned without further incident to the air-strip. The casualty was then airlifted to hospital in Ipoh, and on Flight Lieutenant Fry's return it was necessary to refuel and service the helicopter ready for the return flight to Changi.

Next morning we took off as planned, and after refuelling at Kuala Lumpur were glad to arrive back at Changi. At least there was a good story to relate in the mess that evening.

*

My second recollection again involves Flight Lieutenant Fry. This time we were heading through the Bentong Pass, a wounded Gurkha on board. It was late in the day, not too much time before dark in which to get him to hospital in KL. There was a fair amount of cloud above and we were keeping a wary eye on the weather. When we were just about mid-way through the pass the worst happened: we could see it clamping down ahead, the rearward view just as ominous. In that sort of mountainous area it would have been disastrous to carry on so we looked for a possible landing place.

Our luck was in, we spotted a fenced off compound of huts with a small open area at one end into which we could put down without too much difficulty. Before landing, Flight Lieutenant Fry explained our situation to KL tower and requested arrangements be made to get our quite seriously injured casualty to hospital.

Upon landing in this unknown environment we were relieved to see the uniforms of Malay policemen; we had in fact landed within a few yards of the police post. We explained the reason for our visit and of the urgent need for our passenger to reach hospital as quickly as possible. I am not sure whether it was through the action taken by KL tower or the police, but within an hour an ambulance arrived with an armed escort and took the casualty off our hands. In the meantime the threatened deluge had arrived and darkness descended. I gathered that the rescue party weren't too enthralled about being called out to complete the job for us. Regardless, the major part of the evacuation had been accomplished, the badly wounded man no longer deep in the 'ulu'.

For the rest of the night we were free to worry about the safety of our machine. We assumed the occupants of the huts in the compound had been gathered there for their own safety, indication enough that the area was hostile, and the added attraction of a helicopter might well encourage local 'commies' to take action. The thought made me regard my Sten gun as a comfort rather than an encumbrance. Fortunately the need to use it never arose, the night passing uneventfully.

Come daylight, we were very much in need of something to eat, and the sergeant in charge directed us to a communal eating place at the other end of the compound. On entering the room and seeing the occupants, we wondered whether our assumption about the reason for them being in the compound was correct – their appearance suggested the situation could have been quite the reverse! However, driven by pangs of hunger, we decided to eat. There was no problem with choice: boiled rice or nothing. We quickly ate and went to prepare for our departure. The heavy downpour of the previous evening had caused the machine to sink up to the wheel hubs, so some excavation was necessary.

Eventually we were ready, and thanked the police for our night's shelter. Our one remaining worry was soon dispelled when the engine started on 'internals' and we were able to get on our way to KL, where we could replenish the fuel, and ourselves, before returning to Changi.

*

The final episode to relate again involved the Royal Marine Commandos, this time in the Benta area. Flying Officer Lee was the pilot, and we had been called in to pick up a marine who was not wounded, but who had fallen heavily, damaging a knee, and whose condition was slowing progress of the patrol. The area was not difficult, trees not as tall as usual, most of them dead and spaced fairly well apart, everything to indicate a straightforward evacuation.

The patrol were pleased to see us, and eager to tell of their recent success. They had made contact with a group of bandits and killed four. Apart from the man with the twisted knee, they had suffered no casualties themselves. The platoon commander enquired whether we would be kind enough to take some evidence of identification back to HQ at Benta. This was agreed and the 'evidence' was brought to us in two canvas bags. On enquiring what the bags contained, I was invited to open one and have a look. I did so and was horrified to see two blood-stained heads. The other bag contained similar. My next question was: who had performed the surgery? A young national serviceman, whose features were the personification of innocence, proudly claimed that he was responsible for one and various voices claimed the other three! There seemed to be a great sense of satisfaction in their success which was regarded as a measure of revenge for the murder of some of their comrades who had been ambushed in their truck, their bodies covered in petrol and burned.

At this stage we were grateful that the patrol were anxious to push on. We certainly had no desire to linger, eager to return to the relative safety of Benta airstrip. The casualty and the bags containing proof of identity were loaded, and we attempted to take off. Our helicopter, however, was reluctant to gain height, so we went into forward flight for a short distance – managing to avoid the trees – and put down again. It occurred to us that we were facing downwind, and after a

180° turn the second attempt was successful. On arrival back at the airstrip our casualty, and cargo, were handed over. After a between-flight inspection and refuelling, it was back to Changi with all haste.

The day the CO tangled with the tree tops when exiting a clearing and had to be evacuated himself; the day I was off-loaded in a remote rubber plantation and taken to KL with a Gurkha escort; a survey of the Perak river; a night journey in an armoured scout car; the attack on a police post in Johore; the evacuation carried out from Grik in the middle of the Christmas Day celebrations, and many other incidents, were all part of two eventful years spent with the Casualty Evacuation Flight.

*

Report from an unknown crewman

Took off from Kuala Lumpur 7am for a one hour flight to the LZ of a Malayan Police Field Force unit to evacuate a Malay soldier who had contracted malaria.

Found LZ in a large meadow-like clearing by a river. A small knoll had been flattened, a level section 20ft x10ft had been marked out. It looked like red concrete.

We hovered over the marked area but the pilot would not land. He ordered me to get the casevac on board. I jumped off the step & landed on the 'concrete', went in up to my ankles in the wet mess, which was not sticky. While I was so engaged, the helicopter had risen. It now descended and moved over me, the open door striking me on the head & knocking me to the ground. As I attempted to get up, the step pushed me back down, and as the front wheel was close to my head, I rolled away. I got to my feet, covered from head to foot in the red mess.

I went to the soldiers and spoke to the officer i/c. They had the casualty on a stretcher, but refused to carry him to the helicopter, so I picked him up and carried him myself. I had to put him down while I opened the rear door. The helicopter was rising & falling, but I managed to get the casualty on board and closed the door.

TALES FROM THE HORSE'S MOUTH – CREWMEN

I then jumped on the front step and grabbed the handle on the door frame. The pilot gave the engine full power & banked to stbd. I lost my grip and was flung inside, almost landing on the pilot.

We had words!

Corporal Bob Ashley

Joined the RAF in 1946 after returning to the UK from New Zealand – where he had been evacuated during the Second World War. Completing his training as an airframe mechanic, he took part in the Berlin Airlift, was then posted to FEAF in 1951, returning for a second tour in 1954, when he joined 155 Sqn as a crewman:

After a four week course on the S55 at the Westland factory, Yeovilton, I found myself almost immediately posted to RAF Seletar, Singapore.

As our first six S55s had only recently been handed over to the RAF in the UK, we had to wait a while for them to arrive, a Royal Navy carrier transporting them out. While waiting, we helped with the assembly of some Bristol Sycamores that had recently arrived from UK in crates. These were new and destined to serve with 194 Squadron at Kuala Lumpur. This was happening over on West Camp, RAF Seletar, the RAF's maintenance base for the Far East.

When the carrier HMS Ocean *arrived a few weeks later, it docked at Sembawang Navy base, situated just up the Johore Straits from Seletar airfield. 155 Squadron engineering borrowed a workboat, with a barge lashed alongside, from the Navy, and brought the S55s back down the Straits, two at a time. We then towed them from the wharf by tractor, across the airfield to the West Camp. This was where they were to be cleaned up and prepared to go into service. I seem to remember a lot of problems occurring, and there were many engine runs and air tests before they were ready. The troubles were mainly electrical and instruments (E&I) faults, which required rectification before we could fly them up to KL.*

THE FIRST HELICOPTER BOYS

I was crewman on the first one, flying with the then CO, Squadron Leader Jackson-Smith, on what was supposed to be a one day delivery flight to our new base. The problem was, there had been heavy rain for some time, with lots of flooding in Singapore and Malaya, so we spent the next two days picking up stranded people, or landing in clearings to ferry out police, or whoever.

Once all six aircraft were on line at Kuala Lumpur the real problems began. They weren't suitable for the conditions in which they were intended: high temperature and humidity. The all-up-weight (critical with helicopters) was very high, engines down on power. A change to a lower ratio supercharger helped somewhat, as did removal of all trim, internal panels, and the hydraulic winch system. We even removed the engine fire system and bottles!

One of the first jobs was to get the flight-line maintenance department fixed up. For this an old a/c packing crate was lifted into position at the back of the hangar, tilt-out windows and a door cut out, benches and desks knocked up from any 'gash' wood found lying around, then connect some power. This office was still in use when I left in 1956.

The Pratt and Whitney engine was fitted to the Whirlwind backwards and upside down, at a 45 degree angle so as to drive the rotor on top of the cabin. Such positioning caused the magneto seals on the engine rear to allow oil to leak into the magnetos. Starter motor clutches were also facing downhill, so they frequently oiled up, causing slipping. Just a few of the problems encountered. And six aircraft were never going to be enough to fill all the calls coming in from the army and police, so while awaiting others to be shipped over from the UK arrangements were made for the RAF to 'borrow' three aircraft the Navy had stored in Singapore. The Navy's American-built S55s weighed 200lbs less than the Westland version and had an engine giving 50 more horsepower.

The CO and I flew down to Changi in a Valetta. The CO then left Changi for Sembawang to pick up the aircraft, leaving me at Changi Operations to await his return. As the weather turned very bad, this turned out to be three days later. Here was I, with just a small overnight pack, dressed in jungle greens and jungle boots, carrying a radio headset and throat mike, a parang, a

TALES FROM THE HORSE'S MOUTH – CREWMEN

small tool kit, a Sten gun, three magazines, and the CO's pistol belt he had left with me, and I was wandering around Changi with everyone else in smart, clean, standard RAF uniform!

Anyway, I flew on many ops over my two years, lots of problems to keep us busy, but lots of good memories too, memories that will always be with me.

I recall one Op, out over nowhere when the two tacho needles split. Instant panic until we noted the rotor rpm was normal; the engine rpm was down about thirty per cent, though the engine sounded OK. We carried on until we found a kamong where we could put down. One of the three engine tacho leads had broken. Luckily a guy with us who spoke Malay managed to get a soldering iron from a cycle repair place. After soldering it back together we carried on with the Op.

*

During 1955 negotiations were in progress with the CTs, senior police, government officials, and some ex-members of Force 136 – who knew the people they were talking to, having fought together in the jungle against the Japanese. The CT negotiator was Chin Peng, party secretary to the Malayan Communist Party. The parties concerned mutually agreed to meet at Baling, near the Thai border.

One day Flight Lieutenant Hicks, who seems to have been my regular pilot at that time, informed me we were going up to Butterworth. We flew up via Ipoh, then stayed at RAF Butterworth for a couple of days, waiting to be called out. Eventually, we received word the Op was 'on' and left Butterworth early one morning. Although I was not told our exact destination, we landed on a padang outside Baling, where a secure area had been set up. There was a large tent, with numbers of what were obviously VIPs milling around. We were told to hand in any firearms, then wait to be called. Eventually Hicks was told to go on his own for the pick-up. This did not seem unusual, indeed it was a normal occurrence since our carrying capacity was limited.

After twenty minutes he returned with his Chinese passengers, well dressed in clean, pressed shirts and slacks. They were met by the Force 136 representatives and went over *to the tent where they stayed for a couple of hours or more. They finally came out, climbed into the helicopter and were flown back to their clearing.*

Only after our return to Butterworth was I told what we had been there for [the Baling Talks on Chin Peng's surrender]. *It had been deemed top secret. The negotiations were unsuccessful. The actual dates are in my log book.*

Bob also remembers their being asked to fly 'full chat' down a marginal length airstrip ahead of an Auster, hopefully to create enough of a headwind for the Auster to take off. It worked!

Corporal George Nettleship

An instrument Fitter with 390 MU at Changi in 1949, George had helped to assemble the Casevac Flight's Dragonflys in time for Bob Bowman's arrival. George remembers Warrant Officer Smith who, along with Sergeants Baker and Boag, and Westland Service Engineer Norman Chant, who had supervised assembly of the Dragonflys, and, of course, Chips Fry who later recommended George for aircrew training.

Junior Technician Len Raven

Len Raven with XJ407 and Ken Claydon at Kampong Ulu Klawang.

TALES FROM THE HORSE'S MOUTH – CREWMEN

155 Squadron take a break on Ops at an infant school. Len Raven in the foreground with Al Payne.

20 September 1957, returning from a trooplift operation at Tanah Rata with Eric Leyden, and in company with four other Whirlwinds. Some thirty minutes after take-off, in the Slim River area, a mayday call was received. I looked around and saw XJ 413 spiralling down with bits falling off the end of the tail boom – tail rotor, pylon, who can recall after

Slim River Crash.

such a fleeting moment? My camera was able to record the incident – evidence that would otherwise have been lost. Eric Leyden remained circling the area for as long as he could to help guide rescue parties to the site. A tragic, but thankfully rare, event that claimed the lives of all three crew members: Flight Lieutenant Draper and Corporals Cosens and Simpson. Corporal Simpson was on only his second op as crewman.

*

Another incident in which I was involved happened on 22 January 1958 and concerned Whirlwind XJ407 flown by Flight Lieutenant Ken Claydon. We were returning from a trooplift along with two other aircraft when we suffered an engine failure, accompanied by lots of smoke. Ken immediately put the aircraft into autorotate and selected the only open area in which to put down. It was a rice paddy at Kampong Ulu Klawang, the rice almost ready for harvesting, the field quite soggy. Al Payne, crewman in one of the other aircraft in the formation, circling overhead, reported it looked like a perfect engine-off landing.

Once down, I got out of the cabin, from where I'd been awoken from my slumber. A sightseeing squadron member was

Flight Lieutenant Bultitude (in chair), Brian Swallow (centre) and Len Raven.

up top alongside the pilot and noticed the water was getting close to the bottom of the engine as the aircraft settled, so I took the wooden load spreaders out of the cabin and placed them beneath. Investigation revealed no.2 cylinder had a blown head. Another engine fitter plus new cylinder were flown out from KL, along with Taff Walker, a much more experienced pilot, required to recover the aircraft from the bog. We changed the cylinder, did all the checks then flew back to base.

Corporal David Taylor

My introduction to the rotary world of helicopters: On arrival at RAF Seletar in Sept 1957 I found myself in 390 MU Instrument Section; not my kind of thing at all, I was a first line man, out there with the aircraft. Only this was worse than expected. It was like working for a trade union – one had to clock in and out; on top of which, with the aircon cranked up it was like working in a freezer. Everything went like clockwork – that is, each job was allocated a time. The thing was these times were nowhere near realistic; way overstated in fact. The time allocated for testing an airspeed indicator, say, was probably two hours, when it actually took maybe twenty minutes. Four instruments therefore officially covered my 8-hour day, whereas in real time, just over an hour! So what to do for the rest of the day? We talked amongst ourselves, took long NAAFI breaks from the van which called round, etc. Even school bus guard was a relief! So when a detachment was offered – to 205 Squadron Sunderlands – I accepted indecently quickly. This one month detachment

Author in LH seat, ready to go.

I managed to stretch out for more than a year. Then, with the Sunderlands being phased out – the last of the RAF's flying boats – I found myself posted to RAF Kuala Lumpur, and 155 Squadron with their Whirlwind helicopters; from one totally new environment to another, as different again! Interesting and exciting. From waterborne, to up, up, and away! Was I indeed happy. And before long, despite the qualifying stipulation of engine or airframe tradesmen, many of whom it seemed did not wish to fly, resulting in a shortage, I found myself accepted as a Crewman. Even happier still, despite the fact that we talk about 'run of the mill' troop lifts, it was hard work.

Usually an early morning start – well before the sun had burnt off the mist and low cloud that gathered in the valleys overnight – for a positioning flight to somewhere like Grik, where the troops were already waiting. Most LZs were small, sandy, and dusty. We landed and shutdown, crewmen servicing their aircraft and organising the fuel, while pilots briefed the army as to what was required of them, and vice versa. Then it was start up, load up, and up, up and away. A sortie could be anything from five to twenty minutes, but as the sun rose higher, off would come the jackets and shirts. Hats were never worn, due to the danger of any lose items being blown into the rotor.

Between sorties there was time for a gulp of warm water, then it started again. Hard work beneath a pitiless sun. And the sun's rays not only beat down from above, they also rebounded off the parched earth. Swirling clouds of dust blown up during lift-off and landing would cake our sweat-damped, naked-to-the-waist bodies. And no matter that we turned to face away and protected ourselves, that dust would still penetrate our eyes and fill our noses and mouths. This could go on for hours, aircraft shutting down only if they had a problem, refuelling, and a quick visual inspection as we organised the next load. Sometimes though – especially when Gurkhas were involved – we would get the troops to refuel for us as we kept an eye on things. They seemed keen, and were I suppose otherwise bored, just waiting around. Some troops occasionally lay down to rest, using their pack as a pillow. Good thinking, for there was no telling when the next chance to relax might be.

It was also difficult for the pilots. With such short sector times there was no chance for them to relax. Take-off, a short hop, descent into a jungle clearing – hopefully secure, and away for another quick turn-around. And so it went on, always with the chance of a mechanical problem or of being shot at to keep them on their toes.

It was a relief for us all when the aircraft settled for the last time at the day's end. One more service check, refuel, tidy up, load our kit into the cabin, then climb up into the cockpit, eight feet off the ground. It would still be hot, sun glaring in through the Perspex above and to the sides, and I'd be sweat-stained, weary, and still sweating profusely. I was always aware of that giant fan above my head. Once that began to turn I knew relief could not be far away. Ten minutes and we were a thousand feet up and cool, and down below was spread that verdant carpet of jungle, looking peaceful and calm.

And the troops we had spent all day flying into the interior, what of them? They'd be tired, dirty, and hungry, as was I. It would be so again tomorrow, and probably the next day too. But in between I could look forward to a shower, clean clothes, a decent meal, a beer or two – possibly more – and a relatively soft bed.

Corporal/Tech Al Payne

A posting to the Far East, straight out of training, was almost a miracle, being accepted as a helicopter crewman was the absolute icing on the cake. When it was initially realised that a helicopter pilot could not handle the multi-tasking asked of him, it was decided he needed a helper. The first thought was that the crewman should be an SNCO, for his maturity and experience I presume (but a nonsense as nobody had experience on choppers). However, most SNCOs were married and did not wish to become heroes or fly in these new-fangled machines on which the wings rotated. Therefore the lot fell upon the lower ranks, they being young, unattached, and enthusiastic. In their late teens and early twenties, they were old enough to remember the end of the Second World War. Now, on active service, in a war theatre, emulating their fathers, fighting for Queen and country was exiting and romantic. They would do anything, go anywhere and stay anywhere.

THE FIRST HELICOPTER BOYS

One occasion I specially recall. My aircraft developed a rather serious hydraulic leak which should have required immediate investigation and rectification. However, the pilot's determination to get back at all costs resulted in me kneeling on the co-pilots seat, facing rearwards, gearbox soundproofing pushed back, topping up the hydraulic reservoir as the level dropped. It was an incredibly foolhardy thing to do with only one hydraulic system, but as we made it back before my can of hydraulic fluid was exhausted, it couldn't have been a very long transit.

One advantage of a helicopter is that they can land almost anywhere. One pilot, at the slightest sign of inclement weather would call up KL tower and announce he could not get through and was putting down until the front had passed. Strangely, he always put down on the nineteenth green of Kuala Lumpur golf course, of which he was a member.

One old (compared to us) ex-WWII pilot could not go any length of time without a 'fag'. A one-ship task was no problem, but with a multi-ship, transiting in loose formation, his aircraft always lagged behind. Once he figured there was enough distance between him and the rest he would say to the crewman, 'Come on then, get the fags out.' Pilot would tighten friction on throttle and collective, crewman would light up cigarettes. Pilot would fly with right hand on cyclic, cigarette in left. Crewman would extract empty tobacco tin from flying suit, hold it in right hand. They would flick ash into tin, and when finished, drop in extinguished dog ends. Crewman would then throw contents of tin out of the window. One smug crewman, one satisfied pilot!

There are times when pilots become useful for things other than flying. On one heavy troop lift – a multi-ship involvement from a site which was geographically divorced from civilisation – each aircraft carried two pilots. As Sod's law would have it, one aircraft suffered a clutch failure, requiring a clutch change which meant dropping the engine. This entailed use of an engine transit/servicing stand: a heavy, girder section frame with casters on each corner. On the rear cross member are transit brackets which match up with transit brackets on the engine. Similarly there are transit brackets on the forward cross member and also a lifting eye. The stand *is wheeled into position under the engine, brackets on the rear cross member and engine are aligned, pins inserted. A crane hook is then attached to the lifting eye on the front cross member, the stand forward end is lifted through an angle of forty-five degrees until the brackets on the forward cross member are aligned with those on the engine, and pins fitted, with the crane continuing to take the strain. Engineers then make all the engine disconnections required, and the crane lowers the front end of the stand, complete with engine, until it is sitting on all four casters. The engine can now be worked on in situ or wheeled away to the engine bay for deep servicing. Refitting is the reversal of this procedure.*

In this case there was no access for a crane to get to the site. However, a transit stand and replacement clutch were flown in and the procedure for dropping the engine commenced. At the point where the stand had to be pivoted through forty-five degrees, the spare pilots came into their own, eight or nine pilots gathered round the stand and lifted it until the pins were inserted. When all disconnections were made, these pilots again took the strain and lowered the stand, complete with engine, back to the ground – a supreme effort: the Wasp engine weighs nine hundred and thirty pounds! Once the clutch had been changed, these stalwarts again gathered round, lifted the engine back into position, then lowered the stand once the engine attachment bolts had been refitted. This operation was an absolute sight to see, but unfortunately there is no evidence on record of the achievement (where was Len Raven and his camera when needed!). Ground runs were satisfactory, so the squadron got its aircraft back purely through 'Pilot Power!'

Corporal Peter (Lofty) Dace

Flight Lieutenant Tom Bennett in XJ426 was the first aircraft to land at Fort Betis on 24 September 1959, with myself as crewman.

One incident was an engine failure on 11 March 1960, XJ410 with Flight Lieutenant Hughes at the controls. We were en route from Fort Kemar to Butterworth when there was a bang and clouds of smoke from the engine. We autorotated and landed quite firmly in a deserted area just clear of the jungle. It was Padang Serai, and within five minutes we were surrounded by curious villagers. A cylinder had cracked, luckily one of the upper ones, easily accessible. A replacement was flown in from Butterworth base. I changed it and we were back at Butterworth by 19.15.

Re the Sycamore XL822 crash. A gang of four were involved in the field repair and recovery of this aircraft: Sergeant 'Taff' Huntley, Junior Technician John Pressland (or Pressman), SAC John Runacres, and myself. There was also a group of RAF Regiment Malaya guards, just in case! We were driven up to the Cameron Highlands in a three-ton truck: ourselves, and gear to knock up some 'deluxe' accommodation. Bulk of tools, engine, blades, and lifting gear followed once we had established camp, flown in by Whirlwind, John 'Taff' Walker at the controls. We were in the clearing for ten days. One thing I recall was the butterflies, attracted by the salt in the dried urine. We always used the same place to pee.

I was also involved with the search for the Sabre pilot from Butterworth after two of them disputed the same piece of airspace and collided over the jungle. One made it back to base, the pilot of the other was forced to eject.

It was a last hurrah for the Whirlwinds, which were being replaced by the Sycamore with uprated blades. Three aircraft were held back from shipment to RAF Seletar as they were fitted with SARAH search and rescue receivers, which the Sycamore did not have. The Sabres carried SARAH beacons. I flew in XJ414 with Flying Officer Hurley, and in XJ411 with Flight Lieutenant Stevens. We also carried supplies, and a jungle rescue team. Despite all this, it was a Sycamore, piloted by the inimitable Tom Browning, that ferried the pilot back to Butterworth.

My final job as crewman was to accompany the last of the Whirlwind 4s to Seletar, for transit to UK and conversion to Mk 10 configuration. The lightweight but more powerful and reliable Gnome turbine reinvigorated the Whirlwind considerably; it became a different aircraft altogether.

('Run of the mill' for such as us Pete, though never just another day in the office!)

TALES FROM THE HORSE'S MOUTH – CREWMEN

L-R: J. Pressman, Taff Huntley, Pete Dace, and RAF Malaya Regiment guards.

Site and Deluxe accommodation.

THE FIRST HELICOPTER BOYS

Engine Removed.

Squadron Leader Barnes departs after delivering new engine.

As good as new.

Chapter 7

Tales from the Horse's Mouth
Other Personnel

Above: Corporal Dave Plant, airframe fitter, greasing main rotor head. 31 nipples required greasing after every 5 hours flight time.

Left: Sergeant Roy Laken, airframe fitter, making an adjustment to the tail rotor control cables on the strip at Kuala Lumpur.

TALES FROM THE HORSE'S MOUTH – OTHER PERSONNEL

Recollections of a Westland Rep

Keith Pardoe

As some folks may remember, Keith was the Westland Rep assigned to assist with the introduction of the Westland built version of the S55 to RAF service in the Far East during 1954, by which time the Navy already had a couple of years' experience flying the Sikorsky built version with 848 Squadron.

> *The RAF's Whirlwinds were transported from the UK aboard the aircraft carrier HMS* Glory, *and upon arrival at Sembawang Naval Base, I, along with a fairly senior RAF officer and a party of airmen, was dispatched from Seletar to take possession. Although I and the officer rolled up at the gates in an RAF staff car, this apparently did not impress the navy. We were faced with the usual barrage of questions as to who we were and what was our business, but in this case it seemed these were questions which required to be answered in the presence of a fairly senior naval officer. However, upon arrival of such, we were quickly cleared and given the go-ahead, which is when the RAF officer stuck his head out of the car to politely enquire where HMS* Glory *was 'parked'. The 'fairly senior naval officer' went ballistic, or perhaps 'overboard' would be a more appropriate expression. But once he had managed to control his blood pressure, he apprised his RAF equivalent of the fact that ships don't actually park, they berth!*
>
> *Reminds me of the RAF lads, seconded to a navy base – always referred to as a 'ship', named HMS (whatever was appropriate) – who, upon arriving at the guardroom ready for a night on the town, were informed they would have to await the 'liberty boat', due in thirty minutes. After a short consultation amongst themselves they immediately formed up in single file, backs to the gate and, along with appropriate arm movements, proceeded to reverse through it. When the guard enquired what they thought they were doing, the reply was, 'We can't wait. We're rowing ashore.'*
>
> *To return to the newly arrived helicopters, aboard the recently berthed HMS* Glory, *the Whirlwinds were winched over the side onto lighters, two aircraft per vessel – apparently*

a very unstable load in a choppy sea – for the journey up the Johore Straits to the Seletar jetty. Here they were offloaded by means of the jetty's venerable crane, to be towed by tractor over to West Camp... which is where another problem was encountered. The towing arms supplied by Westland were self-manufactured, to a price dictated by MOD policy – i.e. cheap! Hence they were found to be somewhat wanting; almost useless in fact. Keith therefore found himself heading back to Sembawang, cap in hand, requesting the loan of one of their Sikorsky-built originals, which was up to the job.

*

STUCK IN AN AROMATIC PADDY

More than just a Westland rep, Keith was pretty well a founder member of 155 Squadron as well. If he put his mind to it he could really dish the dirt, and on occasion be on the receiving end too, as he recalls in this tale of the early days of 155:

Squadron Leader 'Jacko' Jackson Smith flying XD 184 B was experiencing a progressive loss of power and elected to land in the only clear area – a very wet paddy field. The squadron and tech wing put their heads together and co-opted me into a three-man team led by Squadron Leader Jack Polehill, and we were flown out by Flight Lieutenant Frank Hicks to sort the problem out. The prospect of a major component change in a wet paddy field did not inspire enthusiasm ... but in the event the problem was sorted out in ten minutes flat.

The technical jargon stuff:

The carb hot air butterfly in the induction system had opened due to the failure of the locking wire, introduced to inhibit the hot air intake – which was not required in Malaya.

Explanation for simple folk: a piece of wire had broken. As a result only exhaust air was admitted to the engine – with dramatic loss of power. A more elegant mod was later embodied.

Problem rectified, the engine was run and found to be satisfactory (posh word for OK). However, despite applying maximum power the helicopter would not lift off; it was well and truly stuck. The wheels had sunk into the paddy and the helicopter was sitting with its flat bottom hard on the mud and the oleos fully extended!

By now, a considerable crowd of onlookers had appeared – as though from nowhere – to watch these intrepid bird-men wallow about in their paddy.

A fag and some ideas were needed to sort out the next move. So we waded across the paddy to drier ground to contemplate the problem.

The crowd now began to smile and giggle, barely disguising, even with hands over mouths, a situation to which they but not us were privy, until suddenly two of us, who shall remain nameless, dropped like stones into a deep sump in the corner of the paddy. The good natured crowd were beside themselves, their day was getting better and better.

Of course it did not stop there. The only way to get 'Bravo' out was to remove the mud from below the fuselage. The crowd were far too well dressed to partake of this game, especially as they so enjoyed seeing the Raj on their knees, raking out the foul smelling mud. Jackson Smith remained firmly in the cockpit: drivers/airframe do not get wet and muddy. And... the problem was that as we removed the mud the machine went down even more. However, in the end all was well and with full power applied 'Bravo' shot up out of the mud like a cork out of a Champagne bottle. Never seen a Whirlwind go like that before. Well, it was empty.

I can still smell that paddy field.

CRASH INVESTIGATION

Wing Commander S. Williams OBE

Each wreck, whatever its condition, becomes the subject of a thorough, on-the-spot technical investigation. At Air Headquarters, Malaya, from which all 'Firedog' or truly operational flying in that country is directed, there is one senior officer who has probably carried out more of these technical investigations in two years than anyone else in Malaya. He is Wing Commander S. Williams OBE, Senior Technical Staff Officer.

THE FIRST HELICOPTER BOYS

Technical investigations in the UK – and I have had my fair share of those – may have been exacting affairs, but in Malaya I was to find things very different. My flight from Singapore to Kuala Lumpur, made upon my appointment as STSO to the Air Headquarters, was enough to confirm my worst fears. During that 250-mile journey, I looked down upon an almost unbroken panorama of jungle-clad mountains, which were to be one half of my new parish. The other half, just as bad, stretched a further 250 miles north of the federal capital. And all that jungle was constantly being traversed by a multiplicity of aircraft types, Austers, Pioneers, light and medium helicopters.

The impression I gained then, which has not been dispelled, was that if a small aircraft became lost, it would not be a matter of looking for a needle in a haystack, but one of first trying to find the haystack.

Initiation soon followed my arrival at Air Headquarters. We were asked to make our way to the site where a Dragonfly light helicopter had made a forced landing in deep jungle near the foothills of the Cameron Highlands. The crew of the aircraft were lucky. They escaped with cuts and bruises, and managed

Small aircraft, large jungle.

to walk out of the jungle. Just how much of a trial that walk must have been we were soon to discover.

The early part of this very first exercise proved absorbing and not too discomfiting. I learned that by using the deep jungle forts, which have their own Pioneer airstrips, and by 'helicopting' to even remoter jungle landing zones, the nearest point to the wreck to be investigated could be reached without much trouble. From that point, however, things were rather different.

I was first suspicious of the pitying smile we got from our helicopter pilot as he waved good-bye to us at the landing zone from which we began our trek into the jungle. Within ten minutes of slinging on our packs and slogging along the narrow trail, our jungle green became black with sweat. The more deeply we penetrated, the more humid the jungle became. As we pressed on, with a heavily-armed escort drawn from No. 22 Special Air Service Regiment, we began to appreciate what unfit weaklings we were compared with men from this tough outfit of veteran jungle-fighters and paratroopers. We were already looking forward to the return rendezvous at the LZ when one of the SAS chaps improved the shining hour by reminding us that bad weather often prevented the return of the helicopters, and precluded air-supply drops, sometimes for days at a time. This cheered us up enormously!

At last the trek, made through continuous rain, was over and we arrived at the site of the Dragonfly. It was lying on its side in a fast-running stream and we had to carry out our investigation up to our knees in leech-infested water. When the work was over, we decided to destroy the wreckage of the aircraft, for if we left it, the terrorists might make use of some of the basic material, or booby-trap it – as they had other wrecks – for the next patrol passing that way.

One hundred pounds of plastic explosive was packed into the engine bay and the detonator and quick-match fuse set. We lit the fuse, which was to give us fifteen minutes to retire and find shelter from the blast. After a lifetime of waiting – actually just twenty minutes – there was still no explosion. A conference was held under shelter to decide who should go forward to inspect the fuse. Somehow I got left well behind in the rush of volunteers!

THE FIRST HELICOPTER BOYS

Eventually the fuse was re-lit and a satisfying explosion completely destroyed the wreckage. We shouldered our packs and began the long trek back to the LZ to await the return of the Sycamore helicopter and the air-lift out. The beat of its rotors up the valley made a wonderful sound and soon we were back at base for the de-leeching ceremony and preparation of the technical reports.

Another typical jungle probe, as we call these technical investigations, was made when an Auster – missing, with its occupants, for three years – was discovered on a hill in primary jungle. The team was taken by helicopter to a clearing where rubber trees ended and the jungle began, and there we started an 8,000-yard climb to a height of 2,500 feet. We climbed over and around boulders to get to the site of the aircraft, often drenched, re-drenched and blinded by the cascading stream which provided the only possible path.

During some parts of this climb, our rate of progress was reduced to 500 yards an hour. In what is jocularly called 'more difficult terrain', jungle patrols are lucky to penetrate at the rate of 1,000 yards a day! As dusk fell, we pitched camp for the night about three-quarters of a mile from the wreckage. After one of the most unpleasant nights I have ever spent, an early morning start was made with a limited escort. The main party remained in camp while we hacked and scrambled up the last 1,000 yards to the wreck. When we reached it, late in the day, we discovered that the occupants had not been as fortunate as some aircrew.

The investigation completed, the grim descent was continued. Back at our LZ near the rubber estate, we found that the batteries of our 'walkie-talkie' had expired. We were out of touch with base and obliged to make another night of it in the jungle. We were greatly cheered however by the high spirits of our Gurkha escort: fine, tough little chaps who made light of their enormous packs and did everything they could to make us comfortable. The following morning brought an enquiring helicopter, which soon had a one-craft shuttle service flying the party back to base. Another 'probe' was over.

I include this story as we worked closely with 656 Squadron, and the end result did involve the use of one of our helicopters.

TALES FROM THE HORSE'S MOUTH – OTHER PERSONNEL

Selatar Team. Crew from Aircraft Recovery and Salvage Flight at RAF Seletar, Singapore, remove blades from a downed Dragonfly prior to recovery from a swamp in 'Up Country' Malaya.

Sergeant Ken McConnell

In 1956 Sergeant Ken McConnell was attached to No. 656 AOP Squadron, his Auster marking targets and dropping leaflets. He was based at Ipoh, about thirty miles from the Cameron Highlands.

On 28 May 1956 at about 8.30 pm there was a knock on the door of his house which Helen, his wife, answered. She recognized Captain Love, one of Ken's officers, and with him was his wife. Helen guessed it was bad news about Ken.

When Ken had taken off there was a little light rain, but he knew his route for the 110 miles to KL would never be far from the road. There were some thunderstorms around the Cameron Highlands, over to port, but his route seemed clear. But after flying for about fifteen minutes, passing Batu Gajah on his starboard side, the horizon was obscured by a massive cloud that stretched across his track. With cumulonimbus ahead he turned to go on the reciprocal, but found the storm had closed in behind him. At 3,000 feet he was drifting eastwards, towards the foothills of the Cameron Highlands.

THE FIRST HELICOPTER BOYS

He started to climb and called Ipoh tower, but static interference swamped his call. The Auster was now being thrown about all over the place by turbulence, being sucked down about 1,000 feet at a time, then propelled upwards again. He managed to attain 6,000 ft on the altimeter but he knew he was drifting over increasingly high ground. Suddenly he was caught in a strong downdraft. At around 5,000 ft he emerged from cloud in hard rain, a grey-green carpet at right angles dead ahead. He made a fierce turn to port on full power and the plane developed a high speed stall before turning on its back and falling in an inverted spin. The Auster powered into the jungle canopy.

Unconscious, Ken was woken by a steady drip on his neck. He was trembling violently and soaked to the skin. He saw the base of a large tree a few feet away so figured he was on the ground, maybe a few feet up. When he finally got out of the wreckage, his ankles, now swollen, would not support his weight, so he started to crawl. He found the wing made a good shelter against the rain.

Taking inventory of his injuries, he had a severe chest pain and a stabbing pain in his side as he breathed. He thought he must have broken a rib. He was afraid of a bone piercing his lung. He thought his left ankle must be broken as he was completely numb, the right was sprained. There were gashes above and below his left eye, which was closed, and there were gashes to his arms and legs.

All he could do was shiver and huddle under the wing till the first shafts of morning light dawned. Ken crawled from under the wing to assess his situation. He had crashed into a mountain with a slope of about thirty degrees. The tops of the trees were 200 feet above. As the Auster plunged through them they had closed tightly back together, leaving no gap. Somewhere amongst the debris were first aid and jungle survival kits, he knew. But all he managed to salvage were several loose items, the kits having broken up on impact. He found his overnight bag, a groundsheet, two signal rockets, a tin of fifty cigarettes and some matches. He also found a compass which had a mirror. On looking at himself he thought he was lucky not to lose his eye. He treated his wounds as best he could. He bound his ankles with shell dressings, put two pairs of socks over these, then fastened them with adhesive tape. He had lost his shoes but found in the survival kit a pair of jungle boots. He cut the tops off these so he could get them on. He changed into the clean set of greens from his overnight bag. He had a survival knife, and food, so he put the groundsheet under the wing, opened some self-heating soup, then had a cigarette. His headache had gone but his side and chest still hurt. His ankles still gave him most problems.

TALES FROM THE HORSE'S MOUTH – OTHER PERSONNEL

With dry clothes, soup, and cigarette, he managed to doze off, until awakened by the sound of an aircraft. The signal rockets were designed to penetrate the canopy and burst above the trees, so he prepared to fire one as the aircraft came close, but the engine sound faded, so he decided to save them.

His more immediate problem was insects, especially the wasps that were buzzing around his head. Others were attracted by his injuries. He found some insect repellent, but better still was a sort of beekeeper's hat from the survival kit. Using fabric torn from the wing, Ken made a fire, boiled some water, and made tea. He searched the wreckage for the smoke generator, Very pistol and cartridges, and the marker balloon, but all he found was the balloon. He took some tablets from the medical kit, plus salt tablets. He then took stock of where he was, slightly confused from the crash. He knew he had been above 3,000 ft, so guessed he was deep in the Cameron Highlands. He figured he was at least 25 miles south east of Ipoh. He'd retrieved his rifle from the wreckage, though the butt was broken. To activate his balloon he needed water, and with his bottles nearly empty he had to get down to the stream below. This would be difficult as his ankles still hurt tremendously, so he waited one more day and tried to build up his strength, but he would have to ration his food.

On the third day he decided to get the water. It was a perilous journey down, even worse trying to get back, and when he finally made it back under the wing he passed out.

It was the sound of an aircraft that brought him round, but when he attempted to inflate the balloon it burst.

He heard aircraft, but they were over to the west, so he decided he would create smoke by burning his aircraft. But because it was rain soaked it would not burn. Only one thing left, he decided, try and walk out to civilization, so Ken collected all he would need. Once on the move, he realized that with the extra weight, and the pain it was causing, he wouldn't get far, so he returned to the wreck. Next day, after a good sleep he set off again, this time with a smaller load: a small amount of food, his compass, machete, and broken rifle. He estimated his trek would take 6 or 7 days. He hobbled in short stages, resting in between. He needed to be watchful as terrorists were active in the area. Because of the light growth on the jungle floor he managed quite well. After the first day he reckoned he had covered about four miles. Next day, now in secondary jungle, his progress slowed. Food was getting low, so he looked to the jungle to provide for him. The next day however, he felt he did not need food, realized he was living off his body reserves. Water was not a problem, there were plenty of clear streams. Ken noticed some old CT camps, so kept his rifle ready, with a round up the spout. Once, he stumbled, and the gun went off right next to his ear. He thought it had fractured his eardrum. He fired a rocket when he heard an aircraft but none came near.

On 31 May the ground search was abandoned, although there was still a reward of £250 for information. Helen McConnell steadfastly held on to the belief that Ken was alive and would find his way out of the jungle as he had always promised. But she was offered the chance to go home on government expenses, so she left on 12 June.

Ken was getting weaker. He did not know how long he could last. He figured he had been in the jungle for about 2½ weeks since the crash. He had eaten nothing for days but had forgotten his hunger. Each night he lay down not knowing if in the morning he would have the strength to get up again. He needed something to boost his morale. It came the next day as he emerged into a clearing near the top of a ridge. The jungle gunongs stretched out before him, but he could make out landmarks. He had seen them from his aircraft. He could recognize outcrops – the Ipoh Plain, a sight he thought he would never see again. He made good progress that day, but it rained and by 4 pm he was drenched. It rained solidly for twelve hours.

On his 21st day Ken got a stroke of luck. He was about to climb a slope when he heard a sound in the undergrowth. He turned to see a brown and white dog coming towards him. His mind was now racing: CTs or aborigines? He could hear voices and saw a shadow move through the forest. He shouted, 'Is that the Security Forces?' There was no reply and the voices faded away.

He slept on top of the hill that night and in the morning kept up his routine of dressing his wounds. He was sitting down in a hollow when the same brown and white dog appeared. He then heard someone talking in Malay and suddenly behind him were two aborigines with blow pipes. They made signs to him to let him know they knew about his plane crash. They sat beside him and made him a cigarette. When he'd had a rest and a smoke they helped him down to their small village. There they bandaged his injuries, gave him a sarong to replace his worn trousers and fed him tapioca and fish. He was not far from the head of the pipeline, about ten miles from Ipoh. One of the villagers ran to the nearest Home Guard post to raise the alarm. The end was in sight, and, twenty-two days after his crash, a helicopter flew Ken out. This was the longest a European had been lost in the jungle.

TALES FROM THE HORSE'S MOUTH – OTHER PERSONNEL

Mike Dalton – Air Britain Historian

My father, Flight Lieutenant Max Dalton, was an engineering officer at RAF Seletar, 1954-57. His section was involved in maintenance and modification work, plus the unpacking of arriving crated aircraft. I was at Seletar school at the time so had a good opportunity to witness base activities.

A couple of interesting things happened. Firstly, a visit by the Duke of Edinburgh was scheduled, and it was expected he would be taken on a helicopter trip round the island. To cater for this my father's section prepared a Whirlwind, complete with 5-star plate. Unfortunately the local political situation deteriorated, with numerous strikes and civil disorder, so the operation was cancelled. My father kept the 5-star plate as a memento. (A round-the-island tour did take place later, in a Sycamore.)

The second, rather sad occurrence was a serious accident involving another Whirlwind (XJ427).

Duke of Edinburgh arrives in a Sycamore, 31 October 1956.

THE FIRST HELICOPTER BOYS

XJ427 Accident.

After servicing, Flying Officer Evans was commencing ground running checks, but upon engaging the main rotor and applying power the aircraft began to vibrate so severely it broke up. One main rotor blade detached, killing a member of the groundcrew. The aircraft rolled onto its side but

Well executed break. Now, show us your diamond nine!

TALES FROM THE HORSE'S MOUTH – OTHER PERSONNEL

Going home at day's end.

Kilo en route.

Roping exercise.

Sam Saunders deplanes Ghurkas.

did not cause any more injuries. It was later repaired. The resulting court of enquiry ascertained the cause to be the incorrect fitting of the blade, the corporal responsible for fitting the blade was the person killed.

TALES FROM THE HORSE'S MOUTH – OTHER PERSONNEL

XE311 at rest.

Chapter 8

Crewroom, Reunions and Lift-Off Chat

Sergeant Jack Feeley, together with SAC Williams and David Vicary, were the 'ubendum wemendum' (servicing) element of the team supporting John Dowling when he carried out the FEAF part of the operational trials with Sycamore Mk 10, WA 578 in 1953. After all that has been said and written about it, it seemed reasonable to ask Jack to tell us about some of these exciting adventures. Jack says:

> *I don't know about exciting but the trial of the original Sycamore did involve me in one or two memorable events.*
>
> *Once, at Gua Musang, in Ulu Kelantan, I had to walk through the bandit infested bush to Gua Chah (Fort Chabai) to replace a faulty booster-pump. This trek of twenty-odd miles was quite eventful for myself and SAC Williams as well as our escort from 3 Malay Regiment. Upon our arrival, John Dowling's reception at Gua Chah was terse: 'Did you bring my toothbrush?'*
>
> *Later I received a good briefing on the history of Ulu Kelantan and the Pulai Chinese who had settled there some hundred years before. This was given by a Mr Banks, John Dowling's mate and the Protector of the Aborigines for Kelantan.*
>
> *And so to Kota Bahru! A survey followed of the border area with Siam. God knows why!* – *'Perhaps you were forgiven for the toothbrush, Jack. After all, you were mentioned in* The First Twenty Years' [John Dowling's book on RAF Helicopter operations].
>
> *Someone else mentioned in the book, though not by name, was George Meyrick – one of the original Casevac Flight pilots but who was temporarily grounded and became officer i/c Labuan Detachment in July 1950. The book suggests that*

CREWROOM, REUNIONS AND LIFT-OFF CHAT

George's deafness was perhaps a consequence of having flown the Hoverfly at the Airborne Forces Experimental Establishment (AFEE) bare headed, 'to detect more easily by ear any significant changes in rotor speed!' Another ex-AFEE, and subsequently distinguished helicopter test pilot, once explained to me that the R-4 Hoverfly Mk 1 was flown without headsets (or helmets) because the cockpit noise level was so low that you could converse (almost) normally and that it wasn't fitted with a radio anyway. He also said that he had much later flown a Sycamore in Cyprus with George, so his hearing defect had been overcome sometime after his brief stay with the Casevac Flight and move to Labuan.

Jim McCorkle says that he too met George when they served together flying Sycamores in Cyprus. So, once again, there are all sorts of versions of the same stories.

For example, Ray Firman's wedding recorded in his 'Thoughts on my Malaya, 1953-56' led to David Jones's fond memories of the wedding which he recalled. Ray, though, is certain that it wasn't his wedding that David attended because he didn't have a formal reception. But David certainly went to one somewhere and had a really good time. But when, where and whose?

Even worse: your nit-picking, supposed stickler for accuracy, Tom Browning, has a confession to make. Two actually, because after having ducked out of last year's reunion to have a hip op, the op was put off because his hydraulic system pressure was off the clock: After Tom paid his tribute to Nobby Clarke, Taff Walker told him he remembered Nobby telling the story about his ditching an Anson – but where? He thought it was off Blackpool, and that they became aware of where they were when they heard the tram bells ringing as they clanked their way along the sea front! While there was no doubt about Nobby having ditched, the question remains, where? Was it Southend, Clacton, or Blackpool? Knowing that he had read about it in *Tee Emm* as a callow youth, Tom set off to the RAF Museum, Hendon, to read all about it. Guess what: nothing at all! So, sorry folks, I got it wrong. But as Taff confirms, it did happen and it had to be during the war because there was a blackout, otherwise they would have been able to see the coast before ditching. But where was it?

One incident that did involve Nobby was the great 194 Squadron para jump. After 194's second Sycamore crash in 1959 an anxious HQ FEAF asked what the pilots would like to do to amuse themselves pending a decision on their future. There was no shortage of ideas. Mostly exotic places to go to: Hong Kong, Australia and all points south – some actually did go. Nobby, though, sitting quietly, reflectively, in the crew room, which was his wont, said, 'I've always wanted to do a parachute jump.' So Nobby's wish was sent on to HQ. 'Great idea,' they replied, 'But we can't really do it for just one, how about getting a few more to go with him?' So we just had to volunteer, didn't we. After all we wouldn't want to be accused of spoiling Nobby's day out – let alone being chicken. There is said to be a picture to prove it, but as yet it has managed to evade all my enquiries.

*

It isn't often that we hear from somebody who can appreciate the before and after of helicopter casualty evacuation. V.A. (Ozzie) Osborne, who won the Military Medal at Dieppe, says,

> *In 1951 I was a Police Lieutenant in command of a small detachment of Jungle Company personnel at Kuala Betis, Ulu Kelantan, when I fell victim to a disease of the typhus/typhoid type and had to avail myself of the sole available method of evacuation. I was taken down the Sungei Negiri to Bertam on a raft constructed by aborigines: a journey of two days, which involving shooting a couple of rapids; and from Bertam, a rail journey on a line still under construction to Kuala Krai, and from thence to Kota Bharu hospital where I was 'interned' for 5 weeks isolation.*
>
> *In 1954 while operating in the Sungei Belum area I was again a candidate for casualty evacuation. This time I was lifted out by Sycamore, deposited on the lawn between my quarter and the bachelor officers' mess of No.7 Police Field Force, driven by my wife in my Morris Minor, and checked in to the hospital. All done in a matter of a few hours.*

*

Ken Crowhurst

Memories
Ken tells Jacko Jacques' story of firing a Verey cartridge straight up through the main rotor blades, and adds:

CREWROOM, REUNIONS AND LIFT-OFF CHAT

Just goes to show how fickle can be the memory at times, for surely this could only happen once! But in the version that featured in Lift-Off for Summer 2000, the Auster is dispensed with, the Dakota is transformed into a Valetta and the chopper was a Dragonfly piloted by Jacko, who related the tale back then, so you'd think he would know!

*

The Safety Equipment airman who dropped a CO_2 cylinder on the aircraft dispersal area at Changi – we watched it fizz around on the PSP like a firework, just missing one of the Dragonflys and an Auster before coming to rest against the Dope Store. The escaping gas cut his hand and he left a trail of blood spots through our hangar on his way to get some first aid.

*

The Group Captain and the Wing Commander who were doing circuits and bumps in a Harvard at Changi and made a wheels-up landing in the middle of the runway – each apparently thought that the other had lowered the undercarriage (and neither thought to check!), fifteen minutes before the BOAC Comet was due to land. Quite a panic to find a Coles crane to lift it off – the only one on the dispersal had a Valetta engine hanging from it!

*

Taking part in Ali Baba and the Forty Thieves *in the Astra cinema at Changi, put on by the Changi Players in Dec 1952. Other Casevac members in the cast were Reg Taylor (Sergeant Bandit) and Laurence Earland.*

*

May 1953 I was sent to Changi to help dismantle non-flying Dragonfly WF315 in preparation for transporting it to Sembawang by road. I seem to remember I spent a lot of the journey standing or squatting on the servicing platform by the rotor head, lifting tree branches over the main rotor driveshaft and making sure that it did not foul any of the overhead electricity wires across the roads.

*

When at Sembawang, an S55 from 848 Sqn was sent to retrieve a wing from a Brigand which had crashed into the jungle, so the wing failure could be investigated at RAE Farnborough (apparently Brigand wings had a nasty habit of folding up when pulling out of diving attacks). The wing was winched up and the S55 returned to Sembawang where the crew asked for instructions where it should be deposited. But it had gone – fallen off on the way! I believe they did manage to recover it.

*

August 1953, a large grass fire at KL got out of hand and was heading for the bomb dump. An SOS was sent out to all available personnel to beat it out – a hot job on a hot day with plenty of sparks and smoke, but we succeeded.

*

Visitors to, or passing through, KL while I was there: Richard Nixon, US Vice President in 1953 – his MATS Constellation was ringed by armed guards as soon as it had rolled to a standstill; Duncan Sandys, Minister of Supply (who inspected us on parade, August 1953); band leader, Xavier Cugat, along with Abbe Lane, his wife and the singer, plus the band, December 1953.

*

Operation Cyclone (Sep/Oct 1953), operating Dragonflys fitted with crop-spraying gear from Kluang/Labis airstrips to kill off crops of tapioca being grown in jungle clearings by CTs. In the evenings we were entertained at Kluang by Gurkhas, who put on a stage show to celebrate their New Year and fed us curried goat's meat.

Corporal David Taylor

Memories

I recall being seated in a vehicle, a Land Rover, I seem to think. Would have to have been, wouldn't it? Back then when we had a well-established manufacturing base and Japan did not. So, a Land Rover; which would

CREWROOM, REUNIONS AND LIFT-OFF CHAT

imply being 'squeezed in' rather than seated. We were being driven out to the aircraft, crewmen and pilots. It was one of those early morning starts – the jungle a mournful blue rather than brilliant green, misty cloud amongst the tree-tops, everything covered in dew – somewhere up country – could it have been Grik? Not only was I quite young and decidedly innocent (relatively speaking!), I was also a fairly recent addition to 155 Sqn then, somewhat in awe of the stick and rudder guys, hung on to their every word. Anyway, a technical discussion was in progress between two or three right-hand seat types – no names, no pack drill. The subject of this discussion apparently centred around the relative merits of various brands of toothpaste, would you believe! (Isn't it strange the things you *can* remember in later years!) It seemed someone had been delving into that poor man's *Medical Journal*, the *Reader's Digest* (today it would be *Saga Magazine*), the conclusion being, the greater the salt content the better the cleaning properties of toothpaste (and how would that go down with today's Health & Safety Gestapo!)

Author in amongst the lalang.

I remember thinking at the time, 'Boy, they know some stuff, these pilots!' Told you I was a bit naive at the time! Well, over the years, a certain amount of worldly wisdom replacing naivety, I came to realise that, probably toothpaste apart, they actually did. They were also, along with everyone else on the squadron – from the CO down – the best bunch of people I ever worked with during my time in the RAF.

I also recall that this was the period – as a 23-year-old lad from the sticks – during which our Squadron NCO at Butterworth, Chiefy Henderson (ex 617 Sqn Dambuster, I believe) taught me to drive. And I never so much as put a scratch on that Standard Vanguard we'd been allocated for transportation – it was quite a way from the domestic site to squadron headquarters, a little shed and piece of grass on the other side of the 'V' Bomber pan.

Most of the aircrew had by this time bought themselves a little Honda 50 moped, a rather neat little machine with a clutchless gearchange, and the roads around HQ began to echo to a rather different sound than the clattering rumble of Pratt & Whitney's Wasp. Not loud in the singular, but a bit wearing when all the aircrew seemed suddenly to get the urge to own one, notable exceptions apart. One patriotic expatriate pilot named Paul opted instead for the BSA Bantam.

'Absolute crap,' was the opinion of Tom Browning, a Honda owner.

Paul, who loved it, replied to the effect that at least it was 'British crap'.

Nobby Clarke's selection was a very posh Vespa, which he almost immediately fell off (probably trying to light yet another cigarette), rendering himself *hors de combat* for quite some time. Then there was Tom Bennett. Tall, young, ginger hair, with matching moustache, good-looking (Ah, but weren't we all?). Tom was different again, being the proud owner of a 'stinkwheel' (a bicycle contraption with a French built motor driving the rear wheel). He had a large wooden box made, which was then fitted to the rear, 'for putting things in'. So one day some of the other pilots did. They filled it with the lizards which were a common feature around the area. That other Tom, the debonair Tom Browning (whom I suspect was the instigator, for this was his kind of thing), says he was quite surprised when, during the round-up, capture, and box-filling phase of the operation, one of the little sods had the audacity to bite him when he grabbed it from behind.

Three rebels then, which left at least half a dozen Hondas; apparently available in any combination of colours, so long as they were cream and blue. Of course the noise became a little more than wearing when they took to riding in formation, round and round the single-storey block which formed Squadron HQ. Maybe they were working off the frustration of never having enough choppers serviceable at one time for them to be able to achieve a decent formation in the air. If the moped formation was anything to go by, the airborne version would have been a sight to behold.

Or maybe the formation idea originated with the monsoon fly, with which we were occasionally inundated. Like large flying ants they would magically appear in their thousands, nay, millions, shortly after a heavy downpour. On arrival they would shed their wings, join up in long trains and wander around like strings of circus elephants playing follow my leader. They'd then disappear, just as suddenly and mysteriously as they had at first arrived, leaving us almost ankle-deep in discarded wings. Where they came from, or went too, who knows, or cares? OK, maybe David Attenborough would.

As with all new toys, there was a slight problem with the scooters: one needed to place one's feet on the road when stopping at traffic lights. It was

CREWROOM, REUNIONS AND LIFT-OFF CHAT

something to remember. Not too difficult a thing, I would have thought, especially for a pilot. And it probably wasn't, at least when sober. You out there, Deke Bradley?

That seemed to be the way of things in the Far East Air Force. Every squadron I served on, people got up to some outrageous deeds at times – stunts that would never be contemplated back home (at least outside of the officers' mess) – but when it came to aircraft, flying them, or servicing them, everyone reverted to being very professional, very serious, very quickly. We wouldn't have had it any other way.

Chapter 9

Brief Notes on Past Members

SAC Howarth 'Jock' Nield

Jock served on Casevac Flight and 194 at KL 1952/54. An engine mechanic, he was persuaded (on the promise of a fitters' course) to sign on by the CO, Squadron Leader Henderson. He served in the RAF for some 25 years, ending his career as Chief Tech. His passion on retirement was walking his dogs in the Cairngorms.

Wing Commander Leslie Leethall Harland

Son of a York station master, Leslie was born on 12 February 1920 and educated at Archbishop Holgate's Grammar School. His passion for flying was triggered when his grandmother paid five shillings for him to have a flight with the Alan Cobham Flying Circus from the Knavesmire, now York, Racecourse. He joined the RAF in September 1940 and trained to be a pilot in Southern Rhodesia.

During the Second World War he flew on 109 operations in North Africa and Italy, being awarded a DFC. At the cessation of hostilities he left the RAF for a brief period before rejoining and accepting a permanent commission in January 1947. For the next few years he specialised as a flying instructor.

In September 1954 he was attached to the Westland Aircraft Company's helicopter school before leaving for Malaya to join No 155 Squadron, operating the Whirlwind helicopter in support of ground operations against the communist insurgents. After a few months, he took command of the squadron and over the next two years flew hundreds of short-range sorties taking military and police forces into jungle areas to flush out the enemy. Return flights often included the evacuation of casualties. On some days he flew as many as eighteen sorties. Many of these involved landing in very small clearings where the clearance for the rotor was minimal. Later in the campaign his helicopters were deployed to spray areas with defoliant to destroy the enemy's crops. These operations were particularly hazardous as the helicopters had to operate over territory with no friendly troops below. Harland undertook many of these sorties and also dropped sticks of SAS paratroopers into the jungle (an exercise pioneered by Lieutenant Commander Breese of 848 Sqn RNAS in 1953). During Harland's time in command of No 155, there was a dramatic increase in the commitments for the helicopter force and his squadron operated at intensive rates. For his services during the Malayan Emergency, Harland was awarded a bar to his DFC.

Flight Lieutenant Jan Walentowicz, by son Paul

A refugee from the Polish Air Force. After the Germans invaded Poland, Jan, along with many other of his countrymen, eventually found his way to England, and joined an RAF Polish Squadron. At war's end they were offered a transfer to the RAF, which Jan took up, his country now part of the Soviet Empire.

In 1954 Jan volunteered to train as a helicopter pilot. Following instruction with Westland at Yeovil he was posted to 155 Squadron, Kuala Lumpur. During his three years in Malaya, he flew 1,000 hours on Whirlwind HAR4s and safely participated in almost 200 operations. Len Raven, a member of Jan's crew on five operations in May and June 1957, wrote after his death, 'It was always a pleasure to crew for him as he was a very competent helicopter pilot and a real gentleman. It was a pleasure to meet him again at one of the helicopter reunions.'

On returning to the UK in 1957, Jan joined 'A' flight of 22 Squadron at RAF St Mawgan, Cornwall, again flying Whirlwinds, in the search and rescue (SAR) role. Shortly after, 'A' flight moved to RAF Chivenor, where Jan became flight commander.

Jan Walentowicz.

Jan's flying career ended in August 1960, shortly after his 40th birthday. He then completed an ATC Course at RAF Shawbury and was posted to RAF Linton-on-Ouse to continue his ground tour.

In January 1964 Jan was posted to RAF Khormaksar, Aden. This was during the Radfan operation, when the station was the busiest in the RAF, nine squadrons based there.

He then moved back to the UK in 1966 for helicopter refresher training and was posted to 202 Squadron, RAF Leuchars as C Flight Commander. He was still flying Whirlwinds, though by now it was the HAR10.

On Boxing Day 1966, Jan was scrambled to fly a doctor to the Isle of Arran to treat a very sick woman; daughter of Robert McLellan, the Scottish playwright and poet. It was eventually decided she had to be flown to the mainland for specialist help. By then the weather had worsened, a snowstorm was raging and visibility was extremely poor. Jan knew it was the only chance to save her life and he took a calculated risk by flying at 100 ft above the waves to get her to hospital in Glasgow.

A year later he was involved in the search for a Lightning pilot who had ejected into the North Sea, fifty-five miles away. In near darkness, the pilot, located almost at the last minute, was rescued. Incidentally the fortunate pilot – Squadron Leader Blackburn – was a neighbour of Jan's at the time! Jan was by then, at 47, the oldest pilot in the RAF. In May 1968 he commenced his last ground tour at RAF Acklington and eighteen months later it was all over: 'On 1 October 1969, I said enough is enough, and retired after 32 years service.'

Together with his family, Jan moved to Essex, where with his wife Wyn he bought and successfully ran the Billericay Bookshop for twenty years. He continued with his antiquarian book business – which he had pursued as a profitable pastime for many years – and developed a picture framing service as a lucrative sideline. Naturally he taught himself how to make and fit the frames.

Now aged 70, Jan and Wyn then had a blissful twenty years of retirement in the village of East Hanningfield outside Chelmsford. For many years they spent the winter months in the charming resort of Dunedin in Florida. In 1998 they were invited by the Polish government to a ceremony in Poland to honour the achievements of the Polish Air Force during the war. In 2010 they received a congratulatory card from the Queen to celebrate sixty years of marriage. Jan remained reasonably healthy past his 90th year.

BRIEF NOTES ON PAST MEMBERS

Squadron Leader George Puddy

George Puddy died in October 1995 after a fall at his home in Suffolk. Born in Somerset in 1924, he left school to join the RAF. He trained in Canada and the US, transferring to the Fleet Air Arm in 1945 where he flew Corsairs, Wildcats, Barracudas, Fireflies and Seafires at naval stations in the UK, India, and Australia, returning for demobilisation in April '46.

He joined the RAFVR in 1948 and flew Tiger Moths and Harvards until rejoining with the RAF in 1952. After refresher training and CFS, he instructed on Harvards, Meteors and Vampires until 1955 when he joined Bomber Command and did tours on Canberras with 104 and 59 Squadrons in Germany.

In 1958 he converted onto helicopters at South Cerney, spending the next three years flying Sycamores and Whirlwinds with 194, 155 and 110 Squadrons. On his return to the UK he completed the SAR course at St Mawgan before commanding 22 Squadron 'A' Flight at RAF Chivenor.

After a short spell at Coastal Command HQ Northwood he served with HQ British Guiana Garrison flying Whirlwinds. Then came a tour on the Westland Wessex at Odiham, followed by long spell instructing on Whirlwind 10s at Ternhill. He left for Cyprus in 1971 for a tour with

Above left: Flight Lieutenant George Puddy.

Above right: George Puddy completes the log.

84 Squadron Whirlwinds, returning to CFS Little Rissington in 1974 for his final year of service with the RAF.

After retirement he joined Bristow's Pilot Administration Department from which he finally retired in 1985.

George was a highly skilled and very experienced aviator, his charm and humour sadly missed by a wide circle of friends.

Lieutenant Commander G.C.J. Knight NAS

Extract from *The Daily Telegraph* 28 May 1996:

> *Lieutenant Commander G.C.J. 'Knocker' Knight was a pioneering helicopter pilot with the Fleet Air Arm, one of a group which first proved the effectiveness and versatility of the helicopter, both in operations and for search and rescue at sea.*
>
> *Knight was senior pilot of 848 Naval Air Squadron, the Royal Navy's first operational helicopter squadron which arrived in Singapore in the carrier HMS* Perseus *in January 1953. Their task was to assist the Army in the campaign against Communist terrorism in Malaya.*
>
> *Operating from Sembawang, on Singapore Island, and with the RAF from Kuala Lumpur, 848 transformed the tactical situation on the ground.*
>
> *Knight was among several squadron personnel who were decorated, being awarded the DFC. On the way home in March 1954, Knight and his family had to take to the boats when the troopship* Empire Windrush *caught fire after an engine room explosion off the coast of North Africa.*
>
> *Gilbert Knight was born 2nd November 1921. Educated at Highbury County Boys School, London. He joined the navy as a Naval airman, went to Canada for flying training, being commissioned as an acting Sub-Lieutenant RNVR.*
>
> *He flew with 717 Sqn, at Crimond Aberdeenshire, 812 Sqn flying Fireflies, from HMS* Theseus.
>
> *In 1950 he joined 705, the Navy's first helicopter squadron, and by 1952 he was a helicopter instructor and senior pilot of the squadron.*
>
> *Knight was appointed MBE in 1959, and retired the same year.*

BRIEF NOTES ON PAST MEMBERS

Commander Sydney Hal Suthers NAS

Jim Suthers, the Association's president 1991-96, known as 'Sunny Jim', sank an Italian destroyer and helped in the capture of Enigma codes in the Second World War. Later he pioneered the use of helicopters in the British armed forces.

Keen to fly and go to sea, young Jim read Captain Marryat, C.S. Forester and Captain W.E. Johns, and used his Sunday exeats from John Fisher School, Purley, to walk to Croydon to watch the flying at the airport. In January 1939 he obtained a short service commission in the expanding Fleet Air Arm and, after four months training on the reserve carrier *Hermes*, was sent to the Royal Naval Air Station at Ford, Sussex, to qualify as an observer. An unhappy few weeks in the destroyer HMS *Malcolm*, where he found prejudice against short-service officers, led him to learn to fly a Tiger Moth at Elmdon, Birmingham.

Following the war he flew at the Empire Central Flying School at RAF Hullavington and the School of Naval Air Warfare at St Merryn.

In 1949 Suthers was 'devastated and depressed' to become commanding officer of 705 Naval Air Squadron, flying helicopters: it took him several weeks to feel safe without wings on either side of him. Flying Hoverflys and then Dragonflys, he introduced a training programme and operational procedures for helicopter work in the British forces. Early tasks involved air-sea rescue, but soon he found himself operating a taxi service for senior officers and ministers.

At short notice, in 1952, he was given command of 848 Squadron, consisting of ten Sikorksy S55 helicopters which had been purchased by the Navy for anti-submarine service and were being diverted to lift troops during the Malayan Emergency. Suthers had to oversee the unloading of the helicopters in Gosport, their assembly and test flights at Lee-on-Solent before the squadron worked up on passage to the Far East in the carrier *Perseus*. Although senior RAF officers judged that he would need six months to make his squadron operational, it was only seven weeks after the arrival of aircraft crated in England that the first trooplift from a clearing in the Malayan jungle took place. Quickly he developed a rule of thumb for the number of troops he could carry: 'six Gurkhas, five British, or three Fijians'.

General Sir Gerald Templer was a frequent passenger, using Suthers' helicopters to visit remote villages, often accompanied by Lady Templer, who insisted upon dressing for these occasions as though for a garden party, complete with high heels. The Sikorsky S55's Pratt and Whitney engine proved as reliable as the Pegasus in Suthers' previous Swordfish, until one failed when he was carrying Adlai Stevenson, the US presidential candidate. When Suthers landed safely in a paddy field, Stevenson congratulated him, but made no comment when told that the failed engine was American-built.

In 1954 Suthers was awarded the DFC, and his squadron won the coveted Boyd Trophy.

Later he held several key staff and planning appointments, including in the aircraft carrier *Ocean*, where he helped plan the first helicopter-borne landing of 45 Commando, Royal Marines, at Suez.

On his retirement his logbook recorded 2,540 hours in thirty-seven types of fixed-wing aircraft and 905 hours in six helicopter types.

Flight Lieutenant George Francis

From the *Bournemouth Echo*, August 2006:

> Air ace, plus jazz and big band enthusiast, George 'Kiwi' Francis, DFC, AFC and bar.
>
> Mr Francis joined the Royal New Zealand Air Force in 1940 and flew Spitfires and Hurricanes in North Africa and on the Dieppe raid. In the 1950s he saw active service in Malaya and Singapore flying rescue helicopters during the communist insurgency. In a past interview with the Daily Echo he recalled being fired on by communist bandits after beaching a Vampire on an island in the China Sea as being one of his most exciting episodes. During his 34-year RAF career, he flew more than 30 different aircraft types, including helicopters on air sea rescue missions, and was involved in trials of Concorde and the Harrier jump jet.
>
> In a letter to Brian Lloyd, 'Darkie' Downing's daughter mentions the time that George 'came to KL station to see us off when we left Malaya. A few tears spent that day, I can tell you.'
>
> She also mentioned that Malaya – 1955-58 – was her father's favourite posting during his RAF service.
>
> As a 17-year-old lad he was posted abroad straight out of basic training. Just a 'country boy' who had never been out of the UK before, he found it a wonderful experience.

BRIEF NOTES ON PAST MEMBERS

Cyril Skinner, who attended George's funeral, says it was attended by members of the local ACA Branch, a former member of the French Air Force, a jazz band, and other friends connected with dancing and music.

Talking to one of George's daughters, Cyril mentioned he had once been quietly reprimanded by George, who told him, 'The name is Kiwi, except when we are not alone.' She replied, 'That was just like Dad.'

Cyril says Kiwi also told him the beaching story – slightly different to the Bournemouth Daily Echo *version – when he had to force land an 'experimental' jet (an early Vampire) on a beach in Communist China, and was surrounded by Chinese soldiers, but was rescued by HMS* Belfast, *who managed to extract both him and the aircraft.*

Chapter 10

More Pilot Tales from the Horse's Mouth

Flight Lieutenant Jim McCorkle

The location of this true story is mainland Malaya, one of the most enchanting countries in South East Asia. Malaya stretches out like an inverted thumb from its border with Thailand in the north to the island of Singapore in the south. Clad for the greater part in a thick green mantle of tropical jungle and mountainous rain forest, it is a land of great beauty and vivid contrast. Rich in massive deposits of almost pure tin ore, Malaya is also liberally endowed with huge deposits of bauxite, gold, and silver. Large tracts of land have been converted into neat plantations for the cultivation of coconut palms, oil palms, tea, and rubber. All of these industries, plus vast sources of valuable timber such as teak, help to give the inhabitants of this country a high standard of living when compared to their less fortunate neighbours. The wet tropical climate also encourages the growth of assorted fruits such as bananas, pineapples, papayas, mangosteens, rambutans, and the hypothetically aphrodisiac durian, much favoured by the Chinese.

   During this troubled post-war period, helicopters of the RAF were called upon to act as aerial taxis for the Crown, giving the troops a fast, flexible radius of action, vastly superior to that of the jungle-impeded rebels. As successive sections of the country were cleared of Communist Terrorists, the harassed survivors retreated into a pocket of jungle just south of the Thai border. Little was known about this seldom-penetrated area, but it soon became the focal point of large-scale operations designed to end the long insurgency.

MORE PILOT TALES FROM THE HORSE'S MOUTH

A platoon of Allied soldiers operating in this section of the Ulu became aware that they were being stalked as they moved around in the green twilight of the jungle. Occasionally there might be tantalizing glimpses of ghostly figures which seemed to dematerialize and vanish wraith-like into the undergrowth when approached. Now and again the soldiers would stumble upon rude lean-to shelters bearing mute evidence of recent hasty evacuation. It was decided that these phantoms must be a group of aborigines known to exist in this area, of small stature, not warlike or unfriendly.

No signs of booby-traps or terrorists so far, so the soldiers started to leave parcels of food and small gifts for the nomads, and were rewarded one day when a group of the tiny people emerged to greet them.

Much smaller in stature, and decidedly swarthier in colour than the Temiar natives to the south, the pygmies gathered around staring in awe at the tall, green-clad warriors. Wonderingly, they fingered the fabric of jungle-green uniforms and examined the weapons and trinkets adorning the men. They themselves were clad only in a brief loin-cloth made of some bark-like material. They carried only small wooden clubs. No other weapons such as the blowpipes used by other tribes further south were in evidence, so there was no danger of poison darts being used here. Now that friendly relations had been established, these tiny native people soon became an integral part of camp life, and assisted as scouts when the troops were on patrol. Initially whenever a helicopter clattered noisily onto the landing pad they were terrified, but soon became accustomed, even assisting in loading and unloading supplies. Nimble fingers were put to use weaving huge mats of bamboo to cover the helicopter landing pad, greatly adding to their safety and durability. They also acted as sentries around the perimeter of the camp, guarding against intruders.

As one of the regular pilots serving the area, I gently alighted onto the mat one day and shut down the engine. As the rotor blades slowed to a standstill I became aware of an air of gloom pervading the camp. Gone were the usual cheerful smiles. When I enquired, 'What's the matter?' I was informed that the natives were planning to vacate the area.

THE FIRST HELICOPTER BOYS

The reason for this apparently was that one of their favoured youths had come down with a mysterious case of poisoning which threatened his life. It was believed that if he died there his spirit (Hantu) would forever be imprisoned there, so they felt it necessary to move on. Naturally we could not just allow this to happen without doing everything within our power to save this likeable youngster.

Because of my ability to fly like the giant hornbills of their forest, I was held in high esteem by the tribespeople, so I was chosen to be spokesman on this occasion. Considering we had no common language, this was no easy task. Using much waving of arms, pointing to myself and the boy then to the helicopter, we finally conveyed the message that I wanted to take this sick boy with me in the helicopter to see if we could save his life. After deliberation, the senior men of the tribe agreed to this, and the semi-comatose boy was lifted on a stretcher and brought to my Sycamore. A ceremony then began which moved me deeply. Each member of the tribe, young and old, filed past the stretcher and touched the youth lightly on the forehead. It was a moving gesture which seemed to combine all the elements of tenderness and get well wishes with a final farewell salute. Plaintive notes of a bamboo flute quivered in the air around us, somehow reminiscent of a lonely kilted Highlander playing a bagpipe lament on a heathered Scottish hillside, as the stretcher was lashed to rings on the floor of the helicopter's cargo/passenger area.

All secure and doors closed, I roared the engine into life and lifted vertically upwards for about 150 feet before heading on my way to the hospital in Ipoh, close to the military brigade headquarters. Winging our way southwest at one hundred miles per hour over the lumpy grey-green canopy of the jungle, I kept track by referring to my map and picking out various landmarks such as river junctions and isolated peaks, all as familiar to me now as the street of my hometown. The shimmering mountains on the horizon swam into focus, each one capped with fluffy white heaps of cumulus cloud. Rising to a little over 5,000 feet above sea level, they marked the last physical barrier between our present position and the tin-rich Kinta Valley, wherein lay my destination. Some thirty minutes later, I radioed my position as being overhead Fort Kemar and gave my estimated time of arrival for Ipoh airport. I said I would require an ambulance to meet my helicopter on landing, and I relayed details about the aborigine boy. I skimmed at low level over the trees, keeping clear of clouds as I navigated my way into a narrow pass between towering peaks. This would lead me directly towards the Ipoh plain and my destination.

On the downslope I passed a huge Flame of the Forest tree, looking as if it were indeed on fire. This was a familiar old landmark which assured me I was on the right path in the correct valley. I mused how strange it was that a single tree could aid navigation over the jungle. I had used it often enough in that role, and taught it to the new pilots I trained. Ahead of me I could see huge scars of tin mines marring the level plain. Here man's search for mineral wealth had simply gone mad. Mammoth dredges looking like the old-fashioned Mississippi steamboats with their wheels churning were chewing their way across the land. They gouged out huge bites of tin ore, leaving behind quarries filled with deeply-coloured pools of water. From my vantage point they looked like a horde of prehistoric monsters, intent upon destroying everything in their path.

The main highway running north-south wended its way between huge outcrops of limestone. They were each honeycombed with caves, many of which housed brightly-decorated temples built directly into the rock.

The sprawling outskirts of Ipoh slid beneath our wheels and I set up my final approach to the landing pad where I could see an ambulance waiting.

The sick youngster had shown little interest in his surroundings as we sped over the high jungle, but became agitated as we neared this town displaying sights he could not decipher. His little face was grey with fear after landing at the airport, and he became almost unmanageable when transferring him to the ambulance. He clung desperately to my hand, and with eyes widely appealing, strove to maintain contact with the one face he knew...mine. There was only one way to pacify him, and that was for me to accompany him to the hospital. I secured my aircraft and climbed into the ambulance.

After he was mildly sedated, I left him to the tender care of the doctors and nurses, returning to the airfield. I refuelled and left for my journey to squadron headquarters, Kuala Lumpur. Later enquiries revealed the youngster to have an infection from some mysterious bite, possibly snake, but he was recovering well with the aid of antibiotics and modern hygiene. Several days later he was fully restored to impudent health and walking around the wards dressed in khaki shorts, shirt, and sandals on his feet. He soon became the pet of staff and patients alike. Sometimes he was taken into town where he saw high-rise apartments, buses, taxis, and market stalls, where food of all descriptions was on display. His palate, used to a simple diet of roots, fish, grubs, and occasional pieces of raw meat, soon grew accustomed to the staple foods offered at the hospital. He especially liked ice-cream and chocolate, quaffing it as often as he could beg, borrow, or pilfer. He even attended some evening film shows at the hospital, where the language could vary between English, Tamil, Malay, or Chinese. It didn't matter to him. He would just sit and stare, round-eyed, like any child, although he could not make head or tail of what was being said.

Eventually, a couple of weeks after his traumatic arrival, it was decided he was fit to go home. But a problem of authority arose. The centre of operations had now moved on from the area he had come from. How could he be taken in a helicopter all the way back to the Thai border? In desperation, one of the head principals at the hospital made a call to 194 Squadron offices and requested to speak to me. I informed him that I was the squadron training officer and had a new pilot to train in jungle procedures: each new arrival had to undergo fifty hours of flying before qualifying for general operations. I told him that I would fly back to Ipoh and would notify his office as to date and time of our arrival. Part of the new pilot's training would be to navigate his way to the area where the lad came from, and we would deliver the boy back to his tribe. No other authority was required.

In a Whirlwind Mk10, we flew out of Kuala Lumpur and headed north. The new pilot was working on his map-reading and navigation etc. I pointed out various landmarks, routes to be followed, with explanations as to various procedures. Arriving at Ipoh around lunch time, we stopped over at No. 2 FIB Headquarters, ate, and informed the Staff Ops of my intended journey. We also volunteered to take any supplies or mail that had little or no priority, delivering it wherever required. An offer like this didn't come along often, and the staff was only too happy to accept. So with one army passenger, bags of fresh mail and supplies, we headed to the hospital to pick up the young boy. He was delighted to see me and to know he was going to be flown back to his tribe. I briefed the army passenger on our intentions and instructed him that, if we did land at the clearing, he was to keep the door closed and the youngster quiet until I personally opened the door. I told him we didn't know if the tribe would still be there or if we would have to search around.

We took off and headed out over the Kinta Valley, where I pointed out the details to the new pilot. Reversing our track into the valley, climbing towards the gap that led to Fort Kemar, I showed the newcomer what a Flame of the Forest tree looked like, pointing out its usefulness in navigation. Doing well, my co-pilot followed the line marked on his map, navigating successfully all the way until we arrived in the former operational area. In due time we flew overhead the old clearing, the matting on the landing pad showing up well. It was not overgrown with greenery and the descent path was clear. I asked my co-pilot how he would recon wind strength and control his descent, all the things a pilot must decide before attempting to drop below the tree tops.

As we circled I noticed some native people assembling and waving up to us from the area in front of the landing mat. Good, the tribe was still there. I told my co-pilot to make the descent. The helicopter approached the rim of the clearing and began slowly to descend while still creeping forward. The final fifty feet or so was vertical above the mat; any further move ahead and the rotor blades would strike a tree, with disastrous results.

'Steady,' I murmured, as the new pilot tensed on the controls, 'You're doing fine.' The four wheels touched down gently, and everyone relaxed as we reduced power to idling. I shouted down to the army bod to stay inside with the door closed and reminded *my co-pilot to keep the controls central as I climbed down. The small group of tribespeople gathered around, touching me and trying to shake my hand, clearly glad to see me.*

I walked back to the sliding cabin door and opened it. There was a loud gasp of awe as the little Jahai Negrito laddie stepped out into the open and ran to the arms his parents. He was still dressed as he was in the hospital and had a little bag of goodies in his hand. To the superstitious aborigines this was like a miracle. He had not died! Here he was, dressed like the white men and obviously in good health. Here he was, a happy boy trying to tell his parents about the things he had seen after flying out of this clearing. But how could he do that? There were no words in their dialect to describe the traffic in Ipoh, ice-cream, or almost any other thing he had experienced.

I had to interrupt to let them know that I had to depart again. I gave the boy a final embrace and shook his hand, waved to the people, and climbed up to the high cockpit of the helicopter. A nod to my co-pilot and he restored the rotor rpm to operational status, then we climbed away. I took one final glance at the little congregation below us.

I wondered then, and have often wondered since, how long did he live in the jungle after we departed? What became of him? How did he settle back into the jungle after what he had seen and learned outside? Would he be happy? Would he rise to become chief of his little group?

We will never know the answers. I only know the satisfaction of having been partly responsible for perhaps saving his life.

From the diaries of Flight Lieutenant Leslie Scorer

The Emergency in Malaya was not going well and there was a call for volunteers to form a helicopter squadron. Not having flown this new type of aircraft I put my name forward. I was sent to the Westland Aircraft Company at Yeovil. The aircraft used was the Dragonfly and my instructor was John Fay. The RAF paid for our flying by the hour.

Being a union controlled factory, at 12 noon the place died until 1 pm – every civilian worker disappearing. By arranging my trips to start at 11 am, for ostensibly one hour, I was able to fly up until almost 1 pm while still logging one hour. The first S51s featured manual control, and hanging onto the control column was a bone-shaking experience. Later, servo controls were fitted, smoothing things out.

Upon completion of the course I returned to Valley to find that a posting had arrived to 155 Squadron, at Kuala Lumpur.

The squadron comprised one room in a hut near the airfield, with one officer: Flight Lieutenant Frank Hicks. The other three pilots had flown to Seletar to collect some S55s which had been shipped out from the UK on an aircraft carrier.

Flying started on 11 November 1955, and we each took a turn to be attached to the army for a week flying Austers to get used to the terrain. More pilots arrived during the next two weeks while we practised on the Whirlwinds. Operations started on 8 December with a spraying job. An army Auster had found a clearing in the jungle where the communists had planted crops. I flew to the map reference and sprayed the cultivation with weed killer. That sounds simple, but to understand the conditions it should be appreciated that the land was densely covered with trees which were around 200 feet high, 8 or more feet in diameter, and had straight stems which branched out only at the top forming complete cover of the ground from the air. To have any space for cultivation, a tree had to fall or be cut down – a large undertaking. A tree of that size, when falling, cleared a path, bringing other, smaller trees with it. The effect of such a fall left a hole in the canopy about 60 feet wide and a vertical drop of up to 200 feet to enable the helicopter to get low enough to spray.

When communists had been contacted, or were suspected, a troop operation was set up to cut them off from supplies, or to surround them. For us this entailed lifting troops who had been trucked as far as a jungle track would allow, into a zone as near the enemy as possible, i.e. a low bush area which could be cleared by machete. If the ground cover was more than 20 feet high the first troops into the spot slid down ropes attached to the helicopter, later arrivals were put onto the ground. Unless the start point for pick-up was large, we normally operated in pairs, lifting four equipped troops at a time. This meant that each helicopter would land 12 troops within 30 minutes. Parties larger than this were impracticable in jungle operations. Later we were on hand when required to lift out wounded troops or prisoners. One of my first troop lifts was with the 1/10 Gurkhas under the command of Major Wylie, who had been 2 i/c on the Everest expedition three years before when Hillary reached the top.

The helicopters operated in all parts of the country for the army as the situation required, detachments from base were common. Our temporary CO, Squadron Leader Jackson-Smith, was replaced by Squadron Leader L. Harland, whom I had known as a ground instructor at another unit. I was surprised to see him back on flying duties. Wing Commander Flying was Frank Aikins, a well-known car racer in the UK.

Operations moved southward, mainly in the centre of the country, and the troops were Gurkhas and Fijians. The Gurkhas were, in my opinion, the best disciplined and finest troops which I had ever come into contact with, and I have worked with many British and colonial regiments, including the Guards. The Fijians were huge men, always smiling and a pleasant lot to be with.

Gurkha Trooplift.

MORE PILOT TALES FROM THE HORSE'S MOUTH

One of our less pleasant jobs was to bring out the bodies of killed CTs. Because of the difficulty of identifying a body, a hand was cut off and brought to KL for fingerprint identification. As communists cottoned on to this, and destroyed their own fingerprints, it was decided the whole body should be brought out. As we were only 2 degrees north of the equator, a body more than 24 hours old was not a pleasant companion. The Fijians tied them by their hands and feet to a pole which was lifted into the aircraft while the engine was running. Airflow from the blades, being downward, took most of the 'aroma' away, but when you approached the ground for landing the downward airflow was deflected back to the cockpit. In the end we were issued with plastic bags to hold the body, but it was never a popular job.

A regular detachment of two weeks was started in the south, at Kluang. The troops were the Queen's Own and 1/2 and 1/6th Gurkhas, and later the South Wales Borderers. Normal procedure was to fly from Kluang to a DZ where the army would have assembled from trucks. On one of these occasions I flew with a crewman and a passenger compartment filled with tins of petrol and oil. About ten miles from the DZ the cockpit filled with smoke, even with the side windows fully open. The pilot of a helicopter has both hands and feet permanently employed, so I told the crewman to look below to see if he could see anything. He said that he could see flames at the rear of the passenger space. We were flying at about 400 ft, but only some 200 ft above the tree tops. I saw a small opening in the canopy, and when overhead shut off the engine. Engine-off landings were not part of our training but I did not want to burn. We came down steeply. When very near the ground I pulled the control column sharply back and we came to a jerking halt a few feet from the ground – then dropped like a brick. The blades were still windmilling and as we hit the ground they flopped down and cut off the tail unit. The crewman and I grabbed our guns and got out fast to take up defensive positions, as we were in communist territory. I expected the aircraft to blow up with all the tins of petrol on board but soon after landing the smoke cleared away. A following helicopter, having seen the smoke and the sharp descent, reported us as going down in flames. This alerted the army who sent out a foot patrol and we returned with them. A later examination of the aircraft showed that an electrical junction box had shorted in the passenger compartment and only a small part of the aeroplane had been burnt. When the engine stopped the source of input to the junction box had ceased – we'd been lucky.

Back to work again, now with the 1/6 Gurkhas in the centre of the country. Whenever possible I liked to stay overnight with the 1/6th at Segamet, where they had taken over a large Malay house as HQ, and mess dinner at night was as near as they could make it to a peace-time meal. Regimental silver covered the table and the china and cutlery were magnificent. The meal was served by Gurkha orderlies in their three-quarter length coats, buttoned to the neck, with broad waistbands and each wearing his pillbox hat set at a jaunty angle. While it was the form to thank the CO, it was not the thing to speak of the high standard of the mess, as that was the standard they always had, and always would maintain.

The Wing Co Flying was posted and replaced by Wing Commander Peter Le Cheminant, who later in life, as an AVM, was knighted and made Governor of Guernsey.

On 1 December I arranged to take a trip as second pilot on a Valetta. First we flew to Labuan, Borneo, a relief landing strip. Then it was on to Clarke Field, a USAF base in the Philippines. Next day we were off to Kai Tak. Kowloon had the highest density of people that I had ever seen, many sleeping and working in the streets. On the 12th we left for Saigon, which was in a volatile state. Very few white faces and crowds of locals with nothing to do. Along from the hotel in which we had stayed, a car which had been left outside a nightclub blew up, reducing car and building to scrap. Two things not to do in Saigon: drive a car and park it outside a house; go into one of the street bars, where, within a minute of going in, 'girls' would settle like flies around you trying to get you to buy them drinks or demonstrate what they had for sale. We left for Changi as soon as we could.

The Senior Air Staff Officer had me attached to his staff at HQ Malaya as helicopter advisor. While at HQ I wrote an article on helicopter operations which was distributed to all units, but of which I failed to keep a copy.

In March '56 I took some leave and flew with 20 Sqn RNZAF in a Bristol Freighter from Changi to Djakarta, then to Surabaya, Keopang in Flores, and on to Darwin. Next day we flew to Longreach, then Charleville for a night stop. Charleville was only a crossroads and a pub. We stayed the night at the pub and I was introduced to my first Australian breakfast: steak and eggs. Next stop was Broken Hill where I encountered the largest mass and most persistent flies in Australia. The last stop on the outward journey was Edinburgh Field, near Adelaide. Here the aeroplane became unserviceable and as my time was limited I flew by DC6 to Melbourne. From here I arranged a flight from Laverton in a Valetta. Then it was back to Broken Hill, with its flies, and on to Alice Springs, from where we departed as soon as the aeroplane was ready, which was only a few hours, but quite enough. Darwin, Keopang, and then Surabya. This was intended to be a fuel only stop, and the aeroplane was left with its nose up to the taxi track to enable the bowser to stay on the hard surface. A good idea, except that President Sukarno's aircraft had just left the terminal building and was taxying round for take-off. As his aeroplane could not pass ours it had to turn around to taxi the long way round the airfield to the runway. Very soon the police arrived and we were all bundled into a wagon and put under arrest. Our incarceration was in the Orangi hotel, the jail being deemed unsuitable. A police guard was put on the entrance but the back was left unguarded. So we left by the back door to look round the local shops. We returned to the Orangi without incident, and after two days, with no explanation, we were released and taken to the airport, from where we flew to Djakarta and Singapore. Back to juggling bumph.

*

Late in 1955 three of us had a break of one week at the Rest Camp in Fraser's Hill. It was intended to give people a break from the never changing weather of the coastal plain. We drove to the base of the hill; the road was not wide enough for two vehicles to pass and up-going traffic stopped at fifteen minutes *to the hour during daylight. Down traffic left between the hour and fifteen minutes past. This was the road on which Sir Henry Gurney and his family had been ambushed and killed in 1952.*

On our arrival at the top, the Officer i/c Defence asked had we met his defenders. Apparently, knowing we were coming up, they had arranged to ambush our car, for practice. I told him they were very lucky to have missed us, as I was travelling with a loaded revolver by my side and would have fired at anyone who had tried to stop the car. A stupid piece of organisation.

For the first time in Malaya we sat around a fire. One visitor to arrive by Sycamore while we were in residence was the governor, Sir Donald MacGillivray. He posed for a picture which I wanted to take.

Much about Malaya can be found in books, but the build-up to why we were there might not be so easily found. As the Japanese moved down the west coast, small pockets of resistance fighters were left behind. A few army and local civilians stockpiled food and arms in quiet backwaters with the intent of causing disruption to the occupying forces until a counter-attack could eventuate. These were organised later into a body known as Force 326. The militant communists mainly from Singapore had filtered up from the south and joined with the resisters or formed their own groups known as the Peoples Anti-Japanese Army, their supplies and money coming from Chinese businessmen in Singapore. These were the forerunners of the bands of terrorists which we were later to encounter in what is known as the Emergency. During the next three years the Allies made air drops to 326 and the PAJA.

After the Japanese surrender, the underground force came in from the jungle and, in theory, gave up the arms which had been supplied to them. But the communists handed in the old and broken weapons, hiding any in working order. Because of the disrupted state of Malaya, the communists had expected to take over the country, but this was opposed. The communists' answer to this opposition was to bring out the hidden weapons and terrorize the locals. The states banded together and the British army held the new enemy at bay. The communists, CTs, slipped back into the jungle.

MORE PILOT TALES FROM THE HORSE'S MOUTH

This situation, groups of CTs coming out of the jungle murdering plantation workers and managers on the rubber estates, culminated in the ambush of Sir Henry Gurney.

The position of governor was now divided into two. General Sir Gerald Templer took control of the military side assisted by Sir Donald McGillivray on the civil side.

The CTs were forcing the local people to produce food and information, and Templer instituted the system of 'new villages' and called for helicopter assistance.

One Sycamore squadron and later one Whirlwind squadron were sent to Kuala Lumpur. The Royal Navy also fielded a squadron of American-built Sikorsky S55s. The Naval aircraft were built of lighter material than the Westland, and were thus able to lift an extra man.

Until the arrival of the helicopters, jungle patrols had been limited to twenty days of operation as they had to carry all food and equipment on their backs. Progress in primary jungle is slow and half of the twenty days were spent travelling to and from the operational area, shortening the area of operation. With a helicopter lifting in the troops to within one day's march of the incident area, eighteen days could be spent in action. Morale was higher and more contacts were made with better results.

The communists did not have many radios and relied on a courier service to carry information. Because of this system, the army were able to form a defended strip of land from the east coast to the west coast through which the communist couriers could not penetrate, in effect cutting the country in two. The CTs were gradually squeezed so that by 1957 the only effective groups were over the border in the north under the leadership of Chin Peng.

My tour came to an end in September 1957 and Peg, Peta and myself sailed on the Empire Fowey *landing at Liverpool.*

I was posted to Wilmslow, and it was here I was approached on the subject of taking early retirement and going to live in Rhodesia – with the same pension I would expect on final retirement, plus a grant of £5,000. The two people who put the question also asked, should I be sent to Rhodesia, would I be prepared to fire on white Rhodesians. My answer was no.

We left it at that. Very diplomatic, and I reported the matter to the CO. I did however apply for the early discharge and the cash. My application was refused with the words, 'There is a continued requirement for your service with the RAF.' I never did find out who the questioners were or who sent them, but I do know they came from a political source.

Master Pilot Gordon 'Wacker' Cox

A helicopter puttered slowly over the undulating green of the Malayan jungle. Stripped to the waist in the steaming heat, Gordon Cox was flying to a jungle fort to evacuate a soldier wounded in the unending fight against the terrorists. Suddenly a puff of white smoke rose from a clearing. This was an RAF landing signal. Cox swept down and hovered over the treetops.

It looked like an army patrol below. 'One of the men,' says Cox, 'was running about holding a towel to his face.' Cox landed and found the section officer had accidentally set off a phosphorus bomb which had badly burned his face. Helicopter pilots are allowed to use their discretion, and Cox knew that the casualty at the jungle fort could safely be left until the next day. 'I flew the officer to Betong,' Cox recalls. 'He would have been entitled to a helicopter evacuation in any case. He was just lucky I happened to be passing.'

The first RAF helicopters arrived in Malaya in 1950. Now British troops regard them as one of the amenities of jungle life, 'a kind of taxi service', says Squadron Leader Ronald Henderson, the officer commanding the Kuala Lumpur squadron. Though troops seldom hail them from the ground, the helicopters have gradually extended their scope from casualty evacuations to every kind of odd job. They have searched for lost patrols, brought back important captured enemy documents, and even, on one occasion, supplied cooked rice to Gurkhas. 'But casevacs,' says Henderson, 'have remained our number one priority.'

Since 1950 the helicopters have evacuated about 450 casualties from country inaccessible to any other kind of transport. They have reduced from two weeks to thirty-five minutes the time taken to carry a sick man through forty miles of dense jungle. Almost more important than getting out the injured man,' says Henderson, 'is the raising of morale. When they see a helicopter, the troops feel they're in touch with the outside world.'

MORE PILOT TALES FROM THE HORSE'S MOUTH

Around noon one day, seven Gurkhas were patrolling a rubber estate. They were not expecting trouble. Suddenly shots rang out and one of the Gurkhas collapsed with severe stomach wounds The nearest telephone was five miles away. Twenty minutes after one of the survivors had signalled for help, a helicopter took off from Kuala Lumpur, a hundred miles away by road. At 4.30 pm the Gurkha was on the operating table.

Aged 32, Gordon Cox is the 'character' of his squadron, and due to his preponderance of addressing all and sundry as 'Wack', he himself became universally addressed as 'Wacker.' One of the most experienced pilots in the squadron, Cox has flown his full share of casevacs. He has carried to hospital a Malayan soldier with an abscessed liver, and a British private injured by a canister of supplies dropped from the air. One of his patients, a Gurkha whose tent had caught fire, was badly burned: 'He died four days later in hospital,' says Cox, 'but, so far, not a single patient has died on the journey.'

From dawn to dusk, a helicopter stands by for immediate take-off to any point in the Malayan peninsula. After sending for help, the wounded man's comrades move him to a suitable clearing, or start to hack one out themselves. The necessary area is half the size of a football pitch, or a circle of fifty yards diameter, with the inner thirty yards razed to the ground and the rest cut to a height of three or four feet. 'By now, most units understand what's required,' says Henderson, 'but at first, some of the clearings were a bit rough.'

Cox was once asked to evacuate a Fijian soldier from a hilltop clearing. An Auster pilot had reconnoitred it in advance and, though he said a landing would be difficult, Cox decided to see for himself. 'It was quite impossible,' he says. 'In the end they had to carry the sick man to the foot of the hill and cut a clearing there.'

Some of the early clearings were so rudimentary that considerable feats of airmanship were called for. The only member of the squadron who has been in Malaya longer than Cox is Flight Lieutenant Greville Jacques, a chubby-faced enthusiast who, at 29, is flight commander and the youngest pilot on the squadron. Some time ago he was asked to evacuate a casualty from a 'clearing' on the side of a hill with a thirty-degree slope. Unable to land, he flew in slowly until the front wheel of his undercarriage rested against the hillside. Then, with the rest of the aircraft projecting horizontally from the slope, he hovered. 'My rotor-blades were almost thrashing the hillside,' he says.' I stayed just long enough for the patient to be hoisted on to someone's shoulders and bundled into the back seat.' Jacques, like some other pilots, has also rescued a patient from swamp country by hovering a foot off the ground while the man was hoisted aboard.

The helicopter ambulance service has been extended to Malays and aborigines in remote villages. Cases such as beri-beri and malaria, and even pregnant women expecting a difficult confinement, are carried to hospital.

'When we first landed on a padang, as they call their village green,' says Cox, 'the natives would run out of sight. After a while, the children would come up shyly and run their hands over the fuselage. Finally, the adults would return and say, "Ah, good". Nowadays they are so used to helicopters they don't even turn their heads.'

Nevertheless, the Malays have come to look on the pilots with something like veneration. Cox was once searching, with a colonel, for the site of a Valetta crash, when they were held up by fog and had to land on a village padang. The headman immediately invited the colonel to his house, and Cox and Corporal Clifford Johnson, who was flying with them as crewman, were left to look after the aircraft. A band of natives gathered round and, anxious to practise their Malay, the airmen struck up a conversation. The headman returned with the colonel. 'In honour of your visit,' he announced, 'we are going to call the street that runs past the padang Jalan Helicopter. The house on this side we shall call Rumah Cox, and the house on the other side Rumah Johnson.'

Cox was lucky that the headman found such an innocent way of expressing respect. Jacques was once staying overnight with an RAF unit in Taiping when the protector of aborigines invited him and his crewman to an exhibition of dancing. 'We intended to creep out early,' he says,' but we found we were the guests of honour.' While the dancing went on, a native drink was passed freely round. Finally, the headman stood up and made a long speech. 'We didn't understand a word of it,' says Jacques, 'but we clapped for all we were worth.' A Malay then got up and said, 'For the benefit of those who don't speak the language, the chief just said that he is delighted with the way our guests dance through the air. He would now like to see them dance on the stage.' Jacques adds: 'We just had to give them a dance, but frankly, I don't remember much about it.'

Perhaps the most spectacular evacuation was made two years ago by Flight Lieutenant John Dowling when a patrol of Cameronians was tracking two bandits through swamp country with a dog. Early in the hunt, a soldier was wounded and Dowling made a routine evacuation. The patrol pressed deeper and deeper into the swamp, convinced that the bandits were trapped somewhere ahead. But they found that the swamp was rising and that the bandits were further away than ever. They turned to go back, but the water was too deep. They were trapped. When their radio call for help was picked up, Dowling was sent out. By the time he arrived, the water had risen to the soldiers' necks and they were desperately building a platform. Hovering as close to the water as he could, Dowling called for one of them to climb aboard. He then flew back to base and returned for his second passenger. Flying almost continuously for the daylight period of two days, he evacuated fourteen men and one dog. The dog thoroughly enjoyed the journey.

The helicopters, which cruise at a mere sixty-five miles an hour and often fly lower than their normal operational height of two thousand feet, would seem an ideal target for bandit gunners. 'But they never fire on us,' says Henderson, 'because they know that where there are helicopters, troops are not far away. An attack would give away their position.'

One pilot who was flying an army major on reconnaissance did have a narrow escape. Flying over a clearing, they both thought they saw something move, and the pilot wheeled round to investigate. They found nothing, but, still not satisfied, the pilot plunged down and circled the clearing four times, still seeing nothing. Then they climbed and made for home. A few days later, a captured bandit was asked to give corroborating evidence for a position he claimed was the site of his camp. 'A helicopter passed over a few days ago,' he said. 'Anything else?' asked a security officer. 'It circled the camp four times,' said the bandit. 'Our leader had a Bren gun mounted on a tree. If the helicopter had circled once more, he would have shot it down.'

A squadron of naval helicopters last year combined with the RAF machines to form a wing. The RAF models carry two passengers, the naval machines can take five and are also equipped to travel by night.

To anyone outside the service, the rivalry between the RAF and Navy seems comic. Henderson's pilots assert, quite seriously, that before the naval squadron sets off on an operation, it sends one of its aircraft ahead with a cine-camera to record its exploits. The naval airmen regard the RAF as enthusiastic amateurs who potter about the jungle in aircraft not really suited for the job.

The use of the naval helicopters for troop-lifting has considerably helped the anti-bandit war. Captain Maurice Sutcliffe, ground liaison officer with the helicopter wing, says, 'They can lift anything from a patrol of eighteen men to a force of a thousand. They can reduce a march of perhaps five days to a matter of hours. The troops are fresh when they arrive, and the enemy is taken completely by surprise.'

THE FIRST HELICOPTER BOYS

In a recent operation against a terrorist camp, an army force advanced from a main road. The terrorists had retreated into deep jungle. But six naval helicopters had in a single day dropped nearly three hundred soldiers into the area. 'The terrorists walked straight into the soldiers' arms' says Sutcliffe. 'In this sort of operation,' he adds, 'the landing is usually in lalang, or long grass. The first load of men swarm down a rope while the helicopter hovers, and start cutting the grass to make a landing-ground. The second batch also swarm down a rope. By the time the third machine has arrived, a large enough clearing has been cut for the helicopter to land.'

Perhaps even more important than surprise attacks on the enemy is the service given to jungle forts. In the early stages of the war the bandits demanded food and shelter from the aborigines and Malays. As the British forces were usually days away, the villagers were forced to obey. Now there is a chain of police posts or jungle forts across the remotest parts of the country. Supplies are dropped by air; the helicopters relieve the garrisons.

The duties of a helicopter crewman mean at the best steady hard work; at the worst, the sort of thing that happened to Sergeant Jack Feeley, a 23-year-old fitter, when he had been in Malaya only a month.

He was with Flight Lieutenant Dowling on a detachment in the far north-east of Malaya. Dowling was an hour overdue returning from a lone flight to a native village. Then a message arrived saying he was stranded with a broken fuel pump. No helicopters could be sent from Kuala Lumpur, and Feeley was told to reach Dowling as best he could. 'And that,' he says, 'meant walking.'

He and a leading aircraftman, an army lieutenant and four Malay soldiers set off through the jungle. 'It should have taken us eight hours,' says Feeley, 'but there were three rivers to cross. Two were in flood with tree-trunks careering down. We had to wait for the water to subside.'

At one point they made a detour to get out of striking distance of an ugly looking snake. As they crossed a river, leeches sucked their blood. 'I held a cigarette to mine.' says Feeley, 'and they just dropped off. One of the men pulled his away, but the jaws were left buried in his flesh and he had five septic sores.' On the evening of the second day they arrived at the village. Next morning they repaired the pump and flew out again. 'The pilot's biggest moan,' says Feeley, 'was that we hadn't brought his toothbrush.'

All the helicopter pilots consider that they have a much more interesting job than the pilots of orthodox aircraft, because the helicopter's manoeuvrability and versatility lets them see much more of the country.

MORE PILOT TALES FROM THE HORSE'S MOUTH

Cox is fortunate in having pleasant, detached married quarters with an excellent view of the mountains and a subsidized rent. With his wife Ruth, he is producing *Arsenic And Old Lace* at the station theatre club, and is also forming a boxing club. He has three young children.

Jacques lives three-quarters of a mile from the camp, in Kuala Lumpur, and pay's £37.10s a month for a four-room, unfurnished flat. 'That's the normal rent here,' he says. To enable servicemen to cope with these rents and the high price of food – a pint of milk costs 2s, a pint of beer 5s 6d – local allowances are paid by the RAF. One of the constant complaints of wives is that when their husbands are on stand-by duty they can never arrange to go out. Cox ruefully remembers the time he was informed late one night that he would have to set off on a casevac the next morning. He got only a few hours' sleep, and at 4 am he was on his way to the airfield. 'I didn't at all mind getting up,' he says, 'because I understood I had to evacuate a man with a broken hip. In the clearing, his mates lifted him gently aboard and I flew him carefully to hospital. But the moment we touched down, he jumped out of the plane and started running across the landing-ground.'

*

This Wacker Cox story told me by 'Taff' Walker refers to a time post-Malaya. Wacker, now commissioned, was flying Whirlwinds at Thorney Island and had been detailed for a late afternoon wet winching exercise in a Mk2 Whirlwind. Wacker asked a pilot friend, Fred, if he'd like to go along for the ride. Fred, having never flown in a chopper before, but well versed in their operation as he was about to convert onto the type, said he would be happy to. He duly hopped into the left-hand seat. Fred now takes up the story:

> *It was a hot, windless day, the sea like glass as we arrived over Chichester harbour and came to the hover – not exactly ideal conditions, I thought, given our all-up weight and lack of power. The heat and humidity only made matters worse, and still air meant an almost total absence of that rotary-craft phenomenon known as translational lift effect. This became self-evident when I looked out, surprised to see the port wheel in the water. As it was still attached to the aircraft, I pointed this out to Wacker, who said it was OK, he was working on it. And it certainly looked like he was, juggling control column, collective, and throttle.*

I looked out again, just checking on progress, but by this time the wheel had disappeared completely, water now lapping at the underside of the fuselage. Not good, eh?

Although I hadn't flown in a helicopter before, I was aware of the pertinent facts: we were overpitching, i.e. rotor rpm too low; as was, therefore, airspeed over the blades. Now, the only way to recover from such a situation is to decrease blade pitch, or gain translational effect by picking up forward speed, both of which called for the sacrifice of a little height; somewhat difficult when part of the aircraft is already below sea level. To put it mildly, lacking any kind of flotation gear, it was obvious we were in deep trouble, or should that be deep water?

'Don't you think it's time to get out, Whacker?' I asked.

'You're right, Fred,' Whacker replied, calmly shutting down the engine, as if at the end of a day's flying. Which, in a way, I suppose it was.

I don't recall the details but I was in the water in record time, heading for the beach at a fair rate of knots. I'd had no problem exiting from the left-hand seat, though I was a bit concerned about Wacker. Well, maybe not Wacker so much as the NCO winchman who was down in the cabin. Wasn't it after all Wacker's duty as captain to remain to the bitter end? Nevertheless, I was about to turn back when I saw this guy waving at me from the shore. He was shouting too, obviously keen to attract my attention, so I continued swimming towards him. I presumed he would have news of the others. The thought didn't cross my mind that they might already be ashore.

I eventually reached the beach and dragged myself out, knackered. 'What is it, mate?' I asked, somewhat breathless.

'Oh, nothing, really. I was just trying to point out, you could have walked from where you were,' came the answer.

He was right, too, the sea was barely three feet deep.

We all survived of course, and the aircraft was eventually recovered, albeit not exactly in pristine condition. In fact it was later struck off charge. Apparently due to the advanced state of corrosion, odd pieces kept falling off. Not really fundamental to the safe operation of an aircraft, that.

*

MORE PILOT TALES FROM THE HORSE'S MOUTH

A couple more Taff Walker stories, if only because Taff has a sackful of them. The first concerns another operation in which he was involved, over the Thai border at a place called Betong, yet another location with which we were becoming quite familiar as the front moved ever northward.

Taff was scheduled to fly some Thai police into a place known by them, somewhat tongue-in-cheek, as Fort Ha Ha, an area of really deep jungle. They were carrying kit-bags, and as they placed them aboard the aircraft, the crewman, ensuring they were positioned with regard to the centre of gravity – rather important in a helicopter – thought he saw one of them move. Being a conscientious type, or maybe just plain nosey, he opened it, and out popped a young Thai girl. Talk about home comforts out on patrol! We were used to the Gurkhas carrying edible livestock in with them – chickens and things – but this was ridiculous. Curried girl? I hardly think that was what they had in mind!

Taff also tells of an event which involved Kiwi rugby players. The op order apparently called for the evacuation of two 'casualties', but when he arrived at the LZ there turned out to be eight, not one appearing to be in desperate need of medical attention. And as they were all healthy, strapping lads, carrying loads of kit, it required four sorties to bring them out. At least they won their game, eventually going on to lift the end of season trophy. Win, that is, not steal.

Renegade Hero

Flight Lieutenant Terry Peet

At a White Rose ACA meeting, one of our members, Tim Nicoll, ex-103 Squadron, was asking about a helicopter presentation I was to put on for them, and he happened to ask if I knew of an ex-Sycamore pilot called............? At this point the age/memory syndrome kicked in and Tim could not recall the name, so he provided me with some basic 'facts' he'd gathered from various sources: the pilot in question had been a comms man in the Royal Navy, flying in Gannets; he then transferred to the RAF as pilot trainee, eventually flying Sycamores in Malaya, crashing one at KL, but was unhurt.

He was presumed drowned while scuba diving off a beach in Anglesey sometime in 1966. But as no body was found he was posted AWOL. Then, in the seventies, he turns up in Hawaii. But his luck was about to run out. He was going to Thailand on honeymoon, or some such, but there was an airline change in Hong Kong (still British at the time). Here he was picked up by the SIB re the AWOL charge, escorted back to the UK, court martialled and awarded two years in the slammer.

A couple of years later, Tim says he was on holiday in Austria when he picked up an airline ticket someone had dropped in the lobby of his hotel. Surprise, surprise, the name on it was familiar, but he handed it in at the desk where the receptionist looked at it and said, ah yes, I'll give it to him, he's over there. Tim says he didn't know whether or not to go over himself, but decided against it, thinking, What do you say to someone like that.

These were the facts as far as Tim recalled hearing them. A plausible story, I thought, I'll give it a mention in the newsletter, some of our members may recall him.

Next morning I receive a phone call. It was Tim and he had recalled the name, Terry Peet. Well, on typing this into the internet all kinds of bells and whistles ensued! There is a book featuring Terry, and the story it tells reveals an entirely different tale, this involving the CIA no less. *Terry Peet, Renegade Hero* – good title, for it turns out he was probably just that.

That was the story as presented to me, but I was able to contact Terry (via email from an address found on the internet) and he gave me the facts.

He began service life in the Royal Navy in 1952 and reached the rank of 'Petty Officer Teleg (Flying)' – on Gannets. He then transferred to the RAF as a pilot, commissioned in 1959. He received a commendation for saving an aircraft in the RN, two green endorsements, plus the Queen's Commendation for services in the air while in the RAF.

After a tour flying the Sycamore in Malaya he returned to the UK, and was an instructor at Tern Hill around 1965.

Then came the James Bond bit!

> *In September 1965 I was asked by a Senior RAF Officer (now deceased) if I would be interested in joining the CIA operation in the Congo as a contract pilot, but under strict secrecy rules, with a clandestine departure arranged through Brussels [Hence the drowning off Anglesey story].*
>
> *I agreed, and was given a travel document to go to Belgium, thence on to the Congo, where I was seen and vetted by local CIA field officers, who apparently cleared everything with London. As a contract pilot for the CIA I was not allowed to disclose my whereabouts to anyone. So I flew with them in the Congo, and with the United Nations as Air*

Operations Manager Biafran War. Then I was asked to go to Laos, which I did, and it was at this juncture that the British government, who didn't agree with American policies in that part of the world, became difficult and asked for my return. The US advised me to go back to UK, which I arranged to do in September 1971, therefore I was surprised to be detained by the RAF authorities while transiting Hong Kong, and flown by special RAF Flight directly to Brize Norton where I was told I was to be court martialled for illegal absence. Being heavily cautioned that I was still under the Official Secrets Act meant I had little material with which to defend myself. I was sentenced to two years imprisonment, which was then halved, and then cut to three months. The American government then gave me the right to return and reside in the States. I have much documentation to back all this up.

Terry (who died in 2015) eventually lived in the UK but, due to his court martial and loss of service pension, only got a very reduced state pension, plus a small pension of about 89 UK pounds per month from the US government.

As he was only one year short of his Naval pension when he requested a transfer to the RAF, he felt badly let down by the RAF, being allowed to go on a so-called clandestine mission, then subsequently disowned when the government of the day decided there was a possibility it was about to be embarrassed.

The full story is really well worth reading: *Renegade Hero* by Michael Kingston.

*

Reports From ex RNAS 848 Squadron Members

Three Bristol Dragonfly helicopters had been brought into operation in Malaya in 1950, but they and the handful of Sycamores that replaced them were too few and too prone to mechanical failure to be effective. The linseed oil applied to the laminated wooden blades of the Sycamore made them 'mightily attractive to the voracious appetite of the white ant', while the low blades themselves meant that if you didn't duck properly you really could get your head taken off. One bizarre accident with a Sycamore was said to have involved an Alsatian tracker dog being carried as a passenger. According to the story-teller (and it sounds like he was!) the dog sat down on the fuel cocks between the seats which turned the fuel off and brought the aircraft down to earth rather suddenly!

A reply to this in the Association newsletter:

> *It makes you smile, doesn't it – especially the thought of the 'crabs' feeding the ants on linseed oil-soaked rotor blades, and letting a dog sit on the fuel cock!*
>
> *According to Jack Feeley, one of the three-man team supporting the 1953 tropical trials with the Sycamore, 'We polished the blades with Simoniz, not linseed oil, although even that could not prevent the continued deterioration, which included dry rot.'*
>
> *So much for the linseed oil. Now for the dog. Impossible, it turns out. The only exposed fuel system control the dog could have sat on would have been the slow running cut-out, but as this requires the control knob to be pulled up..... well yes, extremely unlikely!*

*

The 1953 arrival in Malaya of 848 Royal Naval Air Squadron, flying the American-built Sikorsky S55 (Whirlwind 7), marked the point when the helicopter really began to make its presence felt – although to the very end, demand for helicopters was always in excess of supply. Even with the advent of the more advanced Whirlwind MK10, flying helicopters in Malaya placed just as severe demands on pilots and aircrew as was faced by soldiers on the ground. Sub-Lieutenant (later Rear Admiral) Rob Woodard saw it as a schizophrenic existence:

> *Having spent weeks operating in the jungle, you found yourself in the wardroom of your carrier sipping a gin and shooting the most appalling lines. The jungle interior itself was a terrifying place to be in.*
>
> *Flying helicopters in tropical conditions presented many hazards: Everything got terribly, terribly damp, so the wireless played up. It was not a good thing to fly through a monsoon*

shower. Occasionally one had to, but it could do considerable damage to a helicopter. The engines didn't like humidity and they didn't like heat, which reduced power available, and thus the load. On a good day you could carry up to six Gurkhas or four Royal Marines, plus their basic fighting equipment, on a bad day, it was five and three.

I remember once sitting for twenty minutes at the bottom of a clearing at high power in the hover until I burnt off sufficient fuel to equate to the weight of a man, so I could fly out with four marines rather than leaving one man alone in the jungle. And understand that jungle clearings were only just bigger than the helicopter, not swanky clearings at all. You came down vertically, which is not a good thing for the aerodynamics of a helicopter because you recirculate your own air and it can actually be sucking up disturbed air which comes down through the blades and collapses your lift. So there's quite an art to flying vertically down into a clearing, with 200-foot-high trees just off the tips of your rotor.

By 1955 a combination of helicopters and STOL aircraft working in and out of short landing strips attached to the jungle forts had begun to transform the war in the deep jungle. The way one operated, taking patrols into clearings, was that you'd refuel at the forts. So you would be flying fuel cans into a fort for three sorties and then using them to leapfrog onto another one for another two sorties to the one where you wanted to get to at the end, from where you could fly in and out of a clearing without refuelling. Forts in the main were used as refuelling bases, which we kept topped up. You would climb out and refuel your own helicopter from five gallon tins   not so with the RAF, where it was the crewman's job!

*

A report stated that the RAF pioneered the parachuting of troops from a helicopter in 1956; this is incorrect. 155 Squadron, although carrying out many important tasks during their time in Malaya, did not do this; 848 NAS beat them to it by three years. This was well documented at the time and photographs still exist of the events. I believe US observers who visited 848 during its time in Malaya credited them with a worldwide first in using helicopters for parachuting operationally. In early Malayan troop-lifting operations, the RAF often sent along observers. For the RN, those days were particularly galling, as too many events were reported in UK papers as being carried out by the RAF. The Admiralty, instead of insisting on a correction, chose the 'silent service' approach. This annoyed us immensely. In 1952/3, the *Times* and *Telegraph* did at least give 848 publicity for their forthcoming role in Malaya: '848 Naval Air Squadron successfully pioneered the parachuting of troops from a helicopter on 25 September 1953.'

The SAS were the volunteers! The pilot was Lieutenant Commander J.E. 'Ben' Breese DFC, flying a Sikorsky S55 at Seremban, south of Kuala Lumpur. Initially the SAS elected to drop into bamboo, but as this could be rather painful, they elected to snag the parachute canopy in the tops of tall trees. For this the soldier also carried abseil gear for lowering himself to the ground (yet another special technique perfected in Malaya – the equipment that allowed him to do so being designed and built on the MU at RAF Seletar).

The biggest lift 848 did was on Operation Commodore when on 23 May 1953 over 1,000 troops were lifted in the first 24 hours. During the period 23rd-31st, 453 sorties were carried out; 1,623 troops and 35,460 lbs of freight were lifted, and one casualty evacuated. Nine S55s were involved, and the RAF, who were extremely short of helicopters, used an S51 Dragonfly in an observation role.

'Freddie'. The only place that Flight Sergeant McKeachern could find to put XD185 down in a hurry.

MORE PILOT TALES FROM THE HORSE'S MOUTH

XD185. Difficult to see, especially from the air.

XD185 in the Ulu, close to Fort Selim.

Close cooperation between the RAF and 848 Squadron was demonstrated many times, on one occasion (December 1953), a downed RAF S51 was dismantled by a joint RAF and NAS crew. Lieutenant Commander Roy

XD185 with salvage work underway.

Tony Tamblyn contemplates XD185's engine.

MORE PILOT TALES FROM THE HORSE'S MOUTH

Recovery crew. L–R: Tony Tamblyn, 'Mush' Upfield, Mick Stagg, Len Raven and Dave Duffy.

Recovered parts.

THE FIRST HELICOPTER BOYS

Recovered tail boom; did not help the aerodynamics.

Hawkes, using an S55 as a crane, flew the sections out to the nearest road, only the engine causing a slight problem, but that is another story!

The images shown from page 174–178 are of XD185 (Foxtrot) after an emergency landing on 3 January 1958. At 4,800ft, black smoke starting coming from the exhaust and then the engine stopped. Pilot Flight Sergeant Bill McKeachern, flying with crewman Corporal Colin Upfield, tried to make it to Fort Brookes on aerodynamics alone but failed and had to put down in this jungle-enshrouded riverbed. There were no injuries, but due to the location the airframe was deemed irrecoverable.

Chapter 11

Bits and Pieces

Bucks Free Press **report after the first reunion at which the Helicopter Operations (Malaya Emergency) Association was formed: 27 October 1986 at the George and Dragon, Princes Risborough.**
(*It must have been a slow news week!*)

A crack squadron who performed James-Bond-type antics in the dense jungle and mountains of Malaya and saved hundreds of lives in the fifties got together for the first time in more than thirty years on Saturday. And although the lads were slightly greying, their memories of the dangerous days when they fought a war with terrorists in the swamps were not dimmed by the years.

The sixteen men who got together for a reunion at a Princes Risborough pub were all pilots and groundcrew members of the Casualty Evacuation Flight (Casevac) based in Singapore and 194 Squadron in Kuala Lumpur. Their job had been to go into the jungle by helicopter and pull out injured Malayan police, British forces and Gurkhas who were fighting the terrorists active in all areas.

Operational ground troops had a tremendous morale boost from the presence of the helicopters which they knew could fly in during a critical situation to get them out. And through their brave operations, the pilots and groundcrew, whose job it was to service the helicopters, managed to evacuate well over 1,500 casualties, saving hundreds of lives.

Some of those who got together on Saturday had not seen each other for more than thirty years and the chance to reminisce proved too tempting for many as they travelled from as far afield as Glasgow to be at the reunion.

Tony Clarke, the only one present still flying, said, 'They were tough days. Helicopters hadn't been used before and there were a lot of limitations we didn't know about. We found out the hard way when something went wrong.' Then someone else remembered, 'The campaign had its amusing moments, like the occasion when a helicopter got stuck in a swamp. Support engineers, called in from Kuala Lumpur, had to travel miles in convoy to pull the aircraft out, only to find when they arrived that a quick-witted Malay policeman had done what everyone thought impossible and simply pulled it out with a rope!'

The air was thick with many similar reminiscences when veterans were whisked back thirty years to the dramas of hazardous helicopter operations.

*

AIR OPERATIONS DURING THE EMERGENCY

Anti-terrorist activities began to bear fruit by the mid-1950s. A major element was the relocation to secure settlements of Chinese squatters living on the edge of the jungle. These people sustained the terrorists, either willingly or through coercion, and by moving them to protected enclaves, the terrorists were deprived of their main support. Newly established forts deep in the jungle combined with more aggressive patrolling by specialist jungle-trained units such as the Malayan Regiment, King's African Rifles and the re-formed Special Air Service worked in coordination with the air offensive. These served to restrict freedom of movement in the jungle, bombing being harnessed to drive terrorists into carefully prepared ambushes.

One new development that more than any other had a decisive influence was the introduction of the helicopter. They changed the face of not only jungle warfare but warfare in general. A trio of Westland Dragonfly HC1s formed the Casualty Evacuation Flight at Changi on 1 May 1950 (officially Kuala Lumpur, though it was not to reside there for another two years). Their appearance had an inestimable psychological value to the security forces patrolling the jungle, by assuring them of the prospect of rapid rescue and medical treatment. Vital though the Casevac role was, once the helicopter was used as transport for active troops, becoming a force multiplier, things really began to change. The Royal Navy's 848 Squadron

BITS AND PIECES

848 Squadron on ops.

first gained such a capacity when their Sikorsky-built Whirlwind HAR21s were sent to Malaya in March 1953. During their first year of operations they lifted 14,000 troops, vesting the security forces with a mobility they had previously only dreamt of.

Despite the introduction of further units in 1954 – the RAF's Bristol-Sycamore-equipped 194 Squadron, and the Whirlwind HAR2s or 4s of 155 Squadron – there were never enough helicopters to cope with the demand. This, together with high operating costs, necessitated the widespread use of light aircraft with short take-off and landing (STOL) capability. The initial problem of operating such aircraft in Malaya from the outset was the dearth of airstrips. To begin with there were but a few ex-WWII airstrips, along the coastal strip. Others were quickly constructed inland, and by August 1951 there were many.

*

LETTER FROM ONE OF OUR 'CUSTOMERS'

Dean G. Pursell

> *As I was flicking idly through the teletext recently, I came across your details. I was immediately intrigued as I believe it was your flight which evacuated me in 1952 from Fort Brooke,*

Malaya. I was then a Corporal in 22 SAS Regt (Malayan Scouts), suffering from BT Malaria; I had been jungling for about 110 consecutive days.

My boss tried to reduce my temperature, which was around 104 degrees, by submersion in the river. Though this was quite pleasant, as I recall, it failed. A helicopter was then summoned to evacuate me to BMH Kinrara. On the way, we visited Grik, to pick up another casualty, then proceeded to KL.

This was my first experience of flying in a Helicopter and I was mightily impressed, being more experienced in preparing LZs for your guys in preparation for your visits.

I will always be grateful for my casevac, which probably saved my life. It certainly beats walking.

*

Flight Lieutenant Tom Browning

An abiding memory of crewman 'Lofty' Dace, waiting at Grik for the body of a Gurkha to be brought in for us to fly out in XJ410. The Gurkha had been out with a patrol. Arriving at the banks of a flood swollen river, the patrol decided to supplement their rations with some fishing – using the well proven method of tossing a grenade into the water. Seeing all the dazed fish coming to the surface was so exciting that he jumped into the fast running river – quite forgetting that he was unable to swim.

When they eventually found him, his comrades made a raft and brought him downstream to Grik. Somewhat late in the day Lofty and I watched them carry the raft and its sadly forlorn burden in solemn procession to our waiting Whirlwind. After a short pause they attempted to put it in the cabin but, some ten or more feet long, it was far too big. Eventually, by repeatedly shortening and partly dismantling, it fitted. But by now it was too late to leave and we had to stay for the night. It was several days since the tragic accident and, well, I guess that you will understand why I suggested to Lofty that we (boss-speak for 'he') ought to spray some strong disinfectant around the cabin before we left.

BITS AND PIECES

Next morning Lofty was already waiting for me when I turned up at the helicopter.

'Did you ...?' I began.

'Couldn't get any disinfectant,' he said, 'But an Australian Army medic got me this instead ...' Quick as a flash, and before I could move a muscle, he produced a spray and doused me from head to foot in the sort of perfume that I had been told can only be found in a certain kind of lady's bedroom.

At least that is what I told my wife.

*

Some reports from *Lift-Off* magazine

When All Else Fails

A platoon of troops operating in the heart of the mountains north-east of Ipoh once had occasion to call on a helicopter when during a brush with the terrorists, two of their number were seriously injured. An S55 was airborne within a matter of minutes of the news being received in Kuala Lumpur. The pilot found the troops in deep jungle on the side of a hill just before dusk.

There was literally nothing he could do at the time other than to drop a message asking for trees to be felled so he could land.

When the pilot was back on the scene at dawn, he discovered that one man had died during the night, while a second lay injured. The pilot made repeated attempts to recover the second man from the clearing made overnight, but could find no place to touch down on just two wheels without the tips of his rotor blades striking the ground farther up the slope.

Eventually the casualty was perched atop an eight foot high tree stump; the pilot hovered alongside with remarkable skill, and from there the man was hauled into the cabin. This man's life was saved.

*

The loss of XJ381

On 7 August 1957 bad weather caused Pilot Officer J.F. (Mac) McCorkle to divert from a landing zone in the Cameron Highlands in Sycamore XJ381. Shortly afterwards, his tachometer failed, leaving him, apparently, rpm-less, although, as he was later to relate, he could see vital bits still whizzing round just above his head, and hear faintly comforting mechanical noises round about him. Unaware of actually how fast, or slowly, those 'vital bits' might be rotating, he wisely decided to land at the first opportunity, which happened to be Sungei Menlock, a 3,500ft hill on the top of which was located an LZ. Making an approach, the Sycamore suddenly lost height. Despite Mac taking corrective action, XJ381 hit the ground – only the nosewheel touching down on the neatly constructed landing pad. The main rotor blades flapped down, hit the ground and disintegrated. Happily, Mac escaped unscathed. Sadly, apart from a few recoverable bits and pieces, XJ381 was written off.

*

From a report by Flight Lieutenant Tom Browning

During early years of the Emergency it was common for pilots of the Casevac Flight, and later 194 Sqn, to spend some of their first few weeks with 656 Sqn, learning the techniques of finding their way around the jungle without actually landing in it. Originally this was an arrangement made by the Casevac Flight's CO, 'Chips' Fry, and continued for a while by 194 Sqn. Perhaps by then it was also a way of filling in time for new pilots – especially when flying hours were at a premium.

But not everyone was aware of this. So for me it was mystifying to come across a vague reference in 194 Sqn's records for January 1954 to one of their pilots, Flight Lieutenant Maulden, being absent for the last part of the month and, seemingly unconnected, from an intensive air search that had been mounted for several days – but for what purpose? [The compiler had obviously not connected the absence of Flt Lt Maulden with the missing Auster at the time].

Jacko Jacques provided the first clue: Flight Lieutenant Maulden had gone missing in an Auster. Not during an attachment – he had been declared fully operational long before – but, from 656 Sqn's records, while carrying out a weather recce. To quote from a series of 656 Sqn's newsletters which are kept at the Museum of Army Flying at Middle Wallop:

BITS AND PIECES

Accident VF604

It is with deep regret that we have to announce a fatal accident. VF 604 with Sergeant J Perry as pilot and Flight Lieutenant Maulden of 194 Helicopter Squadron as passenger, took off from RAF Kuala Lumpur at 0830 on 21st January to carry out a weather recce in the mountains east of Kuala Lumpur. No trace of the aircraft or its crew has been seen or heard of since. A very large search was put into operation and the weather was ideal. Had any signals been made from the ground we feel certain that the aircraft would have been found. Sergeant Perry had been with the Squadron a comparatively short time but his cheerful manner and willingness to undertake any task made him a popular member of the Squadron. He also had a reputation for being a careful and skilful pilot. Flight Lieutenant Jack Maulden was popular and well known to the squadron, both operationally and on the sports field. They are both sadly missed and our heartfelt sympathies go to their wives and families.

Without trace of the aircraft it was, of course, impossible to determine the cause of its disappearance: 'At the time of the accident the aircraft was carrying a number of Grenades ... without finding the aircraft it is impossible to say what went wrong ...' – although greater attention was subsequently paid to the storage of all equipment carried in aircraft.

And so, that was the end of VF 604. Or was it? Incredibly, on 1 March 1957 the wreckage was found by a jungle patrol, and visited by a Board of Inquiry on 12th. The cause of the accident remained undetermined.

The other remaining mystery is, where did the Auster crash? It is commonly believed that it was quite close to a road. Perversely, the Museum of Army Flying's 656 Sqn records for the first half of 1957 are missing – everything else seems to be there! But, while there is no specific reference to the discovery of VF 604 in 194 Sqn's records, there are references to a number of missions flown between 7 and 13 March to [grid refs] WQ 094091 and WQ 110901 which, it seems, is a likely area for the Auster to have ended up.

*

THE FIRST HELICOPTER BOYS

Sergeant Chris Tinkler

I well remember the days of fifty years ago and spent some time looking through my log book at some of the hairy moments that I took for granted in those carefree youthful days after 100 casevacs.

I wonder if the crewman is there who accompanied me from KL with full tanks (89 galls) to the Thai border for a double casevac to an incorrect map ref and a square search to correct it. Then having to follow the river to Kuala Krai (because of the probability of having to dunk in the river) as it had got pitch dark after nearly 3 hours. On arrival, with prayers on my mind, and vapour in the tanks, not being able to land on the padang because of hundreds of people milling around celebrating, finally landing on a tennis court by the railway station by the light of the glow from a fortuitously opened firebox from a railway engine just at the crucial time!

Those were the days, now 9,000 hours later I hope I am older and wiser!

*

A report stated that when a Whirlwind helicopter crashed into jungle in remote territory, it took a search party five days to find it because it was concealed by the dense foliage. Subsequently, helicopters likely to be engaged in a similar operation carried a plastic bag filled with toilet rolls. In an emergency the bag could be thrown from the aircraft, scattering its contents over the canopy where they could be clearly seen from the air.

Was this advanced technology ever used in Malaya, I wonder?

*

Corporal David Taylor

Although the role of Crewman was originally intended to be manned by the SNCO ranks it soon became evident there was a dire shortage of such, thus the post became available to the rank of corporal and above. In actual fact, I recall we had SACs and J/Ts too.

BITS AND PIECES

With reference to the subject of crewmen, I have a letter from Squadron Leader George Puddy, forwarded to me by the Helicopter Operations Association secretary, commenting on their role shortly after the Association idea had been proposed.

'The thing that surprises me after all these years is the size of the Whirlwind. It looks a right monster. However, it did us all proud, and had a record second to none in theatre. Any idea on the whereabouts of the crewmen?

'I forget the requirements, but they had to be able to carry out inspections and repair work way outside the confines of their basic trade, all for the "pleasure" of working out in the field under inhospitable circumstances. I was paid a reasonable wage and anyway enjoyed the flying, but what made them stick their necks out, I'll never know! Why would seemingly sane airmen volunteer to work out in the field, under such inhospitable (possibly even hostile) circumstances?'

My reply: 'I can of course only answer for myself, George, but I too enjoyed the flying, especially in the hands of such able and affable aircrew. Also, I was never one for the mundane 9 to 5 life, not that life in the Far East ever was. Or maybe it was the challenge of being able to prove oneself in adverse conditions. There again, maybe we weren't entirely sane... Whatever, it certainly prepared me well for the infinitely more inhospitable environments I was to face when working in oil exploration after leaving the RAF, so was entirely beneficial to my future life. What more can I say?'

Thinking about it later I have to admit it was hard work, and maybe we were taking a bit of a risk, as were the pilots – though the technical risks generally only became apparent in hindsight. But there were risks associated with the environment too, which is why we always carried arms – a Smith and Wesson sidearm for the pilot, US M1 carbine for the crewmen, though this was later replaced by a Sten gun, along with two magazines; I guess they figured we stood more chance of hitting any potential targets with an automatic.

There were times when, taking into account the weight restrictions, the crewman – along with Sten gun – plus part of the load, would be dropped off en route, say to a fort, up in the mountains – less weight being the only way the aircraft *could make the height. Everything would be picked up on the return trip. Even taking as much care as was possible, there was never any guarantee the area was completely safe. It could be a worrying time for a crewman, a pile of supplies, and himself, waiting in a clear area for his helicopter to return. (The supplies might have been out in the open, but I always opted for the nearest cover from which I could observe my surroundings.) All kinds of thoughts run through the mind, and I'll say one thing: I became very familiar with the workings of that Sten gun! I had two thirty-two round magazines, taped back to back (just like in the movies) and I was ready.*

Never was the distant sound of a helicopter a more welcome tune to the ears! Let's face it, although we had control of the skies, and the ground war was being conducted in more or less friendly territory, not all areas were guaranteed to be friendly. That could depend where you set down, and the particular time on a particular day.

But generally, I, along with most, I suspect, pushed thoughts of possible mechanical failure to the back of my mind, only for them to be edged forward, even if only slightly, whenever an incident occurred, which they occasionally did. In fact I seem to recall one crewman felt hard done by because he was one of the few who had not been involved in anything untoward! I remember telling him, 'neither have I Pete, so you are very welcome to any that may be lined up for me in the future!'

In fact the only time I did become slightly more than worried was when we were returning from an op one time. I was plugged in 'downstairs' along with another crewman, two pilots up in the cockpit, when we received a call advising of some possible problem that had suddenly become evident, advising all pilots to land asap to check something or other. All I heard from above were the pilots discussing the situation, wondering what the problem might be, then deciding to chance it and carry on back to base (KL). Apparently all they needed to resolve was whether to gain some height, or drop down low, i.e., was it an engine problem, or rotor head?

Must admit, times like that did get you to thinking!

These minor inconveniences apart, the aircraft were not that reliable – another reason for a crewman to be 'invited along'.

BITS AND PIECES

Despite this there seemed to be no shortage of volunteers for the job, although maybe I am wrong there, for it was officially the domain of the rigger or fitter trades, yet I was accepted, as an ancillary tradesman (instrument fitter). It just meant I had that much more to learn than some. But let's face it, there were often other crewmen around, and if it was anything major, there would likely be a need to fly in parts, along with technicians and tools.

It was to be many years before the post came to be accepted as an official aircrew position (long after the Malayan Emergency), so no brevet was awarded, though we did receive flying pay (M$1 = 2s 4d in 'old' money) for the days on which we flew, were issued with Form 1767, Aircrew Flying Log Book, plus Jungle green clothing, a bone dome and throat-mike, and that Commando-type knife. The throat-mike was a throwback to the Second World War tank days, a standard headset mike picking up too much engine and rotor noise to be of any use. But in those conditions, throat-mikes, which were particularly susceptible to sweat, heat, and moisture of any kind, did not have a long life. The Sten gun and ammunition were collected from the station armoury as and when required.

Apparently Crewman was a FEAF appointment, hence the notification in the front of our logbook: Crewman authorisation: Air HQ Malaya letter – AHQ(M) 7038-1-eng 4/6/53 in accordance with AMO A671-49.

Talking to some of my compatriots, in the early days they were required to take a two week instructional course on the trade they were not (i.e. Engine, or Airframe) plus ancillary trades. Others said they had only been given a couple of hours with the senior NCO in charge of crewmen (who apparently did not fly). I don't even recall there being a senior NCO i/c, and never found myself to be in a position of having to pick the brains of any other crewmen around at the time. Perhaps I was lucky then? But by my time there had been seven years of learning.

Anyway, being young and enthusiastic, we dismissed such thoughts as hard work, and the possible dangers, or at least pushed them to the back of the mind. To me it was something different, exciting, and, who knows, perhaps I felt a need to actually earn that GSM.

*

Letter from John 'Taff' Walker

Dear Dave,
I can hope you'll be able to read what follows. My fingers are a bit arthritic – just like a Whirlwind in manual. [The Whirlwind featured the standard twist-grip throttle on the collective control, which itself featured hydraulic assistance, as did the cyclic controls – powered by a single hydraulic pump! Taff would occasionally practice a hydraulic failure, having me switch off the hydraulics as we flew along. He said he figured he'd be pushed to take more than ten minutes of that. He had both hands on the cyclic, his knee wedged beneath the collective, which had the friction damper fully applied.]

The DVD [Helicopter Ops Malaya, which I had cobbled together] *arrived before Christmas but I wasn't able to view it as Enyd* [Taff's wife] *collared it and ordered that I would have to wait, it would be given to me as a Christmas present. Having now seen it I can present my findings. Great viewing, stirred up lots of memories written by one who has the gen. I shall treasure it. Well done and a big thank you.*

Oddly, a few weeks ago I received another DVD, quite a coincidence, from Tony Tamblyn. I don't know if you remember him, but this second DVD was also about the Emergency and the various aspects, Politics, Special Branch affairs, local issues, the murder or assassination of the High Commissioner Sir Henry Gurney (have I got his name correct?). As it happens I was out there when it happened. I was with 81 (PR) Sqn, Mossies stationed on the holiday camp called Seletar.

So now I am the possessor of two DVDs which complement 'The War of the Running Dogs', by Noel Barber, and a dry as dust official history of 'The Role of the Helicopter', by Wing Commander John Dowling DFC, who I knew very well (now deceased).

Master Pilot John 'Taff' Walker.

BITS AND PIECES

When I look up from this desk I can see a book called 'A Kitbag Full of Orgies' or some such! I have thumbed through and got quite airsick so I am taking gentle sips. Obviously I've read the services bits, and one story which you have included was the one about the damaged blade (Seletar), and stores wanting to dispatch it to KL, to the Squadron, to balance the books. Our CO at the time was Frank Barnes. The chopper was damaged (the blade that is), when operating from Kampong Ha La – just across the Straits. It was being refuelled, rotor turning at this place, when flinging the flimsy aside, caught a finger in the handle, so instead of clearing the rotor disc, went straight up and DONG! I'm not going to tell you who was helping with the refuelling – but have a guess. The damage was slight, and Ken Claydon decided on a careful 15mins return to Seletar. It obviously was not 'S' for an hour and a half to KL.

Page 183 of 'A Suitcase Full of Dreams', Whirlwind in the Ulu, courtesy of Bill McEachern on his way to ? Estate, 5000ft ... engine failure, marvellous reactions, managed a 180 degree turn to return to Fort Selim. On descent, barely clearing jungle canopy, eventually landing in a small creek area, between rocks, no more than a few hundred yards from the fort. This was the last of XD185's adventures in Malaya – as it still was, but only just. What it doesn't include is the post crash 'technical' bit of the F1180: Particles of metal swarf, non-metallic chippings, and fibrous particles were found in the carburettor float chamber. Also a piece of fibrous substance was found on the float control needle valve, preventing it from fully closing, resulting in flooding and high jet levels. This in turn caused the rich mixture cut at 4,700ft. [33-year-old Flight Sergeant W.H. McEachern had flown a total of 2,978 hours at the time of the accident; a total of 669 hours on helicopters, 191 of which were in the last six months.]

There is another story I have to tell you but I forget it at the moment. Thinks! Sycamore XL822, 194, Nobby Clarke, crewman Corporal Thorpe. Different era, I didn't know the lad. I was on 155 at the time. Lifts up Malay policeman from fort for medical – going round the bend – climbs out of fort in the Sungei Telum valley, loses engine, makes for stream, misses, lands in bamboo thicket which cushions impact, but blades shatter. Crewman jumps clear but is hit on head by still rotating blade section and killed. Time I believe mid afternoon. Search commenced, don't know details. Nobby releases policeman from the harness (straight-jacket) with which he has been fitted, spent night in Sycamore. Next day SAS and doctor made a drop to clearing; Nobby, policeman, and crewman's body lifted out.

Nobby's daughter said it had been a terrible time for the family when he went missing, for they did not know whether or not he had survived.

Minimum damage to airframe, new blades, clutch and engine required – this done by working party, then aircraft recovered. See Peter Dace [page 111].

I didn't know Nobby at this time but when 194/155 combined to 110 I got to know him, but it wasn't easy. Silent card.

God bless mate, Taff.

*

Derek Sinden

After six days in the jungle, a fourteen-man army patrol of the Special Air Service bumped into two uniformed Communist Terrorists on a track in the Ulu Keneboi area, Malaya. One of the terrorists fired, the second man in the patrol was hit. The leading man let off a startled solitary burst from his Owen gun. One of the terrorists was probably hit, but both escaped. The time was 8am.

The wounded man was hit somewhere over the eye. He was injected with his own morphine, and bandaged. The patrol commander, a youngish sergeant major, decided the man should be taken out by helicopter – the alternative to four days stretcher march to the nearest road. He radioed his decision and map reference to his battalion base.

Fifty miles away, a helicopter was alerted and an Auster aircraft was dispatched to direct the patrol to a workable helicopter LZ site.

By 10am the Auster had spotted the patrol's smoke signal, and had found a clearing. Under the pilot's direction, the patrol set off. The semi-conscious wounded man was carried in the rear half of the single-file patrol, on a stretcher made out of bamboo and a poncho cape. The 800 yards to the clearing took them one and a half hours. Here, although the 15 foot undergrowth was more dense, the 200 foot trees were sparser.

The use of explosives (certain deep-penetration units always carried them), and *parang* knives, which cut better and blister less than issue machetes, rapidly submerged the ground in a sea of branches and exploded trees, now with stumps like shaving brushes. By 5.30pm the LZ was complete.

Soon, the patrol heard the sound of an aircraft. A smoke bomb was let off, and the helicopter appeared like a great daddy-longlegs over the LZ. After circling twice it came in at a steep angle, making a tremendous noise. The air from its rotor bent trees and hurled up wood splinters. With its engine still running the wounded man was loaded into the stretcher basket, and amid its own whirling gale the machine rose and departed the way it had come. The pilot's moustache had been observed through the Perspex to be exceptionally large. The whole, curious visitation had taken three and a half minutes.

The helicopter landed at Kinrara Military Hospital forty-eight minutes later. By 7pm, eleven hours after he was wounded, the casualty's eye had been saved and his life was out of danger.

*

Flight Lieutenant Tony Freeborn

An obituary in *The Daily Telegraph* for an ex-Wren officer, Leta Frost, recounted her work in pioneering trials for equipment used in rescues at sea; in particular the scoop net (known properly as the Sproole Net) trawled by a helicopter for rescuing people from the sea. The net, in a rectangular iron frame, lay along the starboard side of the helicopter and was lowered and trawled along the surface of the sea to rescue survivors.

In 1962 I was Flight Commander Training on No. 205 Squadron at Changi. Hearing that a naval Dragonfly helicopter equipped with the net was temporarily based at NAS Sembawang, I phoned and arranged for the helicopter to visit Changi and demonstrate the equipment. Of course, I volunteered to be the first to act as a survivor, and boarded the helicopter to be whisked a couple of hundred yards off the coast at Changi Beach. The machine hovered and I was told to jump out into the sea, from what looked like a great height. 'Not on your Nellie,' said I, 'unless you go a bit lower.'

I knew how shallow the water was at this point. The helicopter dropped down a bit and I was again told to jump. I decided to hit the surface in as flat a position as I could manage and out I went. I still hit the bottom quite hard.

Next came the rescue. As the trawl approached I lay on the surface as instructed, was scooped up into the net and whisked up into the air, with nothing but a few bits of string between me and eternity! Wondering if my life insurance policy would cover me for – what? Hazardous sports, perhaps? The trawl was then winched in and, with some trepidation, I clawed my way back into the cabin of the Dragonfly. A quick circuit of the airfield and I was deposited safely back onto the ground. Big sigh of relief! After impressing on the helicopter pilot the shallowness of the water off Changi Beach, the exercise continued in deeper water, with several crews enjoying the experience. Would I do it again given the chance? Not a hope!

*

St John 'Titch' Derbyshire

On my 18th birthday I was posted to Kuala Lumpur based 194 Squadron. Travelling up by train we were required to do guard duty with a short Lee Enfield and ten rounds of ammunition. On arrival at KL I worked on the Alvis Leonides powered Westland S51 Dragonfly, with which the squadron was then equipped.

Later on, the Bristol Sycamore arrived, same engine, but with wooden blades instead of metal. I believe these caused a lot of trouble after I had left, the humidity getting into the wood putting the main rotor blades out of track.

Squadron Leader Henderson was our CO, and I recall that one of our pilots, 'Kiwi Francis' always urinated on the landing wheel before take-off. I never did find out why, although I remember Kiwi Francis well. He was flying the Dragonfly, and I flew into one of the jungle strips with him – first time I met the aborigines. Some of the women were wearing dresses made from supply drop parachutes.

As I was leaving, Westland S55s were arriving (with 155 Sqn). They were badly affected by the humidity, and low on engine power. They were still trying to sort this when I left, the aircraft not being able to carry the required number of troops etc.

While at KL, two of us drove down to Singapore and back, me on a Triumph Thunderbird 650cc, and Peter Hooper on a Matchless G9 500cc.

BITS AND PIECES

We carried Sten guns on our backs, with the magazines in our pockets. No bridges, we crossed the rivers on rafts.

There were a variety of aircraft at KL when I was there. Voice flight had DC3s, there were two Pembrokes, supply drops were by Valetta. The Army had Austers, the Navy Sikorsky S55s, probably fitted with Pratt & Whitney engines. There was also a Beaver.

Best years of my life.

*

Lieutenant Tony Blackwell RA

I was an Artillery Troop Commander normally operating from the edge of the jungle with a Troop of 25 pounders, providing harassing fire to keep the opposition on the move, or spoil their sleep.

In 1958, having just returned to base from an operation, I was called in to my commander who explained that on the following day a troop of 4.2 mortar equipment would arrive at the local railway station. I was to collect and would be choppered into the jungle in one week for use on operations. Simple! Not really, it is a totally different weapon, and no one was trained in its use. A sergeant was found who had used the mortar in Korea, and with his help we were ready to go at the specified time. Even I was amazed.

I was advised that the maximum lift for a Whirlwind Mk 4 was 1,000lbs and that the mortar base plate alone weighed 563lbs and, with metal spikes underneath, would require to be placed on timber supports in the aircraft to stop it going through the floor, which I understood contained the fuel tanks.

The surface area of the mortar base plate was approximately 4'x4'. With the amount of equipment we had to carry it meant weighing everything and working out the individual loads. It didn't help that I had two 17-stone soldiers.

Everything had to be juggled to ensure that I sent enough men in to secure the LZ before lifting in the equipment and still had enough to load and unload the equipment. It was obvious we were going to have a problem loading the base plate because of its size and weight. The aim was achieved, including the lift in of 1,000 mortar bombs weighing 11,250 lbs.

On the second operation the 1,000 mortar bombs were parachuted into the LZ on 125 chutes; all were on target but two roman candled which sent everyone diving for cover and necessitated the change of some knickers. A chopper was sent in the next day to pick up the chutes – wishful thinking on someone's part, the soldiers having become very attached to them. A token number were returned.

All went well until the lift out, when we were told to destroy the bombs which had been buried in the deck and were unsafe to handle. I detailed someone to blow them up with plastic, but it all went wrong. The bombs were not destroyed but the packing cases were burning brightly; the choppers were coming in, and the bombs could go bang at any time; needless to say all the soldiers had their heads down. I had to call up the aircraft and lay them off until some brave but foolhardy soul had put the fire out by smothering it with earth. Then a pilot told me he could only take 800lb lifts, requiring load changes and much swearing, ensuring I didn't travel in that chopper. Very brave. May I take this opportunity of thanking all those involved in our little escapades, for their patience, and for the excellent service that they provided in lifting us in and out of the jungle safely on many occasions.

*

WHERE'S HIS FINGER?

Police Lieutenant John Cromey

The first eighteen months of my service in the Malayan Police force was spent in Gelang Patah district, South Johore. The southwest boundary was the Sungei Pulai, southern boundary the Johore Strait and south-east the Sungei Melayu. The district consisted of several rubber estates with a large pineapple plantation in the northwest. The most isolated police post was on Ming Shu estate and could only be reached by walking a few miles along a rough overgrown and disused logger's track, occasionally used by CTs as a good ambush position. The favoured method of approach was by using a small open boat powered by a Johnson Seahorse 25 hp outboard motor. The skipper was named Adam; he adored the Seahorse so much I think he slept with it.

I normally visited Ming Shu at the end of the month to pay the SCs stationed there. I would set off with Adam and two other SCs down the Sungei Pulai, through the Johore Strait and up the Sungei Melayu to a jetty at the estate compound. We would spend the night there and return home the following day. The estate manager was a middle-aged chap named Seymour, who was privileged to have a bodyguard of seven SCs instead of the usual five. Perhaps it was the isolation of the place that entitled him to such luxury. The majority of his labour force was Tamil, most of who were partial to plenty of toddy – fermented coconut juice – really potent stuff.

On one of these visits I became involved in a domestic disturbance caused by the hypnotic swaying of a young Tamil damsel's derrière as she pranced along carrying two buckets of water, slung at each end of an oscillating bamboo pole resting on her shoulder. This is the usual method of carrying two buckets of anything wet or dry. Young ladies thus bounding along cause eyebrows to rise.

Everything had gone reasonably well that day, and as usual I was invited to have dinner with Mr Seymour, and afterwards partake of some of his favourite tipple. He enjoyed Courvoisier, and who was I to complain. We were putting the world to rights that evening when suddenly the tranquillity was ruined by a loud banging on the door. I followed Seymour to the door and was confronted by one of his bodyguard shouting excitedly, *Tuan! Tuanl, banyak susah dalam kongsi!* (Sir! Sir!, lots of trouble in the workers quarters). I knew it: that blasted toddy again.

On going to investigate we found two drunken sarong-clad Lotharios knocking the betel-nut juice out of each other, all over the winsome wench with the wicked wiggle, who had nonchalantly sauntered by, buckets and all.

I am averse to betel-nut juice stains on my nice clean jungle-green uniform, so hesitated at launching myself into the melée. Not so Seymour. He waded in, thump, thump, thump and then utter silence, one of the assailants holding his left arm aloft, a look of dismay on his weather-beaten face.

'There's something wrong with his left hand,' I said.

'Why?'

'The end of his forefinger is missing.'

Seymour is all for returning to the Courvoisier, but I feel duty-bound to find the missing finger.

Mana jarinya? (where's his finger). A little shuffling around and someone shouts out, *ada benda sanal* (something over there). Nobody will touch this curious bit of something so I have to take a closer look. I think it's the finger-end and someone hands me a piece of white cloth in which I clumsily wrap the shrivelled flesh. It seems that during the brawl one left forefinger found itself in the other fellow's mouth, just as Seymour landed a neat uppercut to a jaw, and snap, forefinger severed at the first joint. A sort of guillotine action you could say. This is proof that chewing betel nut keeps the teeth sharp.

THE FIRST HELICOPTER BOYS

Popeye! Get the Seahorse purring! We're on our way to the Marine Police jetty at Johore Bahru, where we hand over the severed finger complete with owner to a bewildered PC and ask if he will kindly deliver same to the hospital in his Land Rover.

We return to Ming Shu and I continue my interrupted discourse with Seymour. For supper we have horse-piss eggs, fried *ikan bilis* sprinkled with sugar and thinly sliced pickled ginger. Seymour doesn't really need the ginger as he is already well and truly pickled on Courvoisier. This is the life for me.

Next morning we bade farewell to Ming Shu and headed towards the Johore Strait. A change in the weather, it was now raining with a stiff breeze blowing. This was a little unusual but we didn't care, soon to be back in Gelang Patah. The headland that forms the south-east of Ming Shu estate curves round in a nice geometric arc, Adam holds the tiller to take us sweeping around gracefully until we enter the main channel to starboard. We are now in marine mode and, as always, Adam steers a course that will take us westwards, mid-channel, with Johore to starboard, Singapore island to port. I am seated in the prow with two SCs amidships and Adam caressing the tiller while crouched low down in the stern.

We had scarcely altered course to westward when the sea appeared to be very choppy with the wind increasing in strength. Soon we were in the thick of it with our little boat bouncing up and down alarmingly. The waves were growing ever higher, perhaps up to eight feet. We climb up and drop down to wallow in the trough. Adam continues to coax the purring Seahorse along and I'm feeling pretty scared. As we approach the mouth of the Pulai we should alter course to northward, but if we do we will surely be swamped. I turn to Adam shouting and gesticulating wildly: *Terus! Terus!, jangan belok kanan, Aku t'ak mahu mati hari ini, t 'ak boleh renang!* (straight ahead, don't turn to the right, I don't want to die today, I can't swim!). We continue westward hoping to reach shelter on the leeward side of the peninsula that forms the west bank of the Pulai estuary. It juts further south into the Johore strait than the east bank. We continue westwards in the hope that we are far enough north to reach the leeside of the spit of land. If we miss it we will end up on the Sumatra coast, which we do not want.

We were lucky, finally made it to shelter, then followed the Pulai river homeward bound. It was an experience that I would never want to go through again.

I was reminded of the tragic accident in which Police Lieutenant Tozer lost his life when the speedboat in which he was travelling capsized in a storm somewhere along the same stretch of water. I can only assume he was caught up in a set of circumstances similar to my own on that stormy day in the Johore strait.

Service in the MPF occasionally had its tricky moments.

*

Anonymous Memories, Courtesy of an Airman

Fitting out a helicopter for crop spraying. I doubt it would be approved in this day and age.
Grease-gun fights down the strip.

Scrounging new Jungle-Greens whenever we were working with the Army.

Chiefy Moss being taught to fly by CO 'Chips' Fry while at HMS *Sembawang*.

Guard duty on the train between KL and Singapore.

Getting lost with 'Whacker' Cox and having to land to establish a location.

A pilot who shall remain nameless who 'lost' a CT's body over the jungle when the rope snapped because it chaffed against the step. Gurkha in the back was very upset because he thought he would be suspected of having cut the rope!

Another nameless pilot, grounded for chasing a motorcyclist around the airfield at Sembawang, and within an hour found himself on a Casevac.

An 848 Sqn Whirlwind starting up and flying parallel with the runway only for the engine to cough to a stop after quarter of a mile, out of fuel.

On my way from crewroom to dispersal – oil-stained shorts and flip-flops – when a large black car came into view. It contained Sir Anthony Eden, who gave me a grin and a wave. Looked over my shoulder to make sure nobody was watching, and smartly disappeared.

*

CASUALTY EVACUATION SUMMARY, JULY TO SEPTEMBER 1952

Operation Habitual – twenty-five miles NNW of Kuantan
3 July No. 173: A Malay policeman with malaria was lifted from a police post at Bundi and taken to Kuantan hospital.

5 July Nos. 174-7: The medical officer, 1/10 Gurkha Rifles, was taken to a clearing and remained there while the helicopter evacuated four casualties to Kuantan hospital. He conducted a sick parade and then returned by helicopter to Kuantan.

6 July No. 178: The helicopter took supplies to a clearing and then flew to another clearing in the area and evacuated a Gurkha OR with an injured elbow.

9 July Nos. 179-85: Four Gurkhas evacuated from a clearing, three from another clearing. All were suffering from fever and were taken to Kuantan.

11 July Nos. 186-7: Two Gurkha ORs evacuated from a clearing suffering from fever.

13 July Nos. 188-90: The 1/10 Gurkha Rifles called for the evacuation of four more men with fever. Unfortunately the clearing proved too small and the patrol were instructed to move to a dried-up river bed some distance away. Next day, two men were lifted, but bad weather prevented the pilot lifting the other two casualties.

14 July No. 191-2: Remaining two casualties evacuated to Kuantan.

Operation Pilchard – fifteen miles west of Ipoh

9 July No. 193: Helicopter flew into the first clearing that had been prepared in the hills west of Ipoh. Height of clearing was 2,000 feet, and after several attempts at taking off pilot had to leave casualties behind. The patrol moved downstream three miles, and next day a casualty with hysteria was lifted from a clearing en route to the new site.

BITS AND PIECES

11 July Nos. 194-8: In four trips, five casualties were flown out and a replacement patrol commander and men were flown in. One patient had septic tinia, another a parang cut on the knee, one a parang cut on the hand (Captain Hall, the patrol commander). The other two were suffering from piles, bad feet and blood-poisoning. All casualties were taken to Ipoh.

20 July Nos. 199-201: A Gurkha officer who had been injured during a supply drop and two GORs suffering from fever were all evacuated from the same clearing to Kuantan.

23 July Nos. 202-4: Two GORs suffering from fever and dysentery, and one Chinese liaison with fever were evacuated from a clearing to Kuantan.

31 July Nos. 205-6: After a number of abortive take-offs in which increasing amounts of kit were off-loaded, the helicopter evacuated two GORs with fever to Kuantan.

Nos. 207-8: An OR of the 3rd KAR with a sprained hip was evacuated. Since the clearing was an easy one, a KAR officer was carried in to give the patient confidence, this being the KAR's first sight of a helicopter.

A Gurkha OR with fever (or exhaustion) was lifted from a clearing. The trees were 250 feet high, the clearing difficult, but the helicopter lifted out easily.

26 August No. 209-10: Two Malay policemen, one suffering from a septic leg, the other from high fever, were evacuated from a clearing twenty miles SSE of Grik. They were members of 16 Federal Jungle Company.

22 August Nos. 211-12 – Operation Habitual: Two KARs with fever were evacuated to Chukai (Kemaman). Also evacuated were terrorist rifles, documents and ammunition.

24 August Nos. 213-14: A JCLO and a KAR with fever were lifted from a clearing to Chukai.

29 August Nos. 215-16 – six miles north-east of Seremban (Negri Sembilan): Two Gurkha ORs with fever and sores were evacuated to Seremban, also a dog casualty suffering from sore pads, accompanied by his handler.

Nos. 217-18 – Grik: Two Malay policemen suffering from gunshot wounds were evacuated from a clearing (No. 16 FJE) SSE of Grik.

30 August No. 219 – Operation Habitual: A KAR with malaria and bronchitis was evacuated from a clearing to Chukai, and thence to Kuantan Hospital.

2 September No. 220: A KAR was lifted from a clearing to Kuantan. He was suffering from flesh wounds incurred when he fell into a pig trap and got caught on the bamboo spikes.

3 September No. 221 – ten miles north-east of Seremban: A Fijian with cerebral malaria was evacuated from a clearing direct to the grounds of Kinrara BMH.

8 September No. 222 – Operation Habitual: A KAR suffering paralysis in his left side evacuated to Kuantan.

7-8 September Nos. 223-6 – north-east Seremban: Four Gurkha ORs with fever evacuated from a clearing (2/7 Gurkha Rifles).

10 September No. 227: Police Lieutenant Wilson of 20 Jungle Company lifted from a clearing on the Sungei Pulai, north-east Ipoh, and flown to MRS Ipoh.

12 September Nos. 228-30 – north-east Seremban: Our old friend 2/7 Gurkhas, again in same clearing. Three more ORs with fever evacuated to Seremban.

15 September No. 231: A KAR who had been badly burned lifted from Temerloh (Pahang) to Kinrara.

16 September Nos. 232-4 – north-east Seremban: Three Gurkha ORs with fever lifted from the usual clearing. Captain Thornton, 2/7 Gurkhas, moved his company out after this. Eventually, thirty-two men from the company ended up in hospital on this operation.

13 September No. 235 – Operation Habitual: A KAR with fever evacuated from deep primary jungle. A stretcher case, he was flown to Kuantan, via Chukai.

BITS AND PIECES

SIGNAL		MEANING
H	1.	S.O.S. - Ground Party lost and in need of positional fix.
H̲	2.	Ground party in need of supply drop (food and medical supplies)
H̄̄	3.	Ground party has suffered casualties and in need of assistance. (supply drop and ground help)
W	4.	Require wireless set re re wiss ses
WI	5.	Require wireless battery
W̲	6.	Require wireless set and battery
↑≡	7.	Ground party in action with enemy in direction of arrow and in need of air support. (All own troops behind the arrowhead, and horizontal bars denote distance of enemy, one bar for each 100 yards.
▢	8.	Require small arms ammunition
⊠	9.	Cancel airstrike or supply drop not required

Ground to air signals from Forts, LZs, clearings etc.

15 September Nos. 236-8: Two trains collided head on near Gua Musang (Kelantan). Five civilians were injured, one of whom died. One was lifted by Auster, the remaining three taken in two lifts to Kuala Lipis hospital. They were Indian civilians.

17 September No. 239: A GOR who had received a burst of fire in the stomach was lifted from a clearing six miles north-east of Seremban to Kinrara hospital. Unfortunately the man died before he could be transferred to the ambulance.

24 September No. 240 – Operation Habitual: A KAR with fever lifted from a clearing to Kuantan hospital. The clearing was difficult due to unusual wind effects. The pilot carried out a number of take-offs before he obtained sufficient performance to climb away safely.

27 September No. 241: A Chinese policeman of 8 Jungle Company suffering from cellulitis was evacuated from a clearing to Kuantan hospital.

29 September No. 242: A Malay soldier with malaria lifted from a clearing fifteen miles wouth-west of Mentakab (Pahang) to the town.

*

JUNGLE RESCUE

At 8.30 hours on Thursday, 22 August 1957, Vickers Valetta VX491 took off from Kuala Lumpur. Its task was to drop supplies to British troops on anti-terrorist patrols, also to release propaganda leaflets over suspected terrorist hideouts. The pilot was Flight Sergeant Robert Pound, his crew consisted of Master Navigator J.A. Tucker, and wireless operator Sergeant B.T. Boyatt. Four air dispatchers of 55 Company RASC were attending the material to be dropped. At 10.35 hours Boyatt sent a signal to Air Headquarters reporting that the first two drops had been completed. That was the last contact Aircraft Control Centre had with the Valetta.

As time passed it became clear the aircraft was overdue. Orders were issued to launch search and rescue operations, but in the absence of an emergency signal from the aircraft – from which a fix might have been obtained – the searchers were faced with a very large area to cover. More Valettas from Air Supply Force, Pioneers of 267 Squadron, Sycamores from

BITS AND PIECES

194 Squadron, Whirlwinds from 155 Squadron, plus a 656 Squadron, AAC Auster, were scrambled in an effort to search the area before nightfall.

Meanwhile an RAF jungle rescue team was brought from Changi to Kuala Lumpur, and paratroops from 22 SAS Regiment were called in to help. They would be dispatched as soon as anything was sighted. But hours passed with nothing being found, so the call did not come. With darkness descending, the aircraft returned to base, the paratroops stood down, knowing that next day there would be even less chance of finding their comrades, the creeping foliage possibly shrouding the wreckage forever.

Lance Corporal Raymond Travis, 20, was in charge of operations in the back of the Valetta. Three 19-year-old drivers were helping prepare a batch of leaflets for the next drop over a nearby terrorist stronghold. The four were already veterans of the campaign, completing more than 130 sorties between them. Travis, wearing headphones, suddenly heard Pound shout, 'Strap in!' At the same time the alarm bell began to ring. Travis motioned the others to their seats – installed backwards for extra safety – then got into his own seat. The aircraft appeared to be flying normally, but then, through the open cabin door, he saw trees racing by, and realised they were going to crash. The next instant there was a hideous whirl of grinding, tearing metal. . . .

Travis never knew how he got out of the aircraft. The next thing he remembered was standing, dazed, in the jungle, calling to the other dispatchers. As if in a dream, he saw them appear a little way off, and he pushed through the head-high bush towards them. The aircraft had caught fire and Travis was the only one not burnt. Roe suffered most, but Downes had nasty burns on his face and hands, Moore had head and arm injuries.

There was a burst of gunfire and they scattered, trying to run through the clinging bushes. Suddenly, realizing it was not terrorists but ammunition exploding in the blazing aircraft, they burst into hysterical laughter. The flames reached the petrol tanks, which blew up, stilled the jungle into silence and shattered what was left of the aircraft. They too fell silent. Flight Sergeant Pound's warning had undoubtedly saved them, but not the three crew.

Travis and his men moved fifty yards from the wreck and built a basha in which to shelter. It was a painful night. Roe's back was badly burned and he could get no rest in any position. The others took turns to prop him up. Tropical rain poured into their inexpertly constructed shelter, and they lacked any form of equipment, which added considerably to their discomfort. It seemed an age before morning came.

THE FIRST HELICOPTER BOYS

At first light, ground crews swarmed over the airfield at Kuala Lumpur and engines roared into life. Ten aircraft took off to continue the search for the missing Valetta. A Hastings was scrambled from Changi to act as a radio link between aircraft and the control centre. The RAF jungle rescue team and SAS paratroops were once more on stand-by.

Speed was vital. This was not merely a race against the jungle; the searchers had to beat terrorists known to be in the area. Any survivors would have little chance if terrorists found them first. But another factor was entering the drama. The sky clouding over, visibility far from good, and the aircraft was thought to have gone down in mountainous terrain, where clear skies were essential for safety. But meteorological reports from Kuala Lumpur forecast conditions would get worse.

That Friday morning, as aircraft continued their search, Travis and Downes decided to try to find help for Roe. Moore stayed with the badly injured driver, leaving the basha now and again to fetch water from a nearby stream. The others set off, knowing they were probably sixty miles from Kuala Lumpur, possibly quite near Tanjong Malim, Perak. They recalled a road not far away, so assumed they were within a few miles of a village.

With no machete they could only claw their way through the tangled undergrowth. The going was extremely difficult, their clothes being quickly torn to ribbons. That first day they covered little more than a mile. Building another basha at dusk they managed to get some rest.

Meanwhile a 656 Sqn Auster was flying through broken cloud over mountains on the border between the states of Perak and Selangor. The air was rough, the little aircraft being thrown about uncomfortably when, through a gap in the cloud cover the crew caught a fleeting glimpse of the crash site. The pilot signalled this sighting to the Hastings, which relayed the message to the control centre. They were delighted, for the chance of finding the crash in such conditions was one in a thousand. But their joy was tempered by the fact that, in the brief view they'd had, no signs of life had been observed.

The wreckage lay some four thousand feet above sea-level, on a mountainside, seven miles from the Slim River. Control sent two helicopters with five airmen and seven paratroops to a base on the Slim River airstrip. Two medical officers and two nursing orderlies were in the party. The other aircraft were recalled, for now the weather was closing in.

On Saturday morning helicopter engines shattered the dawn at Slim River, and twelve men climbed into the rear of the aircraft. Together the helicopters left the clearing and made their way to the crash site. One by one the passengers stepped into space and parachutes opened. Gently the men

BITS AND PIECES

swayed down to make a landing in the forest, made contact with each other, then began to hack their way towards the burnt-out remains of the Valetta.

At Kuala Lumpur, a parade to mark disbanding of the Glider Pilot Regiment was cancelled, everyone waiting tensely for news. At last it came. The rescuers reported that two soldiers were safe, the other two apparently trying to walk out of the jungle.

'No clearing suitable for helicopter landing,' radioed the rescue team. 'Please send explosives and equipment to make one.'

Within minutes an aircraft carrying these things was on its way, a search being organised for Travis and Downes. The SAS men were following their footsteps along the path of the stream, and a patrol of Malay police were taken to the nearest point on the jungle road to intercept them. Captain L.A. Mack, RASC, CO of the unit to which the four belonged, took off in a Dakota 'Voice' aircraft to try to broadcast to his men.

'Stay near the river,' he told them, 'Don't panic. Moore and Roe have been picked up, and we'll have you out before long.'

It was a shot in the dark, of course. But Travis and Downes were lucky. They heard the message – could not see the aircraft – and it cheered them considerably. That night they made another shelter, and once more spent long miserable hours in it. Downs was suffering considerable pain from his burned hands, and Travis was having to do all the work of clawing a way through the spiked undergrowth. He was dragging his friend up the steep slopes, letting him slide down the valleys. Once, with Downes clinging to his shoulder, Travis grabbed a thick growth and tried to haul himself up by it. The growth came alive and Travis let go, tumbling back with Downes on top of him. A twelve-foot python reared over them. Travis grabbed a stick and snapped it, the noise scared the snake and it slithered away into the jungle.

The two were faint from lack of food. Although Downes had attended a jungle survival course, he was too far gone to be able to tell Travis what was edible and what not. Both were getting hallucinations, and several times thought they heard people talking. At last they made camp by a waterfall and waited.

Suddenly, they heard a shot. They shouted, but the only reply was another shot. Travis and Downes began to fear that terrorists had caught up with them. Then, to their delight, a voice rang out in English: 'We're up on the hill. Just coming down!'

Seconds later a Malay policeman appeared on the other side of the stream, and then a captain and a trooper of the SAS burst through the jungle close to them. 'I've never been so glad to see anyone in my life,' said Travis.

THE FIRST HELICOPTER BOYS

During three days wandering, he and Downes had travelled less than four miles. They were an amazing sight, torn and unshaven. Shortly after they were found, a helicopter spotted the party and dropped food and clothing. The SAS helped them retrace their steps towards the aircraft. Roe and Moore had already been flown out and were in hospital at Kinrara. Travis and Downes had to spend a further night in the jungle before they could join them.

Roe was in rather bad shape, but Moore demanded to be allowed to sit next to Flight Lieutenant Nobby Clarke, the helicopter pilot, on the flight back, insisting that, despite his head and arm injuries, he was perfectly alright.

In England, Mr and Mrs Downes spent agonizing days waiting for news.

Air Dispatch was a job for which their son had volunteered. When told he was missing, she could not help wishing he had not felt it his duty to do so. The day after they learned of the crash Mrs Downes had received a letter from him. Only the night before the mission he had sat cross-legged on his bunk, clad in nothing but a towel, and played cards with two other similarly attired youngsters from his unit. Now he was somewhere out in the jungle and she didn't know whether he was alive or dead. She was unaware of his rescue until her sister-in-law burst in to say she had heard it on a BBC news bulletin. Mr Downes telephoned the War Office, and after a slight delay they confirmed his son had been saved. Later Mrs Downes received a letter from Captain Mack: 'We are very proud of Alfred. Despite his injuries, he set off through some of the world's most difficult jungle in order to get help for his more seriously injured comrades. He has shown courage of the highest order.'

Mrs Downes is inclined to use similar phrases when she speaks of the men of the Army and Royal Air Force who searched for him in that same difficult jungle, found him, and brought him safely back to civilization.

From the Director of Operations: 'Please accept my warm thanks and high appreciation of the stirring efforts of those members of the Royal Air Force who assisted the rescue of the four Air Despatchers.'

Letter from the AOC, Air Headquarters Malaya, to Squadron Leader Turner AFC, OC 194 Squadron:

13 April, 1957

Your Squadron, over the past four years, has flown 15,000 hours in Malaya. That in itself is an outstanding achievement and may well be a record for a helicopter squadron. However, the significance lies in the work you have done. This work has been vital to the Emergency and of inestimable help to the ground forces.

Soldiers, policemen, Home Guards and even those loyal Aborigines who are helping us have learnt to rely on you and you have not let them down.

I am sure you know, as I do, that if it were not for the loyal and unselfish efforts of every single member of the Squadron it would not be possible to make a real success of the job which has been allocated to you. I hope they will all find pride in the achievement of 30,000 operational sorties the Squadron has logged, and in overcoming the difficulties and frustrations which have had to be faced.

Your Squadron has worked together as a team and has done the people of Malaya a great service. Its morale is high and I know you will keep it so. Take pride in your motto 'Surrigere Colligere – We arise to lift up' and keep that before you as a stimulant to greater efforts.

From the Air Officer Commanding: 'I wish to congratulate those who took part in it on an extremely well timed and well flown fly-past at Kuala Lumpur Padang this morning on the occasion of the review of the Federation Forces by the Paramount Ruler. This was a fine demonstration before many important visitors from the Commonwealth and other countries of individual unit and service skill. Pilots and the men of their units should feel proud of the effort.'

From the Commanding Officer, Peter Le Cheminant:

> I would like to express my deep appreciation for the tremendous efforts which have been made by you and by all ranks of your Wing during the past few weeks.
>
> There is no doubt that the RAF part of the Merdeka Celebrations, and in particular our responsibilities for flying HRH the Duke and Duchess of Gloucester, have gone well. I know they have been greatly appreciated by the Duke and Duchess. I realise that considerable extra work has been entailed and rapid changes of programme have had to be contended with, but no hitch has occurred.
>
> I would like you to get this over to the officers and airman and particularly to stress that their efforts have been noticed by myself and have been favourably commented on by others.

Formation Flypast: Practice for the Medeka (Malayan Independence) celebrations in Kuala Lumpur, 1960. There were actually 10 aircraft in the formation.

After the flypast: Aircraft make a run and break over the airfield at Kuala Lumpur on return from the Merdeka flypast.

> *It is very gratifying to think that when an extra effort is called for it comes cheerfully and willingly. Unfortunately I can offer very little relaxation for the next few weeks as we now have to contend with the Battle of Britain Celebrations and the AOC's inspection on October 8th. Particularly for the latter I shall be asking again for a special effort.*

BITS AND PIECES

Your Squadron has been deeply involved in all these operations, and you have every right to be proud of the results which have been achieved, results which reflect the greatest credit on every officer and airman in your Squadron.

Please read this letter to your Squadron. It will, I hope, be the source of the deepest satisfaction to you so soon before relinquishing command.

From 155 Sqn ORB for March 1958:

The outstanding event of the month was the presentation by the C-in-C FEAF, Air Marshal The Earl Of Bandon, of a silver replica of a Whirlwind helicopter on the 10th. The inscription on the plinth reads: Presented to 155 Squadron FEAF for its magnificent record of Helicopter Operations in Malaya by the Westland Aircraft Co. of Yeovil.

Chapter 12

Jungle Forts and Airstrips

High Commissioner of Malaya, General Sir Gerald Templer, said, 'The Aborigines, Orang Asli, hold the key to the outcome of the Emergency.'

They lived in deep jungle, were made up of several different tribes, and had been under Communist Terrorist control. The CTs had even had their own Orang Asli organization since the Japanese occupied Malaysia during the Second World War, when the communist-led 'Malay Peoples Anti-Japanese Army' first coerced them.

The aborigines not only grew food for the CTs, they were also their eyes and ears, alerting them if security forces were in the vicinity.

To try to break the hold the CTs had over the aborigines, it was decided to build forts in deep jungle – not forts in the sense of the French Foreign Legion say, mainly timber, thatch, and corrugated tin, but with secure boundaries. From these remote and isolated outposts, contact could be made with these little known jungle tribes, and thence destroy the propaganda and lies with which the CTs had been brainwashing them for years. Such little things as – should they see an aircraft flying overhead, the CTs would tell them it's one of theirs. Having no means, or reason, to dispute this, the aborigines believed them. Also, whereas before security forces had a trek of several days to reach their operational area, they now had deep jungle bases where they could be airlifted into, and from which to operate.

Writing about his experiences as OC Flying Wing at Kuala Lumpur in *The Royal Air Force: A Personal Experience* (pages 82-3), Sir Peter Le Cheminant says, 'The jungle forts acted as bases from which infantry and Police Field Force (PFF) patrols could operate. There were a number in operation in mid-1955, with more under construction, and by the end of 1957 there were nine completed and fully functional. It was a major achievement on the part of the Sappers and I have never seen it recognised as such in any book or journal. Every bit of material, apart from timber, needed to build the airstrips and the living quarters, and to make them secure, had to be flown in by helicopter, as did the plant such as bulldozers, diggers and earthmovers.'

Flight Lieutenant Tom Browning

From what is said above, it sounds like another case of 'if it isn't written down it will soon be forgotten.' And, in response to some not entirely subtle reminders, when I at last got round to doing something about it, I realised that that is just about what had already happened to me: a mind about as blank as the sheet of paper in front of me. But help was at hand in the shape of Brian Lloyd who, indirectly, led me to making contact with Roy Follows, a distinguished ex-Malay Police Field Force officer who just happened to be writing a book about Malayan jungle forts. If only half as good as his earlier works, The Jungle Beat, *which relates to his experiences with 4PFF, and as OC Fort Brooke, and* Four Wheels & Frontiers, *a journey by Jeep from Malaya to the UK – while this was still possible (just!) – it will be a cracking good read. However, I digress.*

After contacting Roy, I visited the Royal Engineers Museum at Chatham. Although the Sappers had done most of the hard work building the forts – and airstrips – their records of it seem to consist of four pages in the Malaya section of their History of the Corps of Royal Engineers, Vol X, 1945-60, *pages 187-90, which deal with the jungle forts, and two reports by Lieutenant K.W. Newham RE, a national service officer who spent three months (7 April-2 July 1954) constructing the airstrip at Fort Shean.*

Before this, the RE History tells us, forts were 'maintained entirely by helicopter and by airdrop, which was both precarious and uneconomical'. Now, although we all know what a good job our choppers did in Malaya, it may surprise you to know that not everyone shares this view: the fixed wing union was even more dominant back then. So much had been expected of the Whirlwinds (and Sycamores), especially after the first generation Dragonflys, that their relatively disappointing performance (particularly when compared to 848s seemingly more successful, lighter, Sikorsky-built Mk 21 Whirlwinds) was grist to the mill of those who were convinced that no good could ever come of the helicopter – or, as related many years later by one of the first 194 Sqn flight commanders to one of the last, words to that effect. So when Brigadier W.F. Anderson, the senior Royal Engineer at Malaya Command HQ, suggested in late 1953 that the forts could be maintained more economically if provided with an airstrip capable of operating fixed wing aircraft – like the Scottish Aviation Pioneer CC Mk 1, which was to enter service in Malaya with 267 Sqn in February 1954 – it was readily accepted.

Considered to be the easiest and most accessible, Forts Kemar and Shean were chosen to be the first to have airstrips. The RE History says that a working party was flown into Kemar by helicopter and given authority to hire local aborigines as manual labourers using only hand tools. 848's Whirlwinds were used for these first airlifts but, unfortunately, there seems to be no reference to them in the squadron's records. They do, however, refer to WV198 taking airfield construction parties to Forts Dixon and Shean on 7 April 1954 'preparatory to a tractor lift'. While Fort Dixon's D4 dozer was to be taken twenty miles upriver and over several rapids in one-ton loads by dugout canoe, Fort Shean's was, in its way, to be more trail-blazing. A Ferguson tractor was successfully broken down into seven helicopter-portable loads and flown into Fort Shean by WV198 on 13/14 April 1954 – the first operation of its kind. 848's records say that it took 'approx 8 sorties'. Lieutenant Newham is convinced that the job took seven sorties over two days: three the first day and, after delay by bad weather, four the next. Whatever, by the time the last 600lb load was flown in, the tractor had been assembled and was already being tested.

'After 11 weeks of unbroken work' the first Pioneer landed at Fort Shean's 200-yard long airstrip on 22 June. On 8 August 1954 Pioneer XE514 became the first to crash at Fort Shean when landing. The pilot and passengers were evacuated by an old stalwart, WV198.

After the initial tractor lift to Fort Shean it became commonplace to fly the eventual fleet of five Fergusons and eight Fordsons from fort to fort. There were exceptions: three dozers took over two weeks to 'walk' to Fort Langkap which, incidentally, had been a Force 136 drop zone in the Second World War, while Forts Brooke and Sinderut never had airstrips and remained dependent on airdrops and helicopters for their maintenance and resupply.

The History of the Corps of Royal Engineers *says that by 1956/7: 'In all, twelve Pioneer airstrips were built for jungle forts at distances of up to thirty miles from road or rail-head.' Sir Peter puts the number of forts (with or without airstrips) as nine by the end of his second tour – June 1955 to November 1957 – say ten if you include Fort Tapong, which was not completed until 1959/60. As far as I can make out these, in alphabetical order, were:*

JUNGLE FORTS AND AIRSTRIPS

Fort Brooke (VE 38 83): No airstrip. Named after Lieutenant Colonel Oliver Brooke DSO MBE of 22 SAS.

Fort Chabai (VE 50 20): Although 848 NAS took two tractors from Chabai to Qua Musang on 16-17 September 1955, the airstrip was not completed until 1956/7.

Fort Dixon (VK 70 44): Tractor delivered by dugout canoes after airfield construction party had been positioned on 7 April 1954.

Fort Iskander (Loc?): An airstrip existed at the police post in 1949, but both were abandoned in 1951. It is claimed that a new airstrip and police post (fort) were built in 1953, but this seems too soon for the airstrip bearing in mind the airstrip programme didn't begin until April 1954. On 21 March 1955 three 848 NAS Whirlwinds flew in a dismantled 25-pounder gun – claimed as another helicopter 'first'. 'From a pilot's point of view, by far the easiest of the jungle strips', according to OC Flying Wing RAF KL.

Fort Kemar (VE 27 45) the first fort to be established: Although the airstrip was largely built using manual labour, a tractor was flown in by 848 NAS to

Fort Dixon Approach.

Fort Dixon from Airstrip.

Fort Iskander view.

JUNGLE FORTS AND AIRSTRIPS

Right: Building Fort Kemar.

Below: Fort Legap.

compact the surface. Pioneer XJ450 was tipped over and written off after encountering a squall while landing on 4 October 1960.

Fort Langkap (WQ 17 60): Claimed to have been a Force 136 DZ during the Second World War and, afterwards, cultivated and used by the CTs before having a fort and airstrip constructed. The RE History mistakenly places the location around VK 54 56 (Johore Grid).

Fort Legap (VE 12 13): Tractor flown in by WV192 in seven sorties on 22 May 1954. 'The tightest and most impressive of the strips', according to OC Flying Wing RAF KL.

Fort Selim Airstrip.

Probably XE316 at Fort Selim. No names recalled.

JUNGLE FORTS AND AIRSTRIPS

Fort Shean.

Fort Shean aerial.

Fort Sinderut.

Fort Sinderut after being decommissioned.

Fort Selim (VK 12 69): Described as a new fort in December 1954 when it started acting as a Sycamore fly-trap. XE314's pilot and two passengers were recovered to Ipoh by 848s WV190 on 7 December 1954; and XE316 crashed during approach on 30 January '55.

JUNGLE FORTS AND AIRSTRIPS

Bristol freighter overhead Sinderut.

Resupply at Fort Sinderut.

Fort Shean (VK 54 31): The first to have a tractor flown in (see account above). On 15 April 1957 a second Pioneer, XG563, was written off after the undercarriage collapsed on landing. The remains later formed the fort's nameboard.

THE FIRST HELICOPTER BOYS

Fort Tapong, looking west.

Fort Sinderut (loc?): Like Fort Brooke, Sinderut remained without an airstrip.

Fort Tapong (QZ 23 03): The last of the 'Emergency' forts, it now lies beneath a reservoir.

Fort Telanok (VK 46 50): First known as Net when 848 NAS's WV191 crashed here on 30 May 1954. On 17 June 1954 WV194 carried out a tractor lift from Fort Shean to Fort Net.

Well, that accounts for twelve forts. 848 NAS records refer to a thirteenth: Fort Hardcastle (VD 85 44) where, on 2 March 1953 twenty Gurkhas were flown in and an aborigine, who had been mauled by a bear, flown out as a casevac. It is possible that this was not an established fort but, rather, a major landing site/zone which temporarily adopted the codename of a particular operation. As we started off by saying: if it isn't written down it will soon be forgotten. So any more information about Hardcastle will be very welcome. (It was later established – by the person in charge of its construction – that Hardcastle was actually the codename for the operation that led to the building of Fort Kemar, the first of the forts to be built.)

JUNGLE FORTS AND AIRSTRIPS

Fort Telanok.

Despite the economies that were claimed following the construction of fort airstrips in Malaya, helicopters were still essential when it came to trooplift and casevac missions in and out of deep jungle – even if the official line was that they should only be used when no other means were available. Nor should it be forgotten that while airstrips were necessities for the original Pioneers and the subsequent twin-engined Pioneers (Twin-pins), they were not essential for the helicopters, although there is no doubt they made life easier for them.

Curiously though, even today there are still never enough helicopters to meet the operational demands made upon them. So, I guess, after all those years nothing much has really changed.

– An impressive piece of research, Tom, but what of Forts Betau and Betis? I have both in my log book, albeit in 1959/60. There is also a Fort Lebau listed on the internet, whereas Fort Sinderut does not receive a mention. I know it was there as I have photos – taken by myself – of it being burnt down, once it had been abandoned. (David Taylor)

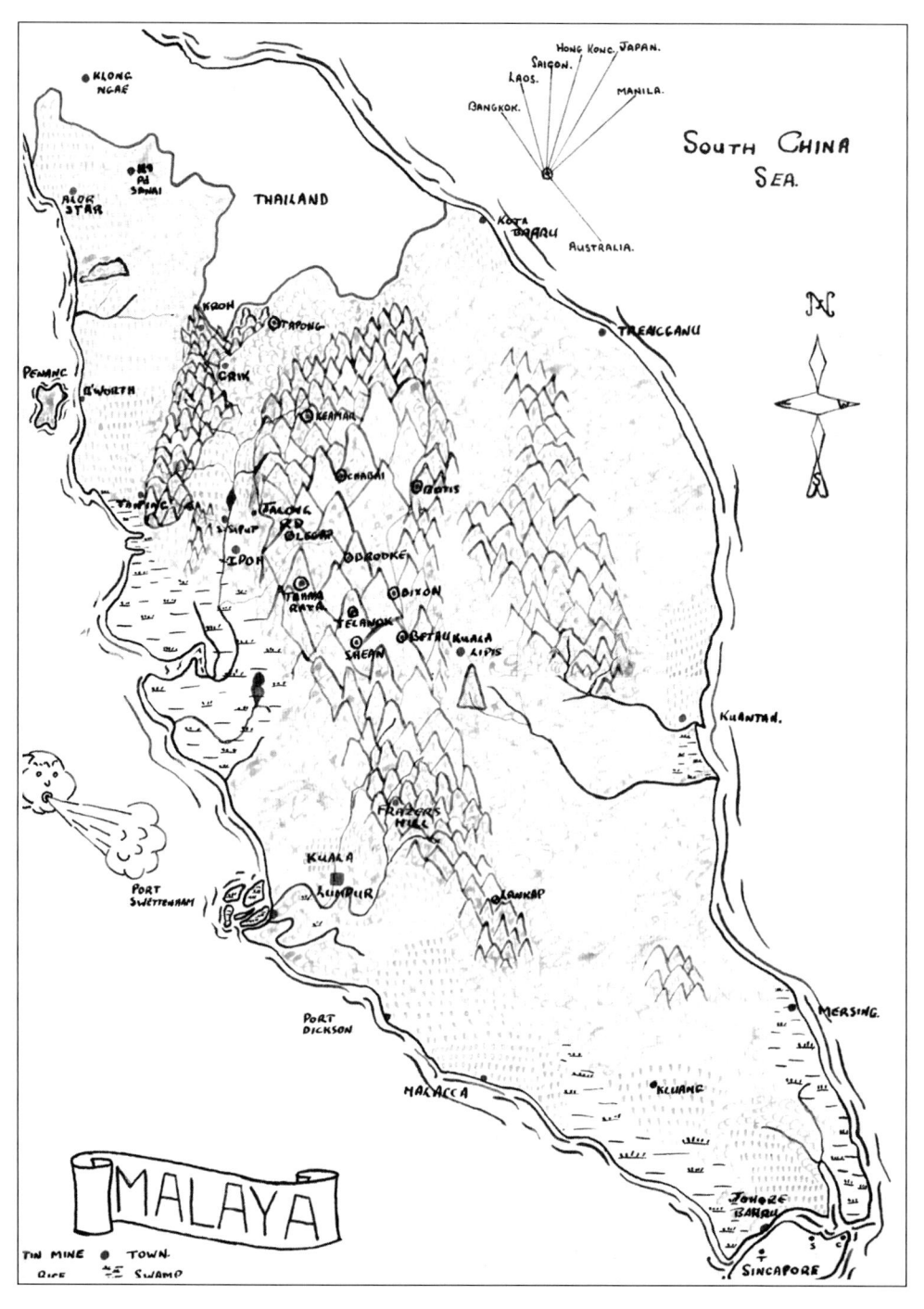

Malaya forts map (personally hand drawn in 1958 – yes, I know it shows!).

JUNGLE FORTS AND AIRSTRIPS

Fort Sinderut being destroyed.

Early Fort Kemar.

Fort Kemar in the 1950s.

The forts became some of the security forces' most important strategic bases. They could be dangerous places. The first of such was Fort Kemar.

THE BUILDING OF FORT KEMAR – 1953

Police Lieutenant Dennis Wombell
Dennis Wombell served in Malaya from 22 September 1951 to 1 May 1956. He served as Platoon Commander 18 Jungle Company in 1953, and Second Team Field Force in Malaya, which operated around the North Perak and Thailand border. He was also involved in the mainline at the border of Thailand (Ops Knot) and was involved in the construction of Fort Kemar. He was assigned to accompany Chin Peng in the Baling Talks in Kedah:

JUNGLE FORTS AND AIRSTRIPS

Browsing one day recently, in 2014, I happened to look up Fort Kemar, and found a site which describes it as it now is. I was incensed to see that on site is a wall with a plaque commemorating the building of the Fort, which, when translated, reads:

FORT KEMAR

DECLARED OPEN BY THE SAS REG IN 1952

TO THOSE WHO SERVED

The fort was neither built nor opened by the SAS, nor did it exist in 1952! What follows is an account of its building in 1953, by the Malays of the Malayan Police 18 Federal Jungle Company.

In the early 1950s, with the Malayan Emergency at its height, the terrorists of the Malayan Communist Party were on the run in both urban and rural areas of the country. Their supplies, especially food, had been severely disrupted by the establishment of defended new villages, where food for the inhabitants was strictly controlled. Life had also been made more tenuous for them by an increase of informers, via build-up of the government intelligence services. As a result, many of them retreated deep into the jungle of the central mountain chain, areas somewhat neglected up to this time by the security forces. In their deep jungle camps the terrorists sought and found the security they desperately needed to grow their own food, to regroup, and to train new recruits. They were largely assisted in this by befriending or intimidating the aborigine tribes who roamed the interior.

The aborigines, the Orang Asli as they are now known, were a shy, timid and simple people, living in stone-age conditions. They were nomadic and lived as family groups in longhouses raised upon stilts in

Fort Kemar, 1953.

small jungle clearings. They grew their staple food crops of tapioca, maize and, in some areas, dry rice, and after only two or three seasons, or a death in the family, they would burn their house and move to new pastures. They fished and, using blowpipes with poison darts, hunted. They were skilled in making traps of bamboo and rattan. Their junglecraft was unequalled, and their tracking skills made it impossible for anyone to move anywhere in their tribal areas without their knowledge.

It requires no stretch of the imagination therefore to understand how valuable these people were to the Communist Terrorists, and how essential it was for the guerrillas to cultivate them; which they did. The Asli knew nothing of the outside world, of government, or politics, and were happy to accept at face value these apparently friendly, Chinese strangers who convinced them they were their friends. It also helped that there had been some contact between Communist guerrillas and the Asli during the war, when these same men had been seen in association with British officers in the fight against the Japanese. This enabled the terrorists to live and cultivate their own crops, largely undisturbed, and to receive from the Asli information on security force movements in the area.

It was obvious that a government presence was required in these areas, so it was decided to establish a chain of jungle forts deep in the interior, manned by units of the Malayan Police. These were not to be forts à la Beau Geste of the French Foreign Legion, but well-defended jungle camps, buildings constructed largely from timber cut from the surrounding jungle. Other requirements needed for construction were to be supplied by airdrop. The role of the forts was to dominate the area in which they were situated, providing a permanent police/military base from which to seek out and destroy CTs and their camps, and to compromise courier routes. An equally important role was to bring government to the Orang Asli by providing the areas of the forts with medicine, schools and shops. It was hoped furthermore to persuade the Asli to abandon their nomadic way of life and settle around the area of the fort where land would be made available for more effective farming of their food crops.

The forts were to be manned by the Malayan Police Jungle Companies – independent police paramilitary units, each identical to an army infantry company in its function and structure, led by both British and Malayan officers. At this time I was a police lieutenant and platoon commander in 18 Police Federal Jungle Company, based on the banks of the Sungei Perak, near Grik, a small remote town fifteen miles south of the Malaya-Thailand border. I, along with my platoon, were allotted the task of establishing the

JUNGLE FORTS AND AIRSTRIPS

country's most northern fort, deep in the jungle of the Sungei Temengor area, close to the Perak-Kelantan border.

My platoon consisted of thirty Malay constables, all conscripts, except for my sergeant and corporals who were members of the regular police force. We had been together for two years and were now jungle-hardened warriors. My sergeant, Mohamed Yusoff, in whom I had total trust, was a sterling character – a first class leader, likeable and highly respected by the men. I had absolute confidence in them all. We were to be accompanied by D Squadron, 22 SAS, British Army. This squadron was to be deployed surrounding the fort, ensuring a security screen during construction. An equally important role was to seek out and make contact with the scattered, isolated aborigine groups, in an effort to persuade them to visit the fort site. They would be advised of our intentions and asked to help with construction, for which they would to be paid.

In order to avoid confusion, every military operation is given its own individual designation. The campaign to locate a site for, and build, our fort, was to be Operation Hardcastle, the name of the fort to be decided at a later date.

In mid-February 1953, my platoon, accompanied by Company Commander Gary Lockington, broke camp and, following the river, marched for the Sungei Temengor, a tributary of the Sungei Perak, deep in the interior of the jungle-covered hills which run like a spine down the centre of the country. We also had with us an advance party of the SAS, the main body to follow in three or four days.

This was just before the introduction of troop-carrying helicopters, and the march, carrying weapons and packs weighing between 40 and 60lbs, was arduous and exhausting. Two words can best describe life in the jungle in these circumstances – wet and stinking. Wet from rain and sweat, stinking because one wears the same clothes for the duration of an operation, changing into a dry set – kept in one's pack – only at night. One of my most abiding memories of life in the jungle, even after half a century, is of getting up in the morning, changing from the warm dry clothes in which I had slept, into my cold, wet and stinking jungle-green uniform, which had hung overnight, dripping, from a bush outside my basha. But God help the man who was tempted to keep his spare dry clothes on!

To march through the jungle in hilly country is especially difficult. More so in a country where there is so much rain. The track, if there is one, is invariably narrow, more often than not on a steep hillside, a precipitous drop down to the river and, for the men in the rear, deep mud churned up by those in front. There are massive fallen trees to climb over – not easy when carrying a full pack and a sidearm – and every two or three hundred yards a stream to wade through, often waist deep. On tracks used by the Asli one would sometimes find a short cut across a long loop in the winding river, but this meant climbing the hill which had caused the river to loop in the first place. The tracks are also infested with mosquitoes and leeches, leeches which hang from the undergrowth waiting to drop onto passing man or animal. One became accustomed and unconcerned – we learnt not to pull them off, which often resulted in a nasty difficult-to-heal ulcer. Touched with salt or ash from the previous night's fire and carried in an ammunition pouch, they would drop off harmlessly. In this way it was possible to remove the more obvious ones from arms, necks and faces on the march, but not those in inaccessible places. They penetrated lace-holes of boots for instance, and were left to gorge themselves until one stripped at the end of the day, removing them from bleeding legs, back and stomach, consigning them to the fire. Mosquitoes, on the other hand, gave one sleepless nights and, if one didn't take Paludrine religiously, almost certainly malaria.

My little Malays took all this in their stride. Not only were most of them kampong Malays who were at home in the jungle, but they had operated in these conditions for over two years and were consequently hardened to it. Not so the SAS. This was by no means the regiment's finest hour. It is well documented that the SAS, revived especially for service in the Emergency, had gone through hard times. Many troopers were well below the standard required of a man with aspirations of joining a regiment which, in future years, would become one of the finest special forces in the world. Most of these guys were unfit, unaccustomed to operating for long periods in deep jungle, and their discipline left much to be desired. Many were what was known in those days as 'canteen cowboys'. On the march, several of them collapsed, and as my Malays casually stepped over one Irish trooper who lay across the track, equipment strewn about him, he called out to me 'Holy Mary mudder o'God sorr, I'm f…ing-well doyin!'

It took almost four days to reach the area in which we were to locate the fort, and upon arrival we set up camp beside the Sungei Temengor, about twelve miles south of Kampong Temengor, an isolated, abandoned kampong surrounded by jungle. Our camp site had in the not-too-distant past been an Orang Asli ladang, thus required little clearing to enable us to receive the much needed airdrop of food the following morning. We wasted no time, and on the morning after the airdrop, leaving the main

JUNGLE FORTS AND AIRSTRIPS

body to clear a larger drop zone, along with helicopter landing zone, Gary Lockington and I took a small party and commenced our search for a suitable site for the fort. In fact the area we had marked on our maps during planning proved to be ideal. It was a flat area on a narrow strip of land between the Temengor and one of its tributaries, the Sungei Kemar, which ran parallel to it for about three miles. At one point the two rivers curved towards each other creating a bottleneck just wide enough for the fort. It then widened again, providing a large flat area eminently suitable for a drop zone and helicopter LZ. The land was 30 or 40 feet above the rivers and not overlooked at any point. It was therefore easily defended, and offered an excellent supply of clean water.

In our absence the working party had completed the clearing of the DZ and LZ, so we were able to receive a second airdrop of food, supplies, and tools required for the construction. It also enabled Lieutenant Colonel Sloane, 22 SAS commanding officer, to arrive by helicopter and visit his squadron HQ in the vicinity of my camp, the main body of the squadron having been deployed in the surrounding area. He departed the same day, taking with him Gary Lockington who, after briefing me and agreeing the location of the fort, returned to Grik.

Once we had the essential tools, work on the fort began in earnest, and I decided we should remain in our original camp until the fort site had been sufficiently cleared. Each day, leaving one section to guard the camp, and make it more comfortable, the working party marched to the fort after an early breakfast, returning before dark. A demanding regime, but it meant every man would be given one day in three of light duties.

Our first task was to completely clear the area of jungle – a formidable task given the number and size of some trees – all done by hand. My Malay boys were completely at home in this environment. Clearing and felling trees, constructing houses of timber, and roofing them with attap was second nature to them, but without the large workforce provided by the Orang Asli it would have taken many months.

Within the first few days small groups trickled in, then the trickle became a flood. Some were led in by the SAS, others, having learned via the jungle grapevine, came out of curiosity – men, women and children, hugely enthusiastic and keen to enlist in one form or another. They are a very friendly, happy and simple people, and it took no time to establish a rapport with them. We explained what it was all about, what we needed, and that they would be paid to help: their enthusiasm knew no bounds. We enlisted those we needed and welcomed their camp followers.

THE FIRST HELICOPTER BOYS

The day after receiving our first airdrop, work started in earnest. My Malays, working alongside the Asli, started to cut, clear and burn the smaller trees and undergrowth with axes and parangs, while those Asli skilled in the use of the beliong, started on the large jungle trees. The beliong is a light axe with a razor-sharp blade, rather like a stone-age axe. The blade is tied to the end of a curved two or three foot long flexible stem, carved at the end to form a cylindrical grip. In the hands of an expert it is unbelievably effective. Some of the trees grew up to 200 feet tall, with a spread of thirty to forty feet. Their technique was to cut the trunk by encircling the tree with a bamboo platform just below the buttress, two men working on opposite sides of the tree. The problem then was the large stump which remained. This was dealt with by another method – explosives! Our expert was Captain Gordon Smith, a Royal Engineer officer serving with the SAS. He and I blew up anything which needed to be blown up. It was great fun. We used Composition C-3, a plastic explosive which looks like sticks of marzipan wrapped in greaseproof paper. It has the consistency of plasticine and is easily moulded into any shape or packed into any hole. Ideal for the job. A bobbin-shaped guncotton primer with a detonator pressed into the C3 with a long enough fuse kept us out harm's way. We also used Cordtex – an explosive in the form of a white plastic cable. Using this we were able to make a 'daisy chain', or ringmain, of C-3, rather like an electric circuit, and blow up a number of connected charges simultaneously. The resultant explosion created huge merriment and awe amongst the Orang Asli as they watched from the protection of trees and trenches. It was also possible to cut small trees by wrapping a length of Cordtex round them and detonating it.

An interlude in my work presented itself when two Orang Asli came running in from their longhouse down-river, telling me one of their men had been attacked and badly injured by a bear. It was an incident that was to end in a Buster Keaton farce! The brown bear of the Malayan jungle is not huge – fully grown, about the size of a man. Seldom seen, they pose little danger. Unfortunately, the injured man had stumbled across a female with cubs: as with all bears, a dangerous situation. I immediately took a small patrol, with food for a couple days, and arrived at the Asli ladang by late afternoon. We found the man had been almost scalped by the bear's claws. While my medical orderly attended to his injuries, I radioed for a helicopter casevac for the following day. The men prepared to make camp on a flat sandy area beside the river, below the longhouse, a little way up the hill. The site was easily cleared, and we started to unpack our kit, light fires, prepare the evening meal, and settle for the night. Then all hell broke loose.

JUNGLE FORTS AND AIRSTRIPS

Two men tore into camp shouting '*Gajah! Gajah! Chapat, mari ka sahaya punya rumah, lari lari chapat.*' Elephant, elephant, come to my house, run, run, hurry up! We wasted no time in unceremoniously stuffing anything we could lay our hands on into our packs, and, with the rest in our arms, fled like a pack of tinkers to the longhouse. The men were given an area at one end to sort out their kit and put down blankets, but I was given a very small room projecting from the rear. Thus far, no elephant. Then, just after I had fallen asleep, I was awakened by screaming and shouting. I felt the floor under me trembling as the earth beneath shook. It took no stretch of the imagination to know that the elephant had not only arrived, but had arrived at the rear, very close to my projecting room. Then the entire population hurtled out of the building, waving burning torches, banging tin cans, and shouting abuse. The elephant, upon concluding there was no female elephant to be found, retreated back into the jungle. Having joined in the general mayhem, my men and I returned to our blankets for a good night's sleep. Or so we thought! The beast continued to snuffle, grunt and thud around for the rest of the night, seemingly much too close to where I lay, but no one could be bothered to get up any more.

I was glad and relieved to see the light of the dawn and, after breakfast, I was called by the Asli headman to go down to see what was to have been our campsite, to find everything, including any tins we had left behind, totally flattened. The helicopter arrived mid-morning and our casualty was safely removed to Ipoh hospital.

By the end of the first week we had cleared enough jungle at the fort area to enable us to move there, to set up a more permanent and comfortable camp. Then we received our first airdrop at the fort itself. We had cleared and levelled the helicopter LZ and were ready to receive visitors.

Life became a great deal easier. It was no longer necessary to split up my platoon to leave a section at the camp, nor did we have to endure the daily trudge to and from the fort. We established a comfortable working routine.

As on all prolonged jungle operations, we received an airdrop every four days, the initial drops being substantial. In addition to normal requirements, we needed a constant supply of construction tools and equipment. We also needed a significant amount of rice, dried fish, salt and tobacco, used as currency to pay our large Orang Asli workforce, to whom cash was of little use. It was an endless list, all to be dropped by parachute from Valetta aircraft. Although most of the time we lived on operational rations, known as 'compo', we also received a supplement of fresh meat and vegetables with every drop. These were very popular given the conditions. I was also able to order personal items through the civilian Rations Supply Contractor in Kuala Lumpur, who, it appeared, was able to procure almost anything. I tested him to the full! He saw this as a challenge, and far from showing irritation or impatience, he supplied me with: Dunhill curved briar pipes, their 'My Mixture' tobacco, and various obscure Turkish cigarettes! The men also were able to order their cigarettes and tobacco, plus other supplements to enhance their basic rations. An account was kept of these personal purchases, to be paid for by the individual at the end of the operation.

There was great excitement and anticipation on airdrop days. They usually took place at about 11.00 am, so after breakfast a bonfire was prepared at the edge of the DZ, ready to provide smoke to enable the pilot to locate his target from a distance, since, in deep jungle, a clearing can be seen only from directly overhead. The smoke also indicates the speed and direction of the wind. Large translucent yellow cloth recognition panels were also pegged out in the centre of the clearing – in my case, in the form of an 'F' – to enable the pilot and his despatch crew to identify us. No one who has lived for any length of time in isolation and cut off from the outside world, will ever forget the drone of an approaching aircraft or the 'chop-chop' of a helicopter. The sound signified news, food, cigarettes, and, above all, mail – letters from friends and family. Initially the pilot would fly a 'dry run', then, having checked the recognition panel and wind, would turn in a wide circle and return to commence his drop. One load at a time, circling until the drop was complete. He'd make a final pass, dipping his wings, a salute from the despatcher at the open door, to disappear over the jungle covered hills. On the ground, excitement would then begin, as the men, helped by hordes of screaming, laughing, Orang Asli children, would run down to the DZ, cut the straps binding boxes which made up the loads, and carry them to a central point where Sergeant Yusoff and I would supervise the distribution. We'd finish on the personal items: the fresh food allowance, the longed-for mail, their even more important cigarettes and various spices, which helped enhance their 'compo' rations. The evening after an airdrop was one of great contentment, when, after the day's work was finished, the fresh food was cooked, the mail read, and the men whose cigarettes had been exhausted, were able to relax in their smoke-filled bashas.

By this time we had established an excellent relationship with the Orang Asli for whom I had both respect and admiration. They were the most primitive people I had ever met, and had the innocence of children. Very few had ever seen a vehicle, an aeroplane, a helicopter, a gun, explosives, or a white man. Witnessing their sheer awe at seeing these things for the first time was a joy. They had nothing which they had not made themselves from materials found in the jungle, nor did they have any food which they themselves did not grow, catch or hunt. Because they had nothing, there was nothing to steal, because they were not violent, there was no crime. They were, in short, a very happy unmaterialistic people. On the other hand, they were masters of the jungle. Their hunting, trapping, fishing and tracking skills were unrivalled. They were marksmen with their blowpipes, armed with poison darts. They were expert house builders, and could navigate their bamboo rafts down the fiercest of rapids. The men wore only a small loin cloth, the women were bare breasted, with never even the slightest hint of immodesty. Happily, their presence was taken for granted by my men who behaved at all times with absolute propriety. It was sad when, eventually, the Aborigine Department in Kuala Lumpur could not accept this situation, and, having decided our Orang Asli ladies should have their breasts covered, sent in, on one of our airdrops, a consignment of bras. Worn without a blouse, these made our pretty, innocent Orang Asli girls look like cheap cabaret girls. I ordered the bras to be collected and burnt! Those girls who wished to cover themselves above the waist and had no blouse were perfectly able to do so in the manner to which they were accustomed, by folding their sarongs above their breasts.

Pretty well all living things were food to the Asli, the ladies especially adept at catching rats. Their technique was to make a squeaking sound by sucking between a finger and thumb over an area of rat holes, listen for the young rats' squeaking reply, then plunge a pointed stick into the ground and catch the rats in their hands as they ran out. They cooked them as they did all their meat, by throwing them onto a large fire. After scraping the burnt fur off the skin, they would pick off and eat the meat.

I occasionally took large groups of men down-river for a fishing trip, using, I am now ashamed to say, explosives. These were either in the form of a couple of sticks of C-3 with a lighted fuse, or a hand grenade. Either, thrown into a large deep pool, would result in an eruption, hundreds of dead fish floating to the surface to be scooped up by cheering, screaming, Asli men and children. I had a slight problem with the grenades, of which there were two types: one detonated 5 seconds after throwing it, the other 7 seconds – allowing it to be fired from a rifle attachment. If we ran out of 5 second fuses, I found 7 seconds frightened the fish away before exploding. My technique in this case was to pull the pin, hold the grenade, and count to three before throwing it. The technique was successful, but decidedly unpopular with those in my immediate vicinity. They were inclined to disappear behind trees until they heard the grenade explode, in the river, not my hand! Fishing days, seen as rest days, were a time for great celebration, not a great deal of work being done by either my men or the Asli.

The most rewarding aspect of the fort-building operation was, to me personally, the medical help we were able to bring the Asli, who, up to that time had only their own, largely ineffective, native herbal treatments. Initially we had only our platoon medical orderly, but even he was able to make a huge difference, treating the simpler ailments, the usual wounds, fevers and septic sores. He was able to clean up very large wounds, but lacked the courage to stitch them up. I took on this role myself with an ordinary sewing needle and boiled strong thread, the patient being held down by two of the beefier members of the platoon. But the greatest scourge among the Asli at that time was yaws – a flesh eating disease closely related to syphilis but not sexually transmitted. It resembles leprosy, in that large areas of flesh are eaten away, causing disfigurement and eventually death. Some sufferers had large septic craters in their faces and I remember one little boy brought in to the fort with most of his backside eaten away. And yet, this dreadful disease was easily cured by the M & B tablets which we carried on operations at all times, being seen as a cure-all. They were produced by May and Baker in 1936 and were the first effective sulphonamides in the treatment of infection before the discovery of penicillin; to soldiers in the field they were a lifesaver. Once we spread the word, we soon had a daily queue of yaws sufferers at our medical hut, and within a very short time theirs sores were seen to be healing. Within months of the completion of the fort, yaws had almost disappeared from the Asli community in the area.

Meanwhile we were making good progress, and on 11 March I was able to report: 'Work on Fort going well. Everybody happy. Moral high and no complaints.'

The clearing of the trees however was painstaking work, and not until the 20th were we able to start erecting the buildings. Once started, and given the skill of my own men, coupled with that of the Orang Asli, these went up in quick succession. So I was able to report on 4 April: 'All buildings completed. Only clearing and wiring one side of perimeter remains.' In three weeks we had built an Admin Block; a Main Dining Hall/Cookhouse; Officers and Orderlies Quarters and Kitchen; three large Barrack Blocks; a Canteen for the men; a Shop and School for the Orang Asli; a Medical Room; an Orderly Room/Office; and, in the centre of the fort, a strongly defended Command Post, for use in the event of attack. The buildings were constructed Malay style, raised on stilts. Small trees were used for the main frames, attap roofs

JUNGLE FORTS AND AIRSTRIPS

laid upon split bamboo laths. Split bamboo was also used for the walls, and for raised sleeping platforms which ran the whole length of one side of the barrack blocks. We also constructed defences: slit trenches with sandbag ramparts on all sides and corners, within the barbed wire perimeter, which had the added protection of a wide barbed-wire 'carpet'.

On 7 April all work on the fort was complete; we were able to clear our temporary camp and move in. At the same time, the SAS, who were no longer needed, were taken out by helicopter. A few days earlier I had received a signal to inform me that the Deputy High Commissioner, Sir Donald MacGillivray, was to visit the fort on the 10th, and was to stay the night. The officer who was to replace me was also to come in with his platoon by helicopter on the same day. I would leave on the 12th. This meant tidying the place up and attempting to ensure that my men, who had been in the jungle for two months, looked reasonably presentable. I had also to prepare for our departure.

A couple of weeks earlier the Asli headmen had put it to me that they were able to take us the entire way back to our camp in Grik by raft – an offer too good to refuse! The journey was to be in two stages: the first down the Sungei Temengor on small 2-3 man rafts, then down the much bigger Sungei Perak, on 6-8 man rafts. After negotiating a price it was agreed that the rafts were to be built and made ready for departure on 12 April. The 10th then, was a busy day. My replacement, John Abercrombie (later killed on an operation in South Thailand), arrived early, and I was able to show him round, then leave him to conduct the arrival of his men and settle them in. Sir Donald arrived in the afternoon with his entourage, and after inspecting the guard, was shown around the fort, and introduced to our Asli population who had arranged an entertainment for the evening. This consisted of our sitting around a bonfire in the centre of a large circle of our entire Asli population, and watching a group of men dance on a low split-bamboo platform. They were accompanied by girls who sat in line on one side, singing and beating out the rhythm with short tube-like sections of bamboo, each of a different length, which they pounded on a long length of thick bamboo which lined one side of the platform. The dancers wore only their loin cloths and crowns of mengkuang, while the girls, who had beautifully painted faces, wore sarongs and covered their breasts with strings of interlaced mengkuang necklaces. As it went on, the dancing became increasingly frenetic, the tempo increased and the dancers worked themselves into a trance, believing themselves to be possessed of spirits of the dead. As the exhausted dancers fell out one by one, the evening gradually drew to a close and we all retired to bed. It was a

Grande Finale, and I felt as I retired wearily to my quarter, our job was done, Fort Kemar now well and truly established.

The following day, after bidding farewell to Sir Donald, I handed the fort over to Abercrombie. On the morning of the 12th we loaded up the bamboo rafts which lay waiting for us on the river below, and set off for home. The Temengor is quite a small river, so rafts for this stage of the journey could be no more than about four feet wide. They could take only two men, seated on a raised bamboo platform in the centre, their kit tied beside them. Each man had his personal weapon tied to his waist, enabling him to use it if required, but ensuring it would not be lost in the event of the raft capsizing. Each raft was navigated by two Orang Asli who stood, one at the bow, the other at the stern, and steered with long bamboo poles. We pushed off in convoy and embarked on a never-to-be-forgotten journey. The Temengor descends steeply downhill from its headwaters in the hills through, a myriad of narrow gorges of cascading, foaming, white water, and I shall never know how we managed to stay on – as did the Asli 'drivers'. But not a single man nor a piece of kit went overboard.

The Asli 'drivers' were remarkable. As they navigated down the rapids, in a state of great excitement they screamed at each other, and to the spirits of the river! They stabbed their poles against rocks on either side and, as we plunged into the water at the foot of each gorge, we were submerged up to the waist until the raft shot up again to the surface like a cork. By late afternoon we emerged onto the calm waters of the Sungei Perak and disembarked onto a large sandbank. Here we found waiting another group of Asli, with five larger rafts. These, again with a crew of two, were able to take six men. But this time the man at the stern had a bamboo rudder with which to steer. After camping for the night and drying off, we embarked again on the following morning, the final stretch home. We floated gently along on the Perak River, something of an anti-climax after the wildness of the Sungei Temengor. By late afternoon we were home, our adventure at an end.

Dennis Wombell York
November 2011

I have to pay tribute to my undervalued young Malay conscript boys, most of them unworldly young men taken from their kampongs to engage in an experience they would never have dreamt of, which they handled, as they did all operations we undertook, with tenacity, courage and loyalty. I pay tribute also to my NCOs of the Regular FMP, especially Sergeant Mohamed Yusoff. They guided and led these young boys with sympathy and understanding, behaved like elder brothers to them. I trusted them all totally and am proud to have led them.

JUNGLE FORTS AND AIRSTRIPS

FORT BROOKE

Police Lieutenant Roy Follows
Fort Brooke, where I took over as commander in Oct 1954, was one of ten jungle forts, all of which were under the command of an officer of the Malayan Police. The most northern was Fort Kemar, then, moving south, came Chabai, Legap, Brooke, Selim, Telanok, Dixon, Shean, Langkap and Iskander which was in north Johore.

Brooke was built by the SAS, along with men from a police jungle company. It was named Brooke after the then CO of the SAS.

Although some forts boasted an air strip on which Pioneers could just about land, Fort Brooke (2,500ft above sea level), being positioned in the mountains, only had a DZ/LZ to take air drop supplies and helicopters. It was garrisoned by police from a jungle company/field force, who also carried out operations from the fort. This meant the fort was sometimes full, on other occasions I'd be left with only just enough men to guard the place.

The complete fort was encircled by a belt of horizontal barbed wire which was only about 2ft high, but 12ft or more wide. Amongst this barbed wire were thousands of sharp bamboo panjis, set in the ground at 45 degrees, 18 inches protruding, ready to impale. But should the fort come under attack, I had assurance (some hope!) that if it was being overrun, I, along with a radio operator plus transceiver, were to make our way to a block house in the centre of the fort – a bit of concrete in a bamboo hut – where all I had to do was repeat over the radio the code words 'Operation Medal' and this would trigger an airborne recapture – just like that!

Often, because of fog, the weekly air drop to the fort was called off, sometimes for several days, so I doubt if paratroops could drop in more or less straight away. And I don't think for one minute they had them standing by just in case.

My main job as fort commander was to win over the hostile aborigines/Orang Asli tribes, who were under communist control. What made the challenge more difficult was that the Department of Aborigines KL had little idea of how many of these little-known jungle people were living in the region. Locked in their deep jungle valleys, stranded in a stone-age time warp, these tribes (Temiar) had, through circumstances outside their control, been bypassed by western civilization. Grubbing out an existence in the jungle, they had no idea of time, distance, miles, yards, or numbers (a few could count to three). This meant they could not tell me how far it was from one place to another, or how many CTs were in a camp when they came across one.

THE FIRST HELICOPTER BOYS

When staying overnight in a tribal longhouse they, having never seen such things as Tommy cookers, canned food, torchlight etc, would marvel at such items as I drew them from my rucksack.

With regards fort defences, no one moved far without their semi-auto. Stand-to was, without fail, carried out each dawn and dusk. Three strategic Bren gun positions were manned twenty-four hours a day. A number of trenches circled the fort, where, in the event of an attack, each man knew his allotted position to take up. Also for immediate use if needed I had a large supply of No.36 grenades always close at hand, plus a small mortar – size 2″ from memory.

Other than for a small petrol generator to power the radio, used to maintain contact with the outside, i.e. patrols on ops, crews of supply aircraft, and the hourly 'all's well' schedule to HQ etc, there was no such luxury in the fort as electricity. For lights it was a case of groping around in the dark with a temperamental oil lamp or candle. Water for cooking came from the nearby river and was carried in several two foot long pieces of bamboo tied on the back of an abo who made many trips back and forth from the river to the fort. I had three 'Gunga Dins' whose job it was to keep the forty-gallon former oil barrel filled with water. Not only did abos carry water, I employed them doing all kinds of work in the fort. But with them having no idea about money, I paid them in beads, rock salt, and loose tobacco, all of which was supplied by HQ. A section of the same river (downstream) was my bathroom and, whenever I took a bath, I never went without my semi-automatic.

Air drop supplies arrived once a week, with items requested at least three days in advance. Everything, from barbed wire, JGs (jungle greens), J boots, crates of rations – including one day of fresh food, meat/chicken – nails, tools, paraffin, petrol, roofing felt, cement – you name it, the RAF/55 RASC dropped it in. Personal items, although permitted, were restricted. All I used to ask for was a weekly bottle of Scotch, and toiletries when I needed them (no toilet paper, shampoos etc). A couple of times the parachute carrying the crate containing my whisky failed to develop, crashing to the ground, shattering the bottle of Scotch!

Fort Brooke was deliberately situated right in the heart of enemy-controlled territory to enable me and my Malay Police platoon to win over local hearts and minds, and to track and attack the enemy, suddenly, from close proximity. Not only had I to try to win over the hostile aborigine tribes, but to speed this up. I also had to try to 'neutralise' two senior Communist Terrorists, who each, with their armed units, controlled the aborigines in the

JUNGLE FORTS AND AIRSTRIPS

area. One with the theatrical name of Fun Ming (no relation to Ah Ming, Commander 9th Platoon, Johor) was in charge of the CTs' Asli-Aborigine organization for the whole region. The other was Pangoi, a domineering tribal headman who, it was claimed, had along with Fun Ming been involved in a number of ambushes against the security forces.

Fun Ming and Pangoi, having known each other since before the emergency, had become firm friends over the years. Consequently Fun Ming, through having such a powerful ally in Pangoi, gave the CTs control over the aborigines.

One thing to my advantage was that Pangoi's tribal settlement was only a few miles west of Fort Brooke, and most days some of his people, including his son Uda, would come into the fort. Using his son as a go-between, I would send Pangoi small gifts, usually of tobacco, along with a verbal message suggesting that we arrange to meet. Also, with his ladang (aboriginal tribal settlement consisting of about four or five longhouses) being not too far away, with a small patrol I did make a couple of surprise visits there, in the slim chance of 'nailing' him. But each time we arrived, we found the place had been quickly evacuated.

We also knew that as we made our way amongst the empty longhouses, unseen eyes were watching our every move. What added to this eerie tension was that I aware that Fun Ming and his unit were regular visitors, and Pangoi's men had a number of firearms, as well as blowpipes. These blowpipes could deliver, nearly silently, a poisonous dart for which there was no known antidote. Death took an agonising hour or more. (The poison is obtained from the Ipoh tree. According to the Temiar, the soil under the branches of this tree is contaminated with poison, so no other plant will grow there. The blowpipe is made from a rare species of bamboo: whereas most bamboo has sectional nodes along its length, blowpipe bamboo does not. A blowpipe, along with a quiver of poisoned arrows, was given to me by a headman. The blowpipe is about 7' long, the arrows between 7" to 8" long.) With this in mind, and being only a small patrol, I would pull out. With no rights to do so, I never set foot inside his house.

I did attack Fun Ming's camp on one occasion, though sadly he and all his unit escaped. But in the end, I am pleased to say that the tyrannical Pangoi surrendered to me.

Edited pages from the fort's monthly report give a snap shot of what life was like there. 'Heavy rain, everywhere sodden, no AD [Air Drop], running out of food, no petrol for the wireless generator,' etc etc. In fact it was not just a normal tropical downpour – they were bad enough – this was a typhoon where the rain came in near horizontal and, together with the violent wind, wrecked part of the fort.

Roy Follows

Unfortunately, Roy passed away in September 2007, so the promised book was never completed.

Fort Chabai

Above: Chabai from the air.

Left: Checking in. Arrival at Chabai.

JUNGLE FORTS AND AIRSTRIPS

Corporal David Taylor

Having visited most of the forts at various times during our helicopter operations from our airfield at Kuala Lumpur, and later RAAF Butterworth, on occasion having to spend the night in one, I, along with fellow crewman Sam Saunders, made the possibly rash decision to spend our next leave with a week at one of these forts. OK, it might have been be a bit risky, though with approval forthcoming we assumed it to be not too much of a risk. Anyway, having previously 'done' Thailand and Hong Kong, and with cash being a bit tight, this seemed ideal. We would learn more about the environment in which we operated, and there was no cost involved. The RAF would fly us in and out on a supply run, and there was no charge for accommodation or messing. Basic living, basic comfort, jungle green dress – which was our normal flying clothing – it was all we needed for a week in the Malayan rainforest. This was truly the 'Ulu'. Nature in the raw. Mountainous, primary and secondary jungle. Absolute peace on earth, so long as you omit the occasional mindless forays during which we discharged a multitude of weaponry on their makeshift range.

Commandant's Mess.

THE FIRST HELICOPTER BOYS

'Got something here for you to try, Dave,' Butch Walker, the Malay Police fort commander said one morning. 'Anti-personnel, semi-automatic shotgun. A fearsome tool.'

True enough I found. It really could devastate the greenery – and, one imagines, anyone, or thing, lurking within – with impunity. All it required was to be pointed in the general direction of a threat and fired. The cartridge was twelve bore size, but as this weapon was intended to deal with somewhat larger prey, the size of the shot was also somewhat larger, maybe a dozen lead balls as opposed to a few hundred. I discharged it at a thick plank of wood. It made fairly neat holes in the face, but the rear was absolutely shredded. Ideal, should a wandering patrol inadvertently stumble into an ambush situation – though stumbling into an ambush in the first place would hardly constitute an ideal situation. Could just spoil your day!

Outside the area cleared for the camp and its barbed wire perimeter was the oh-so-short airstrip – carved out of a nearby hillside, its length effectively further reduced by lack of a straight-in approach, or exit. One way in, same way out; no choice being the choice. No undershoot or overshoot area either, should the pilot get it wrong. But at least he'd be going out lighter than when he came in. This was where the Scottish Aviation Pioneer came into its own, with its low-speed manoeuvrability and STOL characteristics – short-take-off-and-landing – employing as it did such high-lift devices as leading edge slats and full width Fowler flaps. Quite something to watch,

Overnight accommodation whilst out on patrol.

JUNGLE FORTS AND AIRSTRIPS

Awaiting supper.

Pioneer Pilot, 'Butch' Walker (Fort Commander) and his No.2 Des, along with Sam Saunders and myself (taking the photo).

that steep, twisty, terrain avoidance approach, flaps and slats at full stretch, Alvis Leonides snarling defiance. Even more thrilling was the view from inside the cockpit, directly behind the pilot, whose eyes were the only form of ground proximity radar fitted to this machine. I was perched atop sacks

Pioneer about to depart.

267 Squadron Pioneer on finals for Fort Chabai.

of rice and suchlike, attempting to wedge myself in place, hands grasping whatever there was to grasp. Always bearing in mind the pilot required full and free use of his arms, and the controls. It was another very basic aeroplane that did exactly what it had been designed for, and did it extremely well.

Beyond the strip lay an all-encircling wilderness of untamed jungle. A verdant barrier of flora, limestone cliffs and mountains, along with their associated silence. I say silence, because that's the way it often appears – sounds so natural, serene, and comforting, they could usually be disregarded. A background of echoey, tropical-rainforest type music. Nature's nonstop symphony: a cawing, croaking, creaking, buzzing, and whining, with the possibility of an occasional thought-provoking roar thrown in for good measure.

Meandering around two sides of the camp, and twenty feet below our level, ran nature's contribution to our comfort and wellbeing: a small river, or large stream. Fast-flowing, self-cleansing, ice-cold. There is a pureness and clarity to be found in the waters of a mountain stream which is apparent nowhere else. This was our bathroom, ideal for washing, drinking, and, when the sun was at its height, a cooling dip. For anything else – i.e. the bathroom – go well downstream!

Days began early out here. Not with the crowing of your commonplace cockerel, but to the chattering chorus of gibbons and monkeys high in the treetops. Dawn itself was six-thirtyish and, being up in the hills, surrounded by mountains, it was cold, damp, and often misty. So, while the morning shave may not have been one of mankind's more enjoyable experiences, washing in those waters was certainly guaranteed to either kick-start your heart into life, or to end it prematurely. But the first sight of that river in the early morning was something else again, for the surface could be mirror-like. So calm, it appeared to be perfectly still rather than flowing, thus further enhancing the tranquillity of the place.

I say the days began early, not sunrise, you'll note. It would be three or four hours past dawn before the sun was high enough to smile down and chase the shadows and mist out of our valley. I'd realized it would be something like this, for I'd seen it many times on the way to early morning operations, a helicopter being a much better option from which to view this event.

A sea of wispy cloud-like mist would slide down the tree-covered slopes, to collect in the enclosed valleys below, lakes of cloud which obscured everything but the mauve, tree-layered peaks which poked their way well clear. Nothing else to be seen from up there, apart from the

Kitchen stores.

occasional, colourful, yellow-beaked Hornbill, gliding from one area of high ground to the next.

Here at Chabai the air was so fresh it was almost pure oxygen. Tasted like it too: sweet, untainted, regenerative. Just as the days began early, they ended early too, for in the tropics darkness descends rapidly – around seven in the evening – which is when the jungle bursts into life. Patrols apart, that is. They need to be settled well before then, for out here the sun plummets from view rather than sliding below the horizon, giving you bare minutes to prepare yourself. With darkness came the incandescent, pulsing glow of the fireflies.

Our only light was in the form of candles, or flickering oil lamps. The only electricity was a small generator used to power the radio when needed.

It was a vacation you couldn't possibly buy, although maybe most wouldn't wish to. After all, paradise is a personal thing. In fact, it has been said that paradise is often close by where you live, that we don't recognise it as such until we are no longer there.

If not paradise, this was close to perfect tranquillity. Until I once more lost my mind, that is, jumping in with both feet this time. Not the river, you understand.

Infallibility not being within man's scope, Sam and I actually volunteered to go on a two-day jungle patrol, a situation that could well have been positively unhealthy. Talk about crazy, I mean there were people, and things, out there, intent on doing us harm. I just felt it would be something different, something new. There again, let's face it, so is death. A once in a lifetime kind of thing!

It hadn't yet filtered through to my subconscious: the fact I wouldn't have been cleared to take leave in Chabai were it not considered to be reasonably safe. Had I requested a fort that had recently been subjected to an attack, as some of them occasionally were, my extended visit quite possibly wouldn't have been allowed. The thing was, Singapore/Malaya being an 'active service' posting, all intended destinations in this theatre had to be officially approved before leave was granted. Getting killed on duty in the service of your country was one thing. Getting killed while on leave, apparently a different matter altogether. To start with, given such an eventuality, I'd immediately become AWOL (absent without leave). Not that it would be my worry, though it would be that of my squadron commander. But he hadn't appeared too worried when I'd approached him about it. He'd merely waved a finger around his temple and grinned at me. I'd wondered what he'd meant by that?

But volunteer to go on a short patrol we had, and shortly after we were on the way, I wished we hadn't. Okay, we were armed, but so were the terrorists. There was something else to consider, too: death wasn't the be all and end all, there were degrees of discomfort to be endured in the interim.

That verdant barrier for starters. It now turned out to be more than just that, it was a barrier in all three dimensions, each apparently filled with malign intent. We soon found ourselves surrounded by a dense wall of foliage, through which we had to hack our way. By we, I mean of course the Malay police and their Iban trackers who plunged ahead, machetes flashing and slashing. I tagged along behind. It was OK for the first hour or so, as we followed a relatively well defined track. But then we veered off, into the unknown, or so it seemed.

'Naturally, we choose path of least resistance,' Mustafa, the leader, and my self-appointed guide, told me. 'This a kind of track.'

'Could have fooled me,' I said. 'Well disguised and protected, eh?'

'No, Dave. It just not used much. Well-used tracks are the very places ambushes are likely to be set.'

Track or not, that jungle was a green hell that fought back. It whipped, slashed and tore, seemingly intent on preventing any forward progress whatsoever. Branches and barbed vines plucked at my clothes like malevolent hands, flicked dangerously near my eyes. My feet churned up the spongy carpet of the forest floor, releasing its musty fungal smell. Rivulets of sweat trickled down my back. Or were they the feet of insects on the prowl? Difficult to tell. Nor was there any chance of disregarding the sounds when you were in there among them. Sounds which now took on a more eerie quality, as opposed to serene and comforting. Not just the cicadas and bullfrogs, or the whine of a mosquito, for they were always around. Out here there were different sounds to consider: the screech of a monkey, the shrill cry of a bird – echoing – even the roar of a tiger – distant and receding. Mustafa identified them all for me as we moved on. Occasionally he'd suddenly stop, hold up a hand, motioning me to freeze. Pointing to a bush, he'd whisper a name, 'Lesser-spotted gol-gol', or whatever. I'd look, see nothing but still leaves, the bird splendidly camouflaged by splotches of shadow. Then, movement would catch my eye and it was gone. I was lucky if I managed to snatch a brief glimpse. Ah, well, so much for the gol-gol, lesser-spotted or not! By now I was almost ready to give up, too tired to talk.

'Nothing to fear here,' Mustafa advised, 'normal sounds. Those we welcome. It's a silent jungle that spells danger. Nature quietened by human presence. Then is the time to stop and exercise care. Create a matching silence, listen for that tell-tale crack of a branch being stepped on by a carelessly placed foot, the muffled curse, or a negligent cough. They're the kinds of sounds that indicate the presence of unwelcome attention.'

JUNGLE FORTS AND AIRSTRIPS

The sun's light didn't penetrate too well down here: trees over two hundred feet tall (that third dimension), and the almost impenetrable canopy they formed, saw to that. But its effects did, i.e. the heat, as did the frequently heavy rain. If a shower, it continued to drip long after the shower had passed.

'Probably the reason it is known as rain forest, eh?' Mustafa quipped, in reply to my muttered curse as I almost went down.

The ground was wet and slippery, the air as still as a dead man's breath. It was hot and humid. Rather like being fully dressed, trapped in a sauna; a thought that had me longing for a dip in that ice-cold stream back at the fort. Wouldn't even bother to undress first. Wouldn't have mattered anyway, I was wet through already, would remain so until it was time for bed.

Dark thoughts flooded my mind as I tramped along mechanically beneath the shrouding green canopy. Things occasionally squished and crunched beneath my feet. I didn't look, didn't wish to know. We'd only been underway three or four hours, even if it did feel more like a month. Out here, time, days of the week, they were irrelevant.

I was sweat-stained and weary already, facing the stigma of looking defeat in the eye. But I couldn't quit now, be worse off if I did: no one to take me back; sure to get lost on my own. I thought briefly about how that would sound back at the camp. 'Took this Air Force type out on patrol with us, but he couldn't hack it, decided to return to base on his own. Never saw him again.'

Oh that one of our helicopters would make an unexpected appearance; a quick, passing thought. But even had that happened I knew it would depart without me, for there was also ego at stake here. Some of these guys were smaller than me, much older, yet they were carrying twice the gear I was – mine as well as their own – making out quite nicely, thank you. Or so they made it seem. No, I was strong willed, so best to face facts: the aching tiredness, the sweat, the pain, all had to be endured, they would last but days. Failure to carry this through would haunt me for the rest of my life.

So I pushed the dark thoughts to the back of my mind, silently cursed to myself and pushed ahead. And despite the fact my pack only weighed a mere twenty pounds, compared to the fifty or sixty the rest carried, it definitely had the momentum to bring me crashing down more than once.

By the use of hand signals, a halt was called every hour or so. A welcome break, I'd at first thought. Not so.

'Leeches,' Mustafa explained, peering down the inside of my collar. He had me pull my trouser legs out of my socks, and there they were,

A short break whilst out on patrol.

sucking away. He used the glowing end of his cigarette to burn them off, the rest of the patrol assisting each other.

'There'll be more,' he told me. 'Buggers get everywhere. We'll have a full clean-up tonight.'

I didn't like the sound of that, but there was no time to think about it, for in came the next assault: mosquitoes in combat formation, peeling off like fighters diving to the attack. You could imagine they had been awaiting our arrival, lined up in columns of three, presenting arms! And let us not forget the snakes, elephants, and tigers that lived hereabouts, they could do you a lot of no good, too.

Dawn found me jerking awake in my makeshift bed, beneath a makeshift shelter, both thrown together for me by someone far more experienced in these matters. The idea was to get clear of the ground, and to keep as dry as possible. The bed was constructed from two poles and a canvas sheet, the shelter – or basha – fabricated from more poles, ponchos, a plastic sheet and palm frond roof. It had served me well. I had enjoyed a good six hours beneath my mozzie-net. Despite that, after yesterday's slog I felt like I could use another six. Not that I wasn't fit. There were no undue aches or pains, just a lingering tiredness, a boot-full of blisters, and the marks where those leeches had latched on.

JUNGLE FORTS AND AIRSTRIPS

Fortunately we were due for a supply drop that day as not all the patrol would be returning to the fort with us. Most would move even deeper into the jungle, where, close to a trail known to be used by the guerrillas, they would lie in ambush. Whatever the outcome, it was unlikely they would return to Chabai within the week.

So, as preparations were made, I relaxed as best I could. Plenty of time as it turned out, for we first had to await clearance of the usual early morning mist. It hung from the trees in wispy threads. It had the look of rotting lace. At least the associated moisture served to curb the activities of tiresome flying pests.

The rising sun completed its task on schedule, almost as if programmed to do so, for even as it cleared we picked up the distant sound of an aircraft approaching; talked to the crew on the patrol's transceiver – no hand-held, lightweight, microchip-controlled piece of kit this. It must have weighed twenty or thirty pounds, probably the same again for the hand-cranked generator. Despite this, it did have its plus points: it worked well, we had contact, and I wasn't required to carry it. The aircrew had spotted the smoke from our signal fire, had the general area located. Easy to see when flying over the jungle, smoke, a certain give-away. It was what we kept an eye open for when flying towards an operational area. Forewarned is forearmed.

Preparations for an airdrop.

Radio contact with the aircraft.

Now, homing in on the carbide-gas-filled balloon which had been raised above the surrounding treetops to mark our exact position, a Valetta of 52 Squadron dropped fresh supplies and other incidentals. The crew had to be very precise with the drop as the clearing was small. Miss it by 20-30 yards and the chute would never make it to the ground and end up hanging too high in the trees to be recovered. This one didn't do that.

Valetta, green light on.

JUNGLE FORTS AND AIRSTRIPS

The drop, close to our balloon marker.

Received, with thanks.

THE FIRST HELICOPTER BOYS

It was an operation which allowed even more time for me to effect a recovery, although I suspected I wouldn't find it so difficult from now on. It was also an operation which left these guys with even more baggage to lug around for, groceries apart, parachutes had normally to be recovered back to base. Well, on a big drop, a token number. Most would likely be reported as being 'inadvertently damaged', or 'deemed beyond salvage', as this one probably would, well away from the fort. Soldiers, it seemed, became quite attached to the material from which they were fashioned. The canopy made decent bedding, or was useful for keeping things dry, but the soft nylon cord was especially treasured. Handy for lashing things together. Such things as the bed I'd used last night. And it was highly unlikely a team of accountants would be sent in to investigate the loss of a couple of 'chutes.

At times like this, what with excess baggage and all, I was thankful I'd joined the Air Force, and that these guys held us in some regard. Now I could see why. They occasionally had reason to rely on us. A five minute flight could save them a day's walk; less than an hour in the air was equivalent to a week on the ground. So a chopper was appreciated at any time, in an emergency it could mean the difference between living and dying.

Then there was the patrol itself. No stroll in the woods that, bluebells and butterflies kind of thing. Butterflies, yes. Rabbles of them – which, I believe, is the collective noun for butterflies. They were exotic, both large and small. So colourful that, if there was such a thing as a deadly butterfly, these – given nature's propensity to use bright colours as a warning – were clearly prime contenders. As for the blood, of that there was an abundance. An abundant loss, that is. What with mozzies and leeches I was surprised to find I didn't need a transfusion on my return to the outside world. Who needed terrorists on top of that lot?

Anyway, even if the patrol did turn out to be uneventful on the action front, it certainly wasn't boring. Hard graft is what it had been. Absolutely unbelievable my volunteering for something like that, was the way I saw it. Though to these guys, or members of the security forces, yesterday probably *would* have been deemed a stroll. I was nowhere near SAS class; I was an instrument fitter in the RAF, part time helicopter crewman.

But later, back in the relative safety of civilization, I regarded it all as a satisfying, character-building achievement, during which I discovered the limits of my fortitude to be much higher than I'd dared hope. As the saying goes, when the going gets tough, the tough get going. From here on I resolved that I would; get going, that is – in the opposite direction!

*

JUNGLE FORTS AND AIRSTRIPS

RAF PARACHUTES CATS INTO MALAYAN JUNGLE FORT

A *cri de coeur* for cats from the commander of a rat-infested jungle fort in Central Malaya was recently answered with despatch by a Valetta aircraft of the Air Supply Force (Malaya), operating from Royal Air Force Station, Kuala Lumpur.

Valetta overhead.

Kuala Lumpur ASF.

THE FIRST HELICOPTER BOYS

The call, 'Rats getting out of control. Please send cats,' was made by the commander of Fort Telanok, Police Lieutenant L. Trott of the Federation of Malaya Police Field Force, one of two Britons serving with Malays and aborigines in this remote outpost in a mountainous area of Pahang State.

Two large Malayan cats were obtained and accommodated at RAF Kuala Lumpur overnight, ready to be dropped by parachute with the rest of the supplies for the fort the following morning. During the night however, the cats went AWOL and a last minute round-up had to be made for replacements. Fortunately Captain J.E. Bosworth, ground liaison officer in RAF Ops, being due for repatriation, had two cats to spare. These were carefully packed in a padded case drilled with air holes, a tasty snack of fish included to keep the cats going during their forty-minute flight to Fort Telanok, which is accessible only by air.

The drop was made by Flight Lieutenant K.J. Robinson, OC Air Supply Force (Malaya), and the cats parachuted slowly and safely down. They were immediately released and placed on operations.

Chapter 13

Malaya: Circa 1948-60

Although nothing to do with helicopters per se, this interesting piece is written by a Malay citizen who was a schoolboy at the time of the Emergency. A fascinating insight into the way of things from an entirely different perspective, especially when taking into account that English is not his first language. A walk down memory lane, before Merdeka, as remembered from between the cobwebs of time.

Communist uprising, by Chee Leong

The Malayan Emergency was a twelve-year jungle war fought by Commonwealth troops: Malayan Security Forces, British, Australian, and New Zealand Armed Forces, against the communists led by their leader, Chin Peng.

It started with the assassination of three British estate managers at Sungei Siput, Perak. This was later followed by the burning of rubber estates, sabotaging installations, derailment of trains, burning of buses, generating civil unrest all over the country.

The CT (Communist Terrorist) soldier was well used to living in the jungle, having spent the Second World War fighting the Japanese from there. Food and other supplies came from the jungle gardens of the fringe squatters and surrounding kampongs (villages). They had jungle workshops to repair their weapons and equipment, jungle hospitals for first aid treatment, a network of agents and sympathisers in village, town and city, and a cowed rural population to coerce for food, money, information and sanctuary. Discipline, fieldcraft, navigation and minor tactics were good, weapon handling adequate. They relied on surprise in 'hit and run' tactics such as the ambush and (initially) could be ruthlessly cruel in murdering, mutilating or kidnapping people of influence and their families, village headmen, teachers and local government officials.

Most guerrillas were Chinese, though there were some Malays, Indonesians and Indians.

The Malayan Communist uprising circa '40s and '50s when I was young

Going to Singapore during school holidays from Kuala Lumpur took 7 to 9 hours because of the many roadblocks and police checkpoints. The ferry across the Muar river took 45 minutes; ferry across the Batu Pahat river, 30 minutes, subject to currents. If after a heavy rain, add another half hour. The wooden ferry was actually a barge pulled by a motorboat tied alongside, and could carry about five cars and a lorry on each trip. There were no bridges then. Most times the ferry landing ramp would not come down on reaching other side, so passengers had to jump up and down on the ramp to bring it down so the cars could disembark. I had fun jumping, but my weight then did not help any. All the way there were police or military checkpoints, manned by local police or Gurkhas, or British, Fijian or Australian soldiers. Areas or regions with the most communist activity were known as 'black' areas: parts of Selangor, Negeri Sembilan, Segamat, Yong Peng, Johore, whole of Pahang, & Perak. Those areas deemed safe were 'white areas'. New villages were constructed, and a curfew imposed. Rural villagers were moved into the new villages. No food was allowed to be carried in cars, or on bicycles for fear the communists would get it. Rubber tappers on bicycles were frisked. They were only allowed to carry enough for their lunch.

On one occasion, going to Singapore, we had to turn back halfway because of communist activities. There was a communist ambush near Yong Peng, and a bus was burnt. A similar incident took place near Tanjong Bidara, Malacca, when we came across a burning bus. The passengers were safe, waiting for the police or military to arrive. The communists had by then disappeared into the jungle. We turned back.

Curfews were quite common at various small towns in 'black' areas. Thus any trip anywhere had its uncertainties of arrival. Unlike children of today, the moment they leave for anywhere they are asking, 'What time we arriving'? Back then it was '*Will* we be arriving'?

Cooking was with firewood or charcoal. We would get ours delivered by bullock cart. A rolled up lighted newspaper would be used to start the fire.

MALAYA: CIRCA 1948-60

If I did not disappear fast enough, I had to 'volunteer' to help get the fire going by blowing air through a short, hollow bamboo pipe. Needless to say, we sometimes had ash decorating our food, receiving enquiring stares from my mother. I remember one incident, three days before Chinese New Year, the Indian man arriving with his load of firewood (from felled rubber trees). While he was busy unloading the firewood, and carrying it into our kitchen storeroom, I wanted to see how cows behave when firecrackers explode underneath them. Those days firecrackers were the size of cigars, and one can imagine the sound they made! Traffic stopped, people waiting for buses ran for their lives. Some cyclists fell into a drain, all for first time witnessing a driverless bullock cart with two cows stampeding down the road helter skelter, the Indian running behind after them, one hand holding his sarong, other gesticulating frantically, cursing and swearing at his cows' ancestors, while the cyclists were scrambling out of the drains, swearing at *him* and *his* ancestors. I had learnt that cows don't appreciate firecrackers exploding underneath them, and can jump very high, like in a cowboy rodeo, as well outrun a car! It was fortunate no one had seen my experiment, as my mother was quite handy with our house status symbol, the rattan cane. The Indian fellow did however mention on his next delivery of firewood that his cows produced less milk than usual.

Very often while I was still sleeping in the morning, there would be loud screams downstairs, chairs being overturned, pots and pans falling on the floor and my mother or the maid standing on the kitchen table yelling my name. A snake had decided to appear between the firewood while they were about to start the fire to boil water, or a 6 inch centipede, or a scorpion. I could by then differentiate between the kinds of scream. The loudest and longest one would be if their fingers had encountered a mice nest. It was not uncommon to hear similar screams from our neighbours too, as mice seem to love making homes in old, dried firewood. I had by now come to learn my mother could jump on a table without the aid of a chair. Not an easy feat when wearing a sarong.

Telling my mother to wait while I wash my face and brush my teeth would not be an option. She and the maid holding up their sarongs while standing on the table looked like striptease dancers in a cabaret. Laughing was not advisable.

Of course the neighbours would later hear of my prowess at getting rid of snakes, centipedes or mice. The Indian firewood seller would on his next delivery receive a ten minute lecture from my mother, in tones befitting an army sergeant major, of how her first born had risked his life to save her

THE FIRST HELICOPTER BOYS

and the maid. He in turn would swear and promise that we can pee on his grave after he dies of old age if any more snakes appear. Of course on and off my mother and the maid kept improving their table top jumping skills, the Indian mastering his apology skills, and we promising to visit his grave few times when he dies of old age.

It was during this period when the communists were very active with train derailments, burning of buses, ambushes on isolated police stations, and the murder of British, American, as well as local estate owners. Though they lived in the jungle, some did hide out in 'new villages', or towns. All villages on the west coast were now fenced, with security personnel on armed duty ensuring no food was smuggled out or stolen by them. The government was going on a strict 'starve them out' policy.

My grandfather, an estate manager and planter, owned a Ford car. It was armoured, with a steel plate protecting the front screen with two small slots for the driver to navigate and an armed escort to look for any problems when on the road. There were steel plates covering all the windows, and needless to say the car could only achieve 30 mph max because of the weight. You can imagine the heat in the car when travelling anywhere. No travel was done any time after 4pm either due to a curfew being imposed in nearby towns or for fear of a communist ambush. Quite often, if travelling to town to get food supplies, there would be an escort: a small, well-armed convoy of SCs (special constables) or military personnel in their armoured vehicles. We would, during school holidays, be invited to my grandfather's estate somewhere in Central Pahang, especially during rambutan or durian seasons, staying at his huge, rambling, colonial style brick and wooden bungalow.

Coolie lines (later known as labour lines), where the SCs, rubber tappers, or estate employees, Chinese, Malays and Indians lived with their families in wooden terraced homes, were down a laterite road about five hundred yards away. There was also a coffee shop and a small grocery store. The bungalow and surrounding estate homes are isolated, and to reach the nearest neighbour, another estate owner, one had to travel many miles down a small narrow estate road with rubber trees in straight rows on either side, two miles off the main road, as well passing through virgin jungle.

An eight foot high fence with a barbed wire perimeter running along both sides circled the approximate ten acres of my grandfather's bungalow and coolie lines. There would be hundreds of empty cigarette tins and milk cans filled with small pebbles hung on the fence at regular intervals. They rattled when touched or when the fence was shaken. Thus any disturbance or encounter with the fence would attract the many armed SCs on duty

MALAYA: CIRCA 1948-60

around the entire barricaded complex. There were sentry posts: well-armed SCs with their Bren guns or Sten guns in bunkers constructed from coconut or rubber tree trunks at the four corners. As well some located at where the estate workers lived. In between there were powerful spotlights at night, their bright beams directed at the surrounding rubber trees and nearby jungle. Armed SCs would patrol the perimeter regularly, day and night to ensure the fence had not been tampered with or broached.

The double storey bungalow we stayed in had sandbags at every window, upstairs and downstairs. And the thick Chengai (hard wood) wooden windows had slots to look through as well aim a gun should there be a terrorist attack. My cousins and I were given very strict rules never to play near the windows and where to take cover should there be an attack. Even though we were in our very early teens, all of us were taught to handle the guns located in locked cabinets, from .45 calibre automatic pistols, shotguns to sub-machine guns, and had fun when practising at a nearby shooting range.

Should the sentries raise the alarm at night, by banging on a big tin drum, all the lights in the house would be switched off. We had all undergone training where to take cover in the darkness, and to only talk in whispers.

Once a week a British or Australian army patrol would pay us a courtesy visit, we kids getting lovely chocolates, or army biscuits, the SCs getting tins of Woodbine cigarettes. We would offer them drinks and fruits, but they declined our offer of durians when in season. Orang putehs (Caucasian soldiers) never acquired the taste for durians, they being especially not too keen on the scent. 'Like eating a banana in a bloody latrine', they would exclaim.

Once a day, sometimes at nights at different times, there would be a phone call from a police station twenty miles away, testing, ensuring our phone line was not cut and everything was alright. A coded word would be used to identify either party as the communists were known to make phone calls to unwitting estates before an attack. Should the call from the police station not receive a reply, an armed police or military patrol would be despatched immediately to the estate.

Daytimes I would be playing football or badminton with my cousins and friends from the homes nearby, or playing in a nearby stream. Or looking for spiders to fight, always under the watchful eyes of sentries, that we did not stray near the perimeter fence.

Sometimes a plane would fly overhead, its several attached loudspeakers blaring out asking the communists to surrender, at the same time dropping thousands of leaflets. Leaflets were dropped by planes into known Communist areas offering them a safe conduct to surrender to the Malayan authorities.

ATTENTION. ESPECIALLY IMPORTANT MESSAGE. Since the federation of Malaya achieved independence on 31 August 1957, in the first seven months, 215 MCP (Malayan Communist Party) personnel have come out to accept the Merdeka offer. This number includes high ranking personnel who hold posts like Border Committee Secretary, Regional Committee member, etc. Even these high ranking personnel have realized that the Merdeka Offer is a good offer to accept.

The Prime Minister of the Federation, Tunku Abdul Rahman, in a press conference held on 27 march had the following words to say to all MCP personnel: 215 of your comrades have already accepted the Merdeka Offer which is the largest number for any similar period since the emergency began. This Merdeka offer is still open, and is being extended until 31 July. I know there are many more of you who want to come out. If any of you were thinking of holding out in the mistaken idea that operations against you will be relaxed after my target date of 31 August 1958 I give you this warning. **There will be no relaxation whatever after that date.**

Dakotas of the Royal Australian Air Force were used for dropping food supplies or government leaflets asking the communists to surrender. The wind would sometimes blow the leaflets towards where our bungalow was, and we would pick them up...and, as toilet paper was not yet in vogue, they became very useful, right size too. Thus every time we heard a plane flying nearby, we hoped for the wind to blow our direction.

I was also unanimously appointed chief chicken catcher and executioner, at eleven years of age, the eldest among the cousins. This happened when my two grandmothers (grandfather had two wives), mother, plus several aunties and uncles decided to have chicken curry for lunch or dinner. I would select a couple of prospective candidates, all big Rhode Island chickens, my cousins and friends slowly encircling one, I'd then pounce on it. Then the next one.

Apart from being an expert chicken catcher, I was also entrusted with their decapitating, though not without some hilarious moments when one decided to seek freedom, flying all over the kitchen, minus it's head if my aim was not good enough. Imagine the confusion in the kitchen with nine kids, aunties, two grandmothers, my mother all yelling out advice to catch it. Or running away while I stalked the headless chicken, not to mention a couple of sentries rushing over with guns to check out the commotion.

MALAYA: CIRCA 1948-60

During rambutan season my cousins and I would hide under the nearby rambutan trees in the early evening, after first informing the sentries. Armed with our catapults, we'd shoot the many flying foxes eating the fruits. And having the experience of earning money from cutting newspapers, I would sell the two or three flying foxes I shot down for 10 cents each to the Indian tappers who cooked curry with them. My mother was thrilled to learn the apple of her eye had good business acumen at a young age.

The outdoor latrine was situated about thirty yards behind the house. And if nature called at night, we had to inform the nearby sentry post we were making our way to it. It was just a fifteen foot deep hole in the ground.

Spotlights would be switched on as soon as it was twilight, and sentries on duty would be on high alert. Some spotlights would be manually operated and the sentry would move the lights all around his section of the perimeter fencing, while other sentries would stare into the darkness beyond the trees for any unusual movements in the dark jungle outside.

One night I had an uncomfortable tummy and ran to the latrine, forgetting to call out to the nearby sentry. He I guess was relaxing, smoking, looking in another direction. In the darkness of the fairly large, brick latrine, before I could turn on the light switch, I knocked over an empty pail someone had carelessly left near the door. It sure made loud clanging sounds rolling around. As I switched on the light, there was loud clicking of guns being cocked and a very loud, 'BERHENTI! SIAPA DALAM SANA?' (Halt! Who goes there?) I immediately yelled out my name and what I was doing. Again, the loud threatening voice boomed out, 'KELUAR! ANGKAT TANGAN TINGGI!' (Come out with your hands above your head!) My urgent downloading had to be postponed. One hand holding onto my unbuttoned shorts, one hand over my head I stepped out smiling sheepishly, knowing it was my fault not calling out earlier.

There were four sentries aiming their guns at the doorway as I stepped out. They burst out laughing at seeing me trying to hold up my shorts, one hand on my head. Glad they had a sense of humour, at my expense. But not my father. Finishing my business and back in the house I was given a finger in my face lecture about my forgetfulness, and not accepting my explanation it was an urgent call. It's funny how mothers will accept a son's explanation but not fathers.

Jungle night sounds can be intimidating to those not familiar. Cicadas with their shrill mating calls, nightjars giving out their haunting cries, owls softly hooting, faraway monkeys or gibbons calling out to each other. The sentries listening for any unusual or unfamiliar sounds. Outside the perimeter fence, the SCs had laid lots of old dried branches and twigs so that anyone stepping on one would cause a loud crackling sound. Sometimes the noisy night sounds would suddenly all stop and there would be an eerie silence. The sentries would immediately point their spotlights all over checking to see anything suspicious, suspecting most probably a python or king cobra snake out hunting for food.

At night my uncle or one of the sentries would let loose the six half breed guard dogs from their respective kennels, the house's first warning should the dogs start barking at anything moving along the perimeter. The dogs were fed only in the morning and lunch time, nothing at night, so they wouldn't go to sleep.

Quite often we would hear bombs being dropped from planes on suspected terrorist camps somewhere far away beyond the hills, or planes flying low overhead.

One night, around 2am, all of us were woken in a hurry when the sentries sounded the alarm by banging on an empty oil drum. Without waiting for instructions all of us rushed into a room which had sandbags all around, and were told to keep quiet. The men, my grandfather, father, and uncles, all in pyjamas, grabbed their shotguns, pistols and carbines and quickly positioned themselves at their previously arranged, barricaded windows. Nobody talked; they used hand signals.

Seeing a bright orange glow in the sky some miles away, and sounds of gunfire, they assumed a neighbouring estate was under attack, rubber trees being burnt. Everyone was tense, guns at the ready. All us kids, and women, were told to lie down on the floor and keep very still. Nobody made a sound.

The communists were known to attack two estates simultaneously. The dogs were barking like crazy. The SCs were all at their posts, machine guns cocked and ready. My uncle would stand by the phone, first checking to see if the line had been cut. Then, should there be an attack, he would immediately inform the police twenty miles away.

Nobody slept that night. Dawn soon arrived, the first rays of sunlight coming through the small window slots. But terrorists were known to attack at first light too. So no one left their post until the all-clear was sounded: three loud, long blasts from a shrill police whistle. Everyone wondered whose estate it was and whether anyone was killed. The SC sergeant was now instructing the men to be on full alert, and doubling the perimeter sentry duties to two men. All of us were told to play near the house, my father reminding me to call out to the sentry when going to the latrine. An only son does have health benefits.

MALAYA: CIRCA 1948-60

It was a week later, rain had been falling incessantly since afternoon and by nightfall it came down in torrents. Frogs were croaking everywhere, a heavy mist had come up and visibility outside was down to less than twenty feet, the rain mercilessly beating a tattoo on the roof.

We had all gone to sleep around 10pm under our individual mosquito nets. A mosquito repellent lighted coil placed near the window.

It was about 1am when, without warning, loud gunfire somewhere near the house startled all of us from our sleep. There were loud shouts, yelling from the SCs: 'Communist datang, Communist datang, Communist attack!' The dogs barking like crazy.

More gunshots went off as my grandfather and all the men grabbed their guns, rushing to the windows, we kids and the women were asked to crawl towards the sandbagged room and lie down. I heard an uncle saying our estate was being attacked. We were by now trembling with fear from the loud explosions of several machine guns going off next to the house. It sounded like it was coming from near the latrine. Upstairs nobody knew whether the communists had cut the fence and were about to enter the house. All the yelling and gun shots sounded just next to the house. There were loud shouts of 'Sana, sana! Tepi pagar!...Tembak!...Tembak!' (There! There! Next to the fence. Shoot! Shoot!)

More gunshots, the deafening staccato of the several Bren guns drowned out everything else. Several more SCs from nearby bunkers rushed over as reinforcements, all taking cover behind sandbags or lying on the ground.

The spotlights could hardly penetrate through the heavy mist, more shots were fired. We could hear, in spite of the rain, the tin cans strung along the fence clanging away. Obviously the communists were now trying to scale the fence. But my grandfather and uncles held their fire for fear of shooting the SCs below.

More loud yelling from the SCs downstairs, 'Sana, sana! Tembak!...Ada orang sana! Tepi pagar! Chepat tembak!' (There!...Shoot! Somebody at the fence!)

The gunfire continued for several more minutes when we heard shouts of 'Berhenti tembak, berhenti tembak!' (hold your fire!). The silence now deafening, the smell of cordite was strong in the air. My grandfather and the men all rushed downstairs to investigate, guns cocked at the ready. There were SCs everywhere now, some pointing to where they'd been shooting, Sten guns still ready to shoot. Everyone in the house thought the communists had cut through the barbed wire, and we were all going to be killed, houses burned down. A few of us crawled to the windows and peeped through the slots. We could see the SCs lying prone on the wet grass, guns aimed at the fence, all soaking wet from the rain, still coming down in torrents, heavy mist engulfing them like ghostly figures. We could all now hear loud squealing, grunts and screams, the tin cans rattling along the fence. Everyone thought some communists had been shot.

We saw the sergeant slowly crawling forwards, then, still aiming his Sten at the fence, he yelled out, 'Bukan communists, bukan communists!...babi hutan, babi hutan!' (not communists, wild pigs!).

Later we learned some wild pigs had tried to get through the fencing to get at the tapioca, sweet potato and sugar cane plants nearby; their favourite foods. Three of them, all about forty kilos, somehow got tangled up in the perimeter barbed wire, and struggling to get loose causing the tin cans to rattle. And in the darkness, heavy rain, with the mist obscuring the spotlight's beam, the wild pigs, dark brown or black colour, were easily mistaken for terrorists. Altogether seven were shot, four fatally, three lying wounded and squealing loudly. The sergeant then shot them dead. There were a lot of red faces around that night, along with muted laughter. Apparently, when the sentry on duty heard the tins clanging, he had shouted his 'Berhenti, siapa jalan sana, Halt! Who goes there?' And after two warnings, not getting a reply, he, seeing dark shadows trying to break through the fence, immediately opened fire, followed by other SCs in their bunkers. Everyone was still on edge after the previous week's attack on the neighbouring estate.

You can guess what was on the menu for the next few days amongst the Chinese and Indian tapper families, including ours.

My grandmother felt sad when her vegetable garden was dug up and all replanted nearer to her flower garden beside the house.

Chapter 14

Goodbye Emergency, Hello Confrontation
Some views of what followed the Emergency

During 1955 federal elections were held to hasten transition from colonial rule to independence. This was achieved on 31 August 1957, the UK, Australia and New Zealand agreeing to provide assistance during the final phase of the emergency. It was on 31 July 1960 that the emergency was finally over and the country declared 'white'.

British plans to bring a greater degree of independence to the remaining British territories in South East Asia included the incorporation of British North Borneo and Singapore Island into a Greater Malaysia. This aroused fierce opposition from Indonesia which saw its dreams of total domination of Borneo slipping away.

In 1962 elements in Borneo, strongly supported by Indonesia, objected to the proposed Federation, and rebellion broke out on 8 December 1962. Although the initial revolt was crushed early in 1963 an increasing number of raids began to take place from across the Indonesian border.

On 16 September 1963 Greater Malaysia came into existence with the full support of Britain, Singapore and the North Borneo states of Sarawak and Sabah. The arrangement was approved by the United Nations. Indonesia immediately broke off diplomatic relations with Malaysia.

Guerrilla incursions continued, many involving regular Indonesian forces. These were initially confined to Borneo but later there were attacks on the Malayan mainland and Indonesian paratroops were dropped north of Singapore. Since war had not been declared the armed forces were unable to pursue enemy troops or intruding aircraft across the Indonesian border. Hostilities continued until August 1966 when a peace treaty was signed between Malaya and Indonesia.

The experience the RAF had gained in Burma and Malaya stood it in good stead. Air Vice Marshal (later Air Chief Marshal) C.N. Foxley-Norris stated, 'The Borneo campaign was a classic example of the lesson that the side which uses air power most effectively to defeat the jungle will also defeat the enemy.'

The declaration of the end of the Emergency in 1960 did not immediately bring about a reduction in helicopter operations, which was just as well, for more trouble was soon in the offing.

The policy of Konfrontasi, instigated and coined by President Sukarno of Indonesia, began after the Independent Federation of Malaysia was established in 1963.

British North Borneo (Sabah and Sarawak, two of the constituent parts of the island of Borneo, 400 miles east of Singapore) had joined the Federation as East Malaysia. Sandwiched between was the Sultanate of Brunei – a fully independent state, though security and defence remained the responsibility of the UK at the time. The remainder of the island, Kalimantan, was part of the Republic of Indonesia, which deeply resented the establishment of East Malaysia, for it wanted to gain control of the whole of Borneo. To this end, unrest had been brewing among local dissident groups. A frontier of nearly 1,000 miles stretched between the four territories, with ground heights of 8,000+ feet, few roads and an abundance of featureless primary jungle. The climate presented a considerable challenge, being both hot and humid, with columns of cumulus cloud occasionally producing torrential rain. Labuan, part of Sabah, was a small but pleasant island twenty miles off the coast of Brunei.

Trouble began late in 1962 with an internal revolt in Brunei, rapidly suppressed with the assistance of the SAS. Thereafter, offensive activity by the Indonesians consisted chiefly of incursions along the border, which amounted to undeclared war. The British army was deployed along the Kalimantan border in a chain of forward bases, from which patrols were made. Helicopter landing pads were constructed every thousand yards or so for the purposes of resupply, troop movements, and casualty evacuation.

With roads being virtually non-existent, the importance of the helicopter could hardly be overemphasised. Food, water, kerosene, and ammunition were supplied on a daily basis. Troops could be airlifted rapidly to border points where incursions occurred. Flexibility in response to fast developing local situations was a key factor in efficient use of aviation resources.

HELICOPTER OPERATIONS – BORNEO

Flight Lieutenant Tim Nicoll
Youthful reminiscences of a 103 Squadron pilot

These days, holiday brochures for Borneo and Malaya display idyllic scenes far removed from the primitive conditions which prevailed during

GOODBYE EMERGENCY, HELLO CONFRONTATION

the years of Emergency and Confrontation. In areas where previously we ventured only when carrying a gun, people now stroll through beautiful formal gardens. Tarmac roads have appeared where previously there were not even tracks.

Little time elapsed between the end of the Malayan Emergency and Confrontation in Borneo, the third largest island in the world. In the early sixties, Malaya, and for a time Singapore, amalgamated with Sarawak and Sabah to form Malaysia. These two states, which together with the Sultanate of Brunei (all British protectorates, some oil rich!), occupied the northern quarter to third of Borneo. The remainder of the island, known as Kalimantan, belonged to Indonesia, a country which was becoming increasingly communist and expansionist.

Guerrillas, with the backing of the regular Indonesian army, now attempted to annex this northern area of Borneo, thus gaining control of the oil reserves, and so, between January 1963 and August 1966, came Confrontation or *Konfrontasi* – even more of a misnomer than was 'The Emergency' in Malaya!

The catalyst for this was the Brunei Rebellion – December 1962 to May 1963 – during which rebels attempted to seize the Sultanate and its oilfields. But British and Commonwealth forces in Singapore were quick off the mark, basically restoring order within a week or so, though mopping up operations continued for some time.

It was during the Malayan Emergency that RAF (and RN) helicopter operations were first introduced, and gradually improved upon, so when Borneo came along we were well along the learning curve. The underpowered piston-engined Whirlwind HAR4 had given way to the turbine powered Mk 10, a much improved option, better suited to the area. The larger, twin rotor Bristol Belvedere was also in service, as was the twin-engined Wessex; our old friends 848 Squadron, RNAS back in theatre. The main difference this time was the fact that the opposition possessed serious anti-aircraft weaponry, as opposed to a Second World War rifle.

Most fighting took place in Sarawak, to the west, where the mountains were lowest, consequently incursions most easily made.

RAF helicopter units flying the Whirlwind were 103, 110, 225 and 230 Squadrons, while 66 Squadron was Belvedere equipped. Early on, 230 Squadron had been rushed out from the UK, as fast as an aircraft carrier can rush! to confer a degree of mobility on the Australian, British, Malaysian, Singaporean, and New Zealand forces which were seeking to prevent this annexation.

THE FIRST HELICOPTER BOYS

The fact that Allied Forces were crossing the border into Indonesia, effectively carrying the war into the enemy's back yard was, at the time, highly classified, and strenuously denied. However, Denis Healey, Secretary for Defence during the period, has subsequently admitted that he authorised such incursions under the codename 'Claret'. I am therefore now unhindered when writing about the assistance we gave to the troops when fighting on Indonesian territory. In short, wherever the troops went, the helicopters accompanied them. In many cases, to reduce exposure to anti-aircraft fire, the Whirlwinds would fly between, and sometimes even under, the treetops. Under such circumstances the pilots' range of vision would be very restricted. It therefore became practice for a spotter, in an Army Air Corps Bell 47G Sioux helicopter flying above the effective range of the Indonesian 12.5 mm anti-aircraft machine guns, to direct the Whirlwinds to Allied positions. When the troops had been resupplied or extracted, the spotter would guide the Whirlwind back to our side of the border.

The published Rules of Engagement under which we were expected to operate required us to wait until fired upon before we ourselves opened fire. Bearing in mind the short range at which engagements were likely to occur, and the calibre of weapons available to the enemy, this policy can only be described as suicidal. Little wonder aircraft captains interpreted these rules rather liberally when briefing their crews!

In one daring sortie our flight commander, Flight Lieutenant Jim Millar, was faced with the task of extracting Royal Marine casualties from within two hundred yards of Indonesian positions where the Royals were pinned down by heavy fire. The Sioux pilot called for the 105mm howitzers to lay down a smokescreen in no man's land, under cover of which Jim successfully picked up the injured and dead. For this astonishing and fearless feat Jim was deservedly awarded the DFC.

While these carefully planned sorties over the border rarely resulted in damage, let alone loss, to enemy fire, the same was not true of some of the inadvertent over-flights of enemy positions. Bearing in mind that Borneo is at least twice the area of Great Britain you may be able to grasp the scale of the task facing Allied ground forces, and their utter dependence on helicopters for their movement over such a vast, unmapped, inhospitable and largely, impenetrable terrain. Additionally, during the early years, there was the complication of Indonesian paratroops landing in Johore. These too required mopping up by our troops, with their helicopter support. Various military strategists have estimated that the presence of helicopters increased the mobility of the ground troops by a factor of between fifteen and twenty.

GOODBYE EMERGENCY, HELLO CONFRONTATION

I joined 103 Squadron at Seletar in August 1965, aged 27, for a two year tour during which I flew almost 300 operational sorties. Like all new arrivals I had to complete my in-theatre training as a Short Range Transport pilot, along with a jungle survival course before carrying out any productive flying. A little-known but interesting feature of that jungle survival course was that approximately half the students were USAF pilots destined for Vietnam.

In common with about a fifth of our squadron pilot strength I also qualified as an SAR pilot, and later completed a course, becoming one of only four squadron pilots qualified to operate the SS11 air-to-ground missile.

Upon joining 103 Squadron the strength was eighteen pilots and twenty aircraft; by the time I left these figures had doubled.

Squadron headquarters at Seletar incorporated a dedicated SAR Flight, covering Singapore and the southern half of the Malay peninsula, the northern half being covered by 103's Butterworth-based SAR flight; however a majority of the squadron's crews and aircraft were deployed in Borneo.

By the time I arrived in Borneo the main detachment had completed its move from Labuan to Kuching, following the disbandment of 225 Squadron in Dec '65 (225 had been the first squadron to re-equip with the Whirlwind Mk10, in 1961). From west to east it had further forward detachments co-located with Battalion or Commando HQs at Lundu, Balai Ringin, Simmangang and Nanga Gaat. Tasking at the latter detachment was often shared with Royal Navy Wessex, or the Whirlwinds of 110 Squadron. There were normally also four Belvederes of 66 Squadron at Kuching, and a rather greater number of 110 Squadron aircraft at Labuan. With the exception of Lundu which had to be supplied by sea, and Nanga Gaat, routinely restocked by longboats capable of tackling the cataracts on the Lupar River and its tributaries, HQs were generally located on dirt roads, thus accessible from Kuching. While all had helipads, Lundu and Simmangang also had a small airstrip, suitable for the Auster, or single and Twin Pioneers of 209 Squadron.

In several cases, Infantry HQ had a troop of RA Regiment 105 mm howitzers at Seven Mile Bazaar, just south of RAF Kuching. Company positions were usually about ten miles forward of their HQs, often right on the border itself which for most of its length ran along the watershed. These positions were invariably only accessible by helicopter. For this reason they were generally constructed on a small hillock. Trees were allowed to stand on the Indonesian side, to block the view of prying eyes, but removed from the top and reverse slope to provide a helipad with a clear approach. The height of the helipad above the surrounding terrain assisted in our taking off at maximum all-up weight. Some, such as Plaman Mapu and Gunan Gajak, could also be resupplied by parachute, whereas others, such as Biawak, were within range of Indonesian anti-aircraft guns, making para-drops impossible. Sematan, the most north-westerly Allied position in Borneo, could be resupplied via sea, helipad or airstrip, but not by road.

When judged against European standards, communication was fairly difficult, and mobility by the limited troops available would have been well nigh impossible without helicopters.

Squadron presence at Kuching and its forward detachments ran to about ten aircraft. During daylight hours we maintained one aircraft at fifteen minutes readiness at Kuching, but crews flew casevac sorties from all locations in addition to their SRT role. At least two SS11 air-to-ground missile equipped aircraft were based at Kuching. We did not have aircraft and crews specifically dedicated to Special Forces, their sorties being allocated to the most experienced aircrew available, whenever a requirement arose. In addition to maintaining one aircraft and crew at fifteen minutes readiness, all crews were expected to react immediately should an operational requirement arise. An example occurred on 21 November 1965, on the afternoon of which an engagement took place resulting in Rambahadur Limbu of 2/10 Gurkha Rifles winning the Victoria Cross.

With hardly any notice, the SS11-missile-capable aircraft were armed and, together with all other serviceable aircraft, brought to immediate readiness, lined up on the taxiway outside ATC, rotors turning. Hence, aircrew had to remain in the squadron basha, available for tasking from dawn to dusk, not even able to cross the airfield for a meal! Fortunately the catering officer took pity on us, sending boxes of sandwiches. Thirty-five days of such existence, coupled with exhaustion and the tension of operations made a policy of roulement (rotation of military units) unavoidable.

Throughout their tours in the Far East, helicopter aircrew normally spent five weeks in Borneo followed by three weeks in Singapore or West Malaysia. On returning to Singapore we were normally given a 36-hour stand down. Then we completed mandatory training, including night flying, and underwent categorisation and other examinations. Thus, one memorable night while flying the Seletar circuit with Squadron Leader 'Bushy' Clark (he wore a moustache of enormous proportions) of the UK-based Helicopter Standardisation Unit, he suddenly pulled back the speed select

GOODBYE EMERGENCY, HELLO CONFRONTATION

lever effectively disconnecting the engine from the rotor. I immediately went into autorotation and fired off a Schermuly flare which slowly sank earthwards under its parachute. By its light I lined up the runway, went through the practice Mayday procedure and asked the standard question of 'At what height do you wish me to recover, Sir?' Bushy's reply of 'Don't! Just make sure you put it down on the tarmac' caught me rather by surprise. I realise, in retrospect, how he did me a great favour. Quite apart from awarding me a B Cat, he used this incident to inspire my confidence when night flying during the years to come. Furthermore, he stuck his neck out on my behalf since he, not I, would have been left carrying the can had things gone wrong. However, I can't help wondering what today's Health and Safety lobby would make of such realistic training.

After these various commitments, the lucky ones might even have been permitted a few days' leave! In my case this happened just once in my tour when I spent a few days' sightseeing while on detachment to Butterworth. Thereafter it was time to conduct SRT training with the army, or go onto an SAR shift pattern: 15 minutes readiness during daylight, on call at night, then 48 hours off, until it was time once again to return to Borneo.

When all these squadron commitments, their associated specialist requirements and, in some cases, limitations are taken into account, you may begin to understand the vital role played by the flight commanders, and to marvel that they ever found time to fly themselves!

With our area of operations in Borneo being just one degree north of the equator, the climate and weather dominated our way of life. Throughout the year, by day and by night the temperature rarely wandered out of the 80s F, matched by a humidity which, in percentage terms, also remained in the eighties. In short, the climate could only be described as debilitating. In earlier times, Europeans had routinely taken to the high ground – Fraser's Hill, Cameron Highlands – in search of re-enervation. In the sixties, enlightened European firms sent Caucasian staff back to Europe for several weeks a year. British service personnel were expected to grin and bear it for two to three years. In retrospect this may not have been the best policy since most of us undoubtedly slowed down mentally and physically during that time. Weather patterns throughout the year were dominated by the monsoon which arrived in a season corresponding to the European autumn.

Where possible, flying was best completed in the morning, for as the day progressed, cumulus began to build, and could reach 50,000 feet by early afternoon. A deluge of such intensity would follow at about 1600 hours, monsoon drains 10 to 12 feet deep filling within a quarter of an hour. Woe betide if you were still airborne at this time, in-flight visibility reducing to fifty yards! Only thing to do was to open the side window and fly sideways, following a line feature such as a track, or series of telephone poles, until one could land safely. Try that in anything but a helicopter! But every cloud has a silver lining: the sunsets which followed had literally to be seen to be believed!

230 SQUADRON, BACK IN BORNEO

Based on an article by Guy Warner
When 230 Squadron was sent to Borneo in 1965, it was not the first time its aircraft had carried out operations on the island. In the late 1930s, its Short Singapore flying-boats, stationed at RAF Seletar, had undertaken survey flights and transported colonial officers. In January 1946, now equipped with the Sunderland V, they were back at Seletar following war service in many other theatres. This time a detachment was on communications and general duties, including a tour of Borneo and the Celebes, photographing and observing the suitability of flying boat landing areas, returning district officers to their posts in Sarawak and British North Borneo to pick up the reins of an empire on which the sun would shortly be setting, and conveying Japanese war criminals for imprisonment, trial and execution.

In 1958, Sunderlands now consigned to the scrap heap, 230 re-formed flying the Pioneer and Twin Pioneer, converting to helicopters in mid-1962, flying the Westland Whirlwind HAR10, aircraft which were deemed ideal for the Borneo conflict. Early Whirlwinds used heavy, underpowered, Pratt & Whitney piston engines, whereas the Mk10 benefited from the much lighter, more powerful Bristol Siddeley Gnome turbo-shaft. This engine also incorporated an electronic control system, considerably reducing the pilot's workload. It was faster, had longer range, and could carry a greater payload than the Mk4.

The squadron relocated to Odiham, Hampshire, from their base at Gütersloh, West Germany, in preparation for once more serving as part of the Far East Air Force (FEAF). This included fitting the pilot seats with armour plate and installing Bren gun mounts, indications of the expected seriousness of the conflict.

Nine Whirlwinds embarked on HMS *Triumph* on 29 January 1965, collecting, in passing, four more from Cyprus. Air and ground crews were flown to Singapore on 19 February, ready to fly their aircraft to Seletar.

GOODBYE EMERGENCY, HELLO CONFRONTATION

With a break in Singapore, an opportunity was taken to pay a visit to Tiger Brewery, where Flying Officer Anthony Barnetson distinguished himself by consuming a glass boot of Tiger beer (4½ pints) within the stipulated twenty minutes. The CO, Squadron Leader D.M. Thomas, returned the honours, giving the brewery a squadron badge to display in their tavern (appropriate, although they already had one, for the 230 Squadron crest had been based on the label of a Tiger beer bottle).

In the 1930s, the Air Ministry initiated a drive for all units to design their own badges, to be submitted for approval. Most did, though one squadron was experiencing problems deciding on something suitable. Until the night a group of them sat drinking at Seletar, when one glanced at his beer bottle. In that moment, a badge was born. The squadron? Seletar-based 230. Their motto? Kita Chari Juah; We Search Far. Inspiration by Tiger, perhaps? (230 Squadron's crest, along with the story of its creation, is on display in the Tiger Tavern, Asia Pacific Breweries, Singapore).

After a few days local training at Seletar, the entire unit embarked on HMS *Bulwark*, arriving in Labuan on 10 March.

Operations began almost immediately, the first sortie being flown that afternoon by the CO, taking the Director of Operations, Major General W.C. Walker CB CBE DSO, to Muara, then conveying four troops plus 200lbs of freight from Brunei to Labuan. This airfield, a major forward base for the British during Confrontation, was home at various times to many fixed wing aircraft, along with the Belvederes of 66 Sqn, and Whirlwinds of the various squadrons operating in the area, most on detachment from Seletar.

The weather was an important factor in dictating level and intensity of flying activity, particularly helicopters. Morning mist and low cloud were frequent and tenacious, late afternoon thunderstorms widespread and heavy. A further consideration lay in balancing fuel against payload, though in cases of emergency, fuel was available at some jungle clearings. Navigation presented similar problems to those in Malaya, heavily dependent on knowledge of the local topography, while timed runs on specific bearings were also important.

With the central base being back at Seletar, conditions were far from ideal. As for creature comforts, an air-conditioned room was greatly prized, and allocated strictly on a time-served basis. In rooms without air-conditioning, anything of organic origin developed mould fairly rapidly.

The squadron had established detachments at Tawau and Sepulot, where a longhouse had been built by Australian army engineers: eight single rooms, a lounge and bar area, and four washing areas. A hot/cold shower building was alongside. Electricity was intermittent, and the sanitary facility was a genuine three-hole 'long drop lodge' type, comprising of about four cubicles with low rattan sides and a crinkly tin roof, but with a fantastic view. Ingenious automatic vacant/engaged signs were Tiger Beer tin cogs with strings attached to the seat lids. According to one report, the view looked out over the airfield, to the river junction and the jungle covered hills beyond. It was reckoned to be the best 'loo with a view' in the whole of Borneo.

Helicopter landing pads at Sepulot were typically surfaced with lalang grass and hard clay; perfect when dry, but akin to a skating rink when wet. 230's main task was to resupply and reinforce forward patrols along a 120-mile sector of border.

In April 1965, Flight Lieutenant Bill McEachern, with Sergeant G. Ashall as crewman, carried out a difficult rescue on Mount Kinabalu. He landed on a ledge 8,300ft up and waited for nine hours in less than ideal conditions while two injured civilians were brought down from the peak 5,000ft above.

During the first month, nearly 200 sorties were flown, to which the CO noted: 'Comment is superfluous, the facts speak for themselves, I am very satisfied with the squadron's achievement.'

Next month saw a 'hearts and minds' round trip, taking a medical team to immunise local village children, and extracting SAS troopers from a dangerously isolated position. These Australians were fearsome warriors, but tended to smell less than wholesome after a month in the jungle, so it became common for pilots to fly with their heads out of the cockpit window, thus avoiding the aroma wafting up from the cabin.

In July, XR402, flown by Flight Lieutenant Atkinson, was lost when it suffered complete engine failure and crashed into the sea. It had been hovering at low level while holding to take part in a display for a Labuan Red Cross fete. No lives were lost, though three crew members suffered compression fractures to the spine.

Later that month, the Tawau detachment received a distress call from a Saunders-Roe SRN5 of the Hovercraft Unit (Far East), which, having jammed in reverse gear, was forced to anchor. Flight Lieutenant Wood flew overhead and winched down soft drinks to the crew and passengers who were suffering in the midday heat. A tug was summoned to tow the hovercraft back to base.

Another maritime rescue led to Flight Lieutenant Hall towing the station Sub-Aqua Club's dive boat six miles to harbour after its outboard motor failed.

GOODBYE EMERGENCY, HELLO CONFRONTATION

In October, Flight Lieutenant Trevor Wood, Flying Officer 'Dickie' Holmes and Flight Sergeant 'Jock' Hood were involved in a dramatic and dangerous rescue. During a troop lift, a message was received to say four RAF Regiment personnel were drifting down the swollen Talankai River on an air drop container. The container, full of rations and beer, had been swept into the river along with the men. Quickly returning to Sepulot, Wood offloaded his soldiers, picked up the waiting Holmes and Hood, and returned to the river. Soon Jock was dangling over the rushing waters, while Wood manoeuvred as close as he dared to the overhanging trees, rotor blades actually chopping the foliage. One man was rescued, then Hood disappeared underwater, tangled up with the parachute, and a panicky survivor. With some difficulty, he freed himself and gestured to Dickie, acting as winchman, that the helicopter should tow them 200 yards to the bank. Trevor landed and took both exhausted men on board. The third was saved by a Wessex of 848 Naval Air Squadron, stationed at Labuan.

As 1966 wore on, rumours began to grow of an end to Confrontation. The flying tasks continued, except for moving patrols into the combat areas on the border, this having diminished in line with the decrease in Indonesian incursions. Detachments at Sepulot and Tawau were brought to an end in July, though the Whirlwinds were still in action from Bario where Flight Lieutenant Roger Wain was detachment commander. Whirlwinds from Bario, in conjunction with two pairs of Wessex from 848 NAS, were given the task of the last operation, to sweep up Indonesians involved in the fighting in the Long Semado area. Refuelling was required, for which an engine driven pump was supplied at the airstrips. Fuel was air-dropped by Beverley, four 50-gallon drums to a pallet, supported by three parachutes.

Roger Wains' memories of this time included: The occasional 'chute failure. Quite spectacular, caps being forced off the drums on impact, sending plumes of fuel 100 feet into the air. One day, Elsan fluid was carried on the same pallet as vegetables, another 'chute failure doing nothing to improve the flavour of the veggies. The Gurkhas' rum ration was air-dropped on the odd occasion, the bottles almost always surviving. Fresh food was usually brought in by Twin Pioneer – uphill landing, downhill take-off. Fresh meat was supplied by the duty water buffalo!

One afternoon, ferrying 105mm shells – two to a box (165lbs in weight), ten boxes per load – between Long Semado and Ba Kelalen, two Whirlwinds consumed thirty barrels of fuel! Typically they would take off from Long Semado with enough fuel to fly to Ba Kelalen and return, upon touch-down the crewman would hop out, supervise loading to maximum permissible all-up weight, the aircraft would low hover, glide down the strip, fall off the end gaining air-speed, and on to Long Semado, unload, put in about a barrel of fuel with the Kelson pump, no stopping, no refreshments, and don't forget the crewman on the last flight! Helicopters never returned empty, the golden rule was always to load something useful; parachutes etc.

If the air-drop was on time and you were scheduled to fly, you missed breakfast, unless the first stop was Long Semado, where the company commander would appear with fried egg sandwiches and mugs of tea. With 'hearts and minds' being an integral part of overall strategy, it became policy to generate goodwill, so when possible, locals (and pigs) were given lifts.

The strip at Long Banga, about forty nautical miles south east of Bario, featured a particular hazard; a tree some 200 feet tall had not been felled when the air-strip was built because of the risk of it falling the wrong way and blocking the runway. The root buttresses were enormous, you could park a Land Rover between them. One afternoon at Bario, Roger was having a shower when a messenger appeared and summoned him to see the colonel. He was asked to fly the medical officer to Long Banga as a matter of urgency. Flight Lieutenant Hood and Sergeant Leggatt rounded up the crew while the aircraft was pre-flighted in the gathering gloom. As they flew over the dark jungle, lightning flashed in the sky behind. Arriving at Long Banga, the strip was shrouded in ground mist. Ever mindful of that b...dy great tree, the Gurkhas lined up along the river side of the strip with paraffin lamps. Setting up a constant attitude powered approach, Flight Lieutenant Hood monitoring the instruments, Sergeant Leggatt looking for the ground, hoping it would be illuminated by the landing light, and on landing, the helicopter was shut down on the spot. The sick officer received treatment and was flown back to Bario the next morning.

Sukarno lost power in a coup, a peace treaty with Malaysia was imminent. By the end of August 1966, the undeclared war was over, and plans were formalised to move the squadron back to the UK.

ESCAPE FROM COASTAL

Flight Sergeant Gerry Sage
The RAF started to become involved with army support helicopters during the Malayan Emergency using Dragonfly, Sycamore and Mk2 Whirlwinds. By the early 1960s these older helicopters were being replaced

GOODBYE EMERGENCY, HELLO CONFRONTATION

by Gnome-engined Whirlwind 10s and the Belvedere. The next altercation involving the helicopter force started in earnest in 1963 when, after the formation of the Federation of Malaysia, President Sukarno of Indonesia saw it as a direct threat to his country. He started to make military noises which, with help from the Soviet Union, could not be ignored, so a gradual build-up of UK and Commonwealth forces began.

Whirlwinds from 103 and 110 Squadrons were detached to Kuching and Labuan with 230 Sqn from Odiham eventually being posted in, their crews rotating on a one year unaccompanied tour.

In October '65 I had completed a three year tour as flight engineer with 120 Squadron's Shackletons and was biding my time. 230 Squadron had been at Labuan for almost a year, the original crews in need of replacement, which is where I came in.

So, step forward Flight Sergeant Sage (not a volunteer!). The call came: Report to Ternhill for training as a crewman (it was at this time Crewman became an official aircrew post, warranting a brevet) on Belvederes before a posting to 66 Squadron, Labuan. But on arrival at Ternhill they said, 'Oh no! It's 230 Squadron at Odiham, detached to Labuan on Whirlwind 10s!'

The OCU at Ternhill was for pilot conversion from fixed wing to helicopters, and for crewmen to learn a completely new type of flying activity. Our duties comprised: co-pilot, navigator, winchman and operator, loadmaster, and we had to be able to carry out in-field refuelling and daily inspections (DIs) of the aircraft. We would also operate as air gunners as the aircraft could have a GPMG fitted in the doorway.

Unfortunately the course for crewmen proved to be a disappointment. We were told very little about what was expected of us, consequently we had to do a lot of on-the-job learning when we got to the Far East. We eventually completed our three-month course learning to operate the Gnome-engined Whirlwind, which proved to be my only jet type!

Part of the course took place at Valley, search and rescue training, as when in Borneo we would have to function as the only SAR unit in the area. The course eventually finished and the eight very young, first-tour pilots, and six signaller/crewmen were whisked off to Changi by RAF Britannia for a short period of acclimatisation before travelling to Labuan.

Before 1963, Labuan had been a small transit airfield, but with the escalation of the Indonesian problem it was upgraded to a fully operational base with permanent technical and domestic buildings. It was reasonably comfortable, although, the RAF not into air conditioning, it was punka cooled, with mosquito nets at night.

THE FIRST HELICOPTER BOYS

Most Confrontation activity took place in the form of border incursions, the long border between Borneo and Indonesia being poorly defined due to the mountainous land being covered by primary jungle. The main objective of the Indonesians was to cross the border, rape, pillage and cause general mayhem in the villages of the local Ebans and Dyaks. These tribes live in communal longhouses, made of wood and bamboo and built on stilts, a single longhouse home to a whole village. I believe the longest was nearly a quarter of a mile in length.

The villagers lived the most basic existence, growing just a few crops where they had cleared the jungle. Their main source of food was fish from the many rivers, and hunting animals, using poison tipped darts from their blowpipes. Although they were only a generation away from being head-hunters, they were a very gentle people. Most had never seen a car or a bicycle, but helicopters and aeroplanes were becoming commonplace!

In order to try to secure the border, our forces had constructed a series of outposts, with a chain of helipads hacked out of the jungle. Usually built on high ground, these featured a hole in the jungle canopy just big enough to allow a helicopter to land vertically, the pad itself a platform of felled trees approximately thirty feet square, just big enough to allow a chopper to settle. A few miles further in from the border a number of small airstrips had been constructed, again hacked out of the jungle and often beside river beds.

Sepulot was the place I knew best during my tour. It was a small airstrip built by the side of a river junction with the domestic site built on the side of the adjacent hill. It was home to a company of Ghurkhas and a detachment of border scouts – locally employed levies. 230 Squadron had a permanent detachment there, usually comprised of four Whirlwinds, four pilots, and two or three crewmen. Our accommodation was a single all-inclusive building constructed on bamboo stilts, air-drop wooden baseboards, wriggly tin roof and roll-up canvas walls. There were about ten separate bedrooms and a common room with a wooden bar and a paraffin-operated fridge. Electricity, by diesel generator, was only available between 1800 and 2200 hours. But we did have hot showers, locally constructed out of old 45-gallon oil drums on poles and heated by a wood-burning clay oven.

The main drawback of these airstrips was the fact that they were inaccessible by road, therefore nearly all supplies had to be parachuted in. The drops, always exciting to watch, took place every few days, mainly from Beverley or Hastings. All fuel was airdropped, together with fresh food, so a candled drop could be a disaster. Even Landrovers and bulldozers were airdropped as the strips were being built: mind your head!

GOODBYE EMERGENCY, HELLO CONFRONTATION

Our main tasking up country was to ferry patrols of Ghurkhas and border scouts to the helipads, from where they conducted two-week patrols searching for infiltrators. We would pick them up later. Another unit we operated with was the New Zealand SAS, who would appear and disappear at regular intervals.

We'd also airlift Royal Artillery chaps and their 105 mm Howitzers, which could be broken down into four aircraft loads. They would set up, lob a few shells across the border, then leg it back to base. Sometimes we even took them across the border!

Courtesy of Gerry Sage and the Shackleton Association, from their newsletter the Growler & used with permission.

Appendix

Introduction & transcript of a talk given to the Royal Air Force Historical Society

Squadron Leader HHJ Browning

Tom Browning graduated from the RAF College in 1951, his first flying tour was on Shackletons with 220 Squadron. Following a CFS helicopter conversion course on Dragonflys he was posted to 155 Squadron (Whirlwinds) at Kuala Lumpur in 1958, transferring to 194 Squadron (Sycamores) the following year. Shortly after the two helicopter squadrons in Malaya moved to Butterworth, where they merged to become 110 Squadron.

After 848 NAS had been withdrawn, leaving 155 and 194 Squadrons to provide helicopter support in Malaya, is just about the point where I came into the picture.

With the end of the Emergency distantly in sight, and taking account of competing requirements for helicopters elsewhere, it had been decided to run down the helicopter squadrons in Malaya to the point where only 194 Squadron, with its Sycamores, would be left. Fate decided otherwise. Following two fatal accidents in February and April 1959, the Sycamores were grounded. On 3 June 155 and 194 were combined to form 110 Squadron which took over 155's remaining Whirlwinds. By September the squadron had moved to RAAF Butterworth. In April 1960 the first three restored Sycamores were received. The last Whirlwind left on 26 July and the Emergency was declared at an end five days later – although there remained work for 110 to do.

Although helicopters were THE short range transport force in Malaya, it would be churlish not to mention the Single and Twin Pioneers, which were used for troop lifting, fort re-supply and casevac. 'Economy of Effort' was paramount in Malaya – helicopters were only to be used in the absence of alternative methods of transport. It also had a financial ring about it and at only £35 per hour, the Pioneer was cheap and cheerful, especially when compared with £53 per hour for the Sycamore and £73 for the Whirlwind.

APPENDIX

Helicopters operated between first and last light. It was common for three or four to leave ground 7.00 am and return by 6.00 pm, having spent most of the day, apart from two to three hours positioning time, lifting troops and freight from an assembly area to a jungle clearing and/or bringing troops out – flights of no more than ten to twenty minutes or so, covering distances that could have taken days to walk. Sometimes the start of an operation might be delayed by low cloud, sometimes the flight home would result in a hectic tail chase down mountain valleys in a desperate race to beat the lowering clouds and reach the open plains before our escape route was closed. Much of the time it was just another sunny, hot, humid day.

There were no air defences for us to worry about. Although there were rare instances of terrorists being seen in clearings as a helicopter was landing or overflying, I know of no occasion when a landing was opposed, let alone actually fired on.

All three types used in Malaya were in the early stages of helicopter development. The Dragonfly especially so. Even stripped down, it could only be expected to lift about 200 lbs out of a clearing, plus 30 minutes fuel – and the pilot, of course.

To get the best possible payload it was stripped of everything that could be considered expendable – from the winch down to cockpit lighting. A locally manufactured stretcher unit weighing 35 lbs replaced the original external pannier attachments that weighed 210 lbs and which would have virtually precluded carrying any casualties at all!

Pilot techniques and approach criteria for helicopter clearings were established as the result of these early operations.

The Whirlwind set the general configuration for transport helicopters for many years. The weight of the tail end off-set by the nose mounted engine, leaving a large, box-like cabin capable of seating ten passengers – but unable to lift anything like that number in Malaya – directly beneath the main rotor.

Much has been said and written about the poor serviceability of, particularly, the Whirlwind. In fairness I think it should be said that all three types had their fair share of problems. Remember too that we were at the bottom of the learning curve with regard to helicopter operations and maintenance.

But, despite all the problems, the ground crews were untiring in their efforts to keep the squadrons flying. This involved them flying on missions as crewmen, refuelling, turn-round inspections and rectification – such as engine or rotor blade changes – in the field. Crashed aircraft, where they could be reached, were repaired and eventually flown out – thanks mainly to maintenance unit personnel.

THE FIRST HELICOPTER BOYS

One thing all three types had in common was a need to reduce weight. Consequently role equipment was kept to a minimum: no winches or external cargo hooks – not even seats in the Whirlwind. However, the lack of role equipment was not necessarily a bar to, say, carrying external loads on one occasion at least.

Our attempts to recover a 656 (AOP) Squadron Auster in 1960 were made by tying it on with a length of target banner cable. A block of wood was placed between the cable and the floor by the cabin door sill and a crewman, armed with a crash axe, constituted the emergency release gear! The Auster pilot had made a superb forced landing on a narrow track without any damage to the aircraft. Our attempts to carry the wings to a more open area less than a mile away soon put an end to that, although we were more successful with the engine and fuselage.

Other work for the helicopters included communications flights – particularly between the many forts that had been established in jungle areas; what could grandiosely be called tactical reconnaissance; and search and rescue – the latter almost always over land.

Between the end of 1953 and early 1954, Dragonflys were used for spraying terrorist cultivations in the jungle, with a view to denial rather than promoting husbandry. Other operational techniques that were introduced included roping, the purpose of which was to enable troops to land safely in unsecured or unprepared areas where the surface was either obscured by undergrowth, or whose load bearing was suspect. 848 NAS carried out the first experiments using equipment that had served the Royal Navy well over the centuries – scrambling nets! They soon settled on what became the generally accepted knotted rope.

Not that the RAF didn't have its moments of madness too. At some time the rope ladder was thought to be a suitable alternative to the winch. Film taken at the time seemed to suggest that if the survivor had the strength to climb the ladder, he didn't really need rescuing in the first place.

The following list of helicopters operated during the Malayan Emergency by the Casualty Evacuation Flight, 194 Squadron, 155 Squadron, and 110 Squadron, was compiled by Tony Tamblyn, ex 155 Squadron Engine Mechanic Crewman:

Whirlwind aircraft allocated to 155 Squadron FEAF:

XD163 A	XD186 G	XJ410 N	XJ428 P
XD165 B	XD187 H	XJ412 O	XJ431 L
XD182 C	XD188 J	XJ413 P	XJ437
XD183 D	XJ407 K	XJ414 Q	XJ723
XD184 E	XJ408 L	XJ426 S	XJ724
XD185 F	XJ409 M	XJ427 T	XJ761

APPENDIX

XD184 in Kuala Lumpur hangar.

XJ410 ready to begin a lift.

THE FIRST HELICOPTER BOYS

XJ428 crashed, probably near Fort Brooke.

XJ723. Emergency landing after hydraulic failure

APPENDIX

Sources:

RAF Museum Hendon: AM Form 78 (Aircraft movement cards) and AM Form 1180 (Aircraft accident summaries).

Public Records Office, Kew: AM Forms 540 & 541 (Operational Record Books).

*

Some nostalgic place names

2 FIB Ipoh
Benta
Bidan – bombing range
BMH Taiping
BMH Kinrara
Cameron Highlands
Dusan Tua – jungle warfare school
Fraser's Hill – jungle warfare school
Grik
Ipoh
Jalong Road
Kampong Padi Sanai (Thailand)
K K Medang
Kroh
Kuala Kangsar
Kuala Lipis
Kuantan
Lasah
Malacca
Paddy's Ladang
Port Swettenham
Serdang   KL training area
Sulva Lines
Tana Rata

*

848 Squadron NAS

Where are they now?

A	WV189	Crashed in primary jungle, 1 August 1955. Pilot (Lt S.L.C. Thompson) and 4 Ghurkas flown to BMH Kinrara. Malay 6 Regt flown in to guard wreck. Engine failure. A/F Hours 803.00
B	WV190	Transferred to UK for recon, 10 January 1957. RNAS Stretton, RNAY Donibristle, RNAS Arbroath as class 1 intructional A/C and arrived incomplete on 3 July 1957. A/F Hours 1335.00
C	WV191	A/C record lost.
D	WV192	Crashed, operation 'Termite' area of Perak at 3,000ft. Blown up as could not be salvaged. Elephants tried 6 weeks. First S.55 to be totally written off. A/C records lost.
E	WV193	Transferred to UK for Recon 10 January 1957. RNAS Stretton, RNAY Donibristle, RNAS Manadon, RNAY Fleetlands 17 July 1961. A/F Hours 1572.45
F	WV194	Transferred to UK for recon 10 January 1957. A/C records lost.
G	WV195	Transferred to UK for recon, 10 January 1957. RNAS Stretton, RNAY Donibristle, RNAS Arbroath, RNAY Fleetlands, RNAS Culdrose. A9 actions 3.63. A/F Hours 972.05
H	WV196	A/C crashed on op with S.W.B's near Segamat, 12 November 1956. Pilot (Lieutenant John Bawden) killed, no passengers. Failure of free wheel unit. Burnt on impact. A/F Hours 1501.15
J	WV197	A/C crashed on op, 13 October 1956, lifting out 2 police. Pilot, Lieutenant Commander J.T. Stanley. Engine failure, caught fire on impact and burnt out. A/F Hours 1039.55
K	WV198	Transferred to UK for recon 10 January 1957. RNAS Stretton, RNAY Donibristle, RNAS Arbroath, RNAS Lee on Solent 10 October 1962, class 2 instr. Partially restored at Carlisle Airport. A/F Hours 1423.45

*

APPENDIX

HOW MANY FLIERS REMEMBER THIS?

Many, many years ago, the following 'Ten Commandments for Helicopter Flying' appeared in the Far East Air Force's Safety Summary. While being amusing – much in the way of those Second World War TM reports – they outline admirably the factors that spell the difference between life or death for a rotary wing pilot:

He who inspecteth not his aircraft gives his angels cause to concern him.

Thou shalt not become airborne without first ascertaining the level of thy propellant.

Let infinite discretion govern thy movement near the ground, for thy area of destruction is vast.

The rotor RPM is thy staff of life. Without it thy shall surely perish.

Thou shalt maintain thy airspeed between ten and four hundred feet, lest the earth rise and smite thee.

Thou shalt not make a trial of thy centre of gravity, lest thou dash a foot against a stone.

Thou shalt not let thy confidence exceed thy ability, for broad is the way to destruction.

He who doeth his approach and alloweth the wing to turn behind him shall surely make restitution.

He who alloweth his tail rotor to catch in thorns curseth his children, and his children's children.

THE FIRST HELICOPTER BOYS

Helicopter Operations (Malaya Emergency) Association

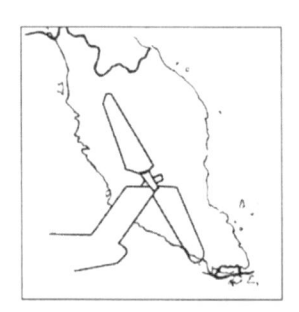

Helicopters used during the Malaya Emergency by Casualty Evacuation Flight

194 Squadron

155 Squadron

110 Squadron

APPENDIX

Westland Dragonfly HC Mks 2 & 4 Operated by the Casualty Evacuation Flight and No 194 Squadron

Of the seventeen Westland Dragonflies that went into service with the Royal Air Force, fourteen were sent to Singapore and Malaya. Outline details of their operational life with the Casualty Evacuation Flight (Casevac Flt) and/or No 194 Squadron are given in the following table. Initially, three Mk 2 Dragonflies made up the Casevac Flt's establishment when it was officially formed on 1 May 1950 but, to meet the need for replacements due to attrition as well as increases in establishment, a total of nine Dragonflies - 5 Mk 2s and 4 Mk 4s - had been flown by the flight before it was disbanded on 2 Feb 1953. The six surviving Casevac Flt Dragonflies were transferred to 194 Sqn when it was reformed the same day. A further six Dragonfly Mk 4s were brought on strength by 25 Apr 53. By the time that 194 Sqn was ready to become an all Sycamore squadron on 28 Jun 1956, only two serviceable Dragonflies remained to be flown back to Singapore: the rest had all been written off as the result of accidents.

Serial No	Mk	Unit	Taken on Strength	Struck off Strength	Notes
WF 308	2(i)	CF	22.5.50(ii)	25.10.51	(i) Ex G-ALMC. (ii) There is some confusion over this date: WF 308's first flight was on 22.4.50, the Casevac Flt formed on 1.5.50 and moved to Changi on 22.5.50. It seems that the Maintenance Base, Far East (Seletar) has used the date that the unit left Seletar as the date the helicopter was taken on strength. On 24.10.51 WF 308 crashed in deep jungle near Raub but was not recoverable. The pilot, Flt Lt K Fry, and casevac, Rifleman Krishna Badhur Thapa, both escaped with slight injuries.
WF 311	2	CF & 194	12.6.50	18.5.53	To 194 Sqn 1.2.53. In April 1952 Flt Lt A J Lee '...strafed bandit's clearing ...' using a bren gun - the first reported instance of the operational use of an 'armed' helicopter by British forces. Whilst on a ferry flight from RNAS Sembawang on 16.5.53 WF 311 crashed 3 miles SW of Kuming after engine failure due to fuel starvation. Cause: bevel drive slipped causing a mis-match between the fuel selector and the fuel cock. The pilot, Flt Lt W Pinner, was unhurt. The accident summary (F.1180) refers to WF 311 as a Mk 4 at the date of the accident although there is no record of such conversion in its F.78 (aircraft movement card).
WF 315	2	CF & 194	22.5.50	31.3.54	To 194 Sqn 1.2.53. Taking off from Fort Chabai on 3.3.54, Fg Off D E Batten had moved into forward flight and reached an altitude of about 25 ft agl when the helicopter adopted a sudden and violent nose down attitude. Failing to respond to full backward movement of the cyclic stick, WF 315 struck the ground in an almost vertical position and rolled over on to its side: Cat 5. Fg Off Batten, received slight injuries. Crash location reported as VE 491207.

© Helicopter Operations (Malaya Emergency) Association.   Page 1   All rights reserved   November 2001

THE FIRST HELICOPTER BOYS

Westland Dragonfly HC Mks 2 & 4 Operated by the Casualty Evacuation Flight and No 194 Squadron

Serial No	Mk	Unit	Taken on Strength	Struck off Strength	Notes
VZ 960	2(iii)	CF & 194	26.2.52	3.11.55	(iii) Ex-RN Mk 1, later converted to Mk 4 standard. Had been plane-guard on HMS Glory off Korea in April '51. To 194 Sqn 1.2.53; to Maintenance Base (MB) as reserve 31.8.53; to 194 Sqn 9.12.53. VZ 960 acquired a reputation for having a poor performance and was eventually used for training only. On a training flight on 3.11.55 Fg Off K W Woodcock and Flt Lt W F J Stevens heard a bang in the rear fuselage. Fg Off Woodcock, who was the first pilot, headed towards KL to make a precautionary landing. At 300 ft the engine failed completely and the aircraft was turned in an attempt to make a forced landing on a sports field at the Federation Police College, Gurney Road, Kuala Lumpur. During the approach another bang was heard and the helicopter landed in a tail down attitude. The tail rotor hit the ground and broke off. VZ 960 continued to run forward and mounted a bank at the end of landing run where a rotor blade struck and severed the tail cone. Both pilots were uninjured.
WZ 749	2(iv)	CF & 194	30.4.52	26.9.52	(iv) Ex G-ALEG. First registered 10.10.48 and operated by *Pest Control Ltd* May 49 - Apr 51. On 26.9.52, after touching down on sloping ground in a clearing at WQ 026512, the helicopter began to slip back and to the right. The pilot, Fg Off B F Walters, lifted off, applying left cyclic to correct the drift. As he did so the starboard wheel hit a tree stump, WZ 749 swung through 270 degrees and sustained extensive damage: Cat 5. Although the pilot was uninjured Major Walls, who was in the clearing, was struck in the face and injured by flying debris.
WT 845	4	CF	21.10.52	21.1.53	In-flight rotor failure approx 1 mile N of Chemor. Pilot, Fg Off B F Walters, and two passengers, Major Barker and Mr Toulson, killed. First fatal helicopter accident in Malaya.
WT 846	4	CF &194	10.10.52	25.11.53	To 194 Sqn 1.2.53. Landing on sloping ground in a clearing at VK 622575 on 25.11.53, the starboard wheel began sliding backwards as soon as it touched the ground. As the pilot, Flt Lt C C Verry, attempted to take-off the starboard wheel struck a tree stump. With full power applied the helicopter adopted a nose up attitude, the tail rotor hit the ground and the helicopter crashed: Cat 5(C). The pilot was unhurt. Before the helicopter made its attempt to land, the marshaller had noticed that the nose wheel was swivelling. This was thought to have been a contributory cause to the helicopter sliding back and to the right after touchdown and FEAF subsequently proposed modifications to incorporate a lockable nose wheel.

APPENDIX

Westland Dragonfly HC Mks 2 & 4 Operated by the Casualty Evacuation Flight and No 194 Squadron

Serial No	Mk	Unit	Taken on Strength	Struck off Strength	Notes
WX 953	4	194	25.4.53	15.5.54	Landing at an LZ at VP 987501 on 14.5.54, WX 953 was in the final stages of approach to the landing pad when the tail rotor struck an obstruction. The helicopter swung violently to the right and ended up on its left side. The pilot, Flt Lt C C Verry, was unhurt although his passenger, Lt Cremin, Royal Hampshire Regt, received slight injuries. Both men walked to a nearby clearing at WL 002506 and were evacuated by a Whirlwind Mk 21 of 848 Sqn. Initially assessed Cat 3(R), arrangements were in hand to repair the helicopter when a tree fell across it: Cat 5(C).
XB 251	4	CF & 194	28.1.53	(22.3.62)	To 194 Sqn 1.2.53. On 14.6.54 Fg Off K W Woodcock and Cpl Brian Falle were making supply drops at VP 806124 - the Waterworks Gap region - and had to make a forced landing in the DZ at 1530 hrs. Cpl Johnson, tools and a new tail rotor were winched in by an 848 Sqn Whirlwind Mk 21 and Fg Off Woodcock winched out. The next day Sqn Ldr Henderson, OC 194 Sqn, was winched in to the DZ by another 848 Sqn Whirlwind and tools, stores and Cpl Falle winched out. At 1540 hrs Sqn Ldr Henderson and Cpl Johnson flew XB 251 back to KL. XB 251 was one of the two Dragonflies to survive Malaya. Stored at MB 28.6.56; to UK 3.10.56; CFS 28.8.58; Stn Flt RAF Gutersloh 21.12.60; Handling Sqn Boscombe Down 7.12.61.
XB 252	4	CF & 194	19.1.53	(11.9.63)	To 194 Sqn 1.2.53. On 16.2.53 Flt Lt J R Dowling, with Lt Marshal RN acting as gunner/liaison officer, led three Mk 21 Whirlwinds of 848 Sqn in an assault on a hut believed to be occupied by Siew Hoong, a senior terrorist, at VU 250720. XB 252 was the other, and longest, survivor. To MB 28.6.56; UK 3.10.56; Handling Sqn 15.6.59; Stn Flt Gutersloh 21.12.60; sold for scrap 11.9.63.
XB 253	4	194	5.3.53	7.11.53	Crashed after taking off from a clearing at VK 384538 and about 2,300' asl' on 7.11.53. The pilot, Flt Sgt G T Manson was unhurt. The wreckage has recently (mid-2000) been rediscovered by a group of Malaysian air historians.
XB 254	4	194	2.3.53	27.10.54	Shortly after climbing to about 35 ft after take off from Grik on 16.10.54, the helicopter assumed a pronounced nose down attitude, yawed violently to the right and dived into the ground nose first: Cat 5(S). The cause was considered to have been due to structural failure of the tail cone, perhaps following previous unreported heavy landings. The pilot, M Plt G Cox, was uninjured.

© Helicopter Operations (Malaya Emergency) Association. All rights reserved

THE FIRST HELICOPTER BOYS

Westland Dragonfly HC Mks 2 & 4 Operated by the Casualty Evacuation Flight and No 194 Squadron

Serial No	Mk	Unit	Taken on Strength	Struck off Strength	Notes
XB 255	4	194	4.3.53	4.3.56	Forced landing in 3-4 ft of water at VP 3468 on 21.1.54 after the engine lost power: pilot Flt Lt W Pinner. Cat 3 (R); returned to 194 Sqn 4.5.54. Taking off from the police post at Gambir (WR 089602) on 5.5.55, Fg Off T Carbis was unable to prevent the nose dropping and the helicopter from moving forwards. After lowering the collective pitch lever the helicopter crash landed straight ahead, landing heavily on the nose wheel and tearing the complete assembly away from the fuselage: Cat 3. Lost power and sank back into trees shortly after take off from Paddy's Ladang on 3.3.56: Cat 5(S). The pilot, Sqn Ldr C R Turner, and crewman, Cpl P W Lumb, were both injured. Their casevac, Trooper Watkins, was unhurt.
XB 256	4	194	4.3.53	14.9.54	Following a practice autorotation at the end of an air test at KL on 15.9.53 the pilot, Flt Lt A J Clarke, struck the ground with the tail rotor, breaking the blades and damaging the tail cone: Cat 2. Whilst returning to KL from an air test on 14.9.54 Fg Off M Caldow heard a grinding noise followed by vibration. After stopping momentarily, the noise re-occurred and the helicopter began to lose height rapidly. After going into autorotation XB 256 landed heavily and rolled over on to its side: Cat 5 (C). The cause of the incident was gearbox failure due to oil starvation.

Sources:
RAF Museum, Hendon: AM Form 78 (aircraft movement cards) and AM Form 1180 (accident summaries).

Public Record Office, Kew: Forms 540 and 541 - Operational Record Books.

Fleet Air Arm Museum, RNAS Yeovilton: 848 Sqn diaries.

Revised   4.11.01

APPENDIX

Sycamores HR Mk 14 Operated by 194 and 110 Squadrons

In addition to the twenty-six Sycamores listed below, the sole Sycamore HC Mk 10, WA 578 (ex G-ALSU), was detached to Malaya for trials in January 1953. Flown by Flt Lt Dowling, whose tour had been extended for that purpose, WA 578 remained attached to 194 Sqn for a few months from March 1953 after the trials team had returned to Boscombe Down. Although these trials are often described as 'tropical' they were, in fact, simply 'theatre' trials. The official tropical trials had been carried out in Khartoum and Nairobi between 28 June and 25 September 1951 using Sycamore HC Mk 11 WT 933 (ex G-ALSW).

Excluding WA 578, Sycamores served with first 194 and then 110 Sqns for, roughly, five and a half years during the Malayan Emergency: from 20 September 1954 until 31 July 1960 - the official end of the emergency. During that time 13 were written off.

Serial No	Taken on Strength	Struck off Strength	Notes
XE 310	6.10.54	(8.6.65)	Cat 3 on 5.10.56 after hitting a goal post whilst landing in poor visibility at Ipoh airfield: pilot, Flt Sgt L J Baker. On 19.4.57, 6 nm north west of Serendah, Flt Lt T Carbis experienced loss of power due to failure of No.1 cylinder and made a successful forced landing near a tin dredge. On 25.7.58, Flt Lt J A Hughes experienced failure of the torque limiting clutch at about 100 ft agl whilst carrying out a vertical climb during an air test. Despite raising the collective pitch lever, Flt Lt Hughes was unable to prevent XE 310 falling freely from about ten feet and receiving substantial damage: assessed as Cat 4(R). After repair at Seletar to 194 Sqn 13.3.59. To Seletar for storage and modification 31.7.59. To 110 Sqn 30.5.60. **Post Emergency:** to UK 8.6.65.
XE 311	28.9.54	(30.4.64)	To Seletar Cat 4(R) 7.10.54; no other details. Returned to 194 Sqn 10.2.55. On 21.8.57 Flt Lt J W Peckowski experienced excessively high main rotor gearbox (mgb) temperatures and made an immediate landing without further damage at KL. Cause: failure to check mgb oil level during 2nd line servicing. On 15.10.57 Flt Lt Peckowski noticed a change of engine noise in-flight and during his approach to a successful precautionary landing at Segamat school padang experienced loss of power: non-ferrous particles found in oil pressure filter. To Seletar for storage and modification 31.7.59; to 110 Sqn 10.6.60. **Post Emergency:** caught fire after landing at RAAF Butterworth on 4.4.64, assessed Cat 5(S) and struck off 30.4.64.
XE 312	20.9.54	5.2.57	On 15.12.55 Sqn Ldr C R Turner experienced blade sailing during shut down resulting in damage to the main rotor blades and tail cone. Initially Cat 4(R) but re-assessed as Cat 3(R) at Seletar on 31.12.55. Returned to 194 Sqn 1.3.56. Crashed at Tanah Rata 5.2.57 when the pilot, Flt Lt L J Wittin-Hayden, found himself unable to maintain height whilst manoeuvring to avoid nearby children shortly after take-off. Whilst attempting to land the main rotors hit a tree. Assessed Cat 5(S) and struck off.

THE FIRST HELICOPTER BOYS

Sycamores HR Mk 14 Operated by 194 and 110 Squadrons

Serial No	Taken on Strength	Struck off Strength	Notes
XE 313	20.9.54	6.1.58	Ex G-AMWK. Whilst climbing away from a clearing at VK 113987 on 4.1.58 a severe downdraft was encountered and height could not be maintained. Crashed into thick secondary jungle: assessed as Cat 5(S) and struck off on 6.1.58. The pilot, Flt Lt S R Kendal, and passengers, Capt Wyld RN and Lt Col A J Drummond, received slight injuries.
XE 314	20.9.54	7.12.54	Ex G-AMWL. Whilst taking off from Fort Selim on 7.12.54 Fg Off J R Barlow was unable to maintain height despite application of full power. The tail rotor struck a tree stump and XE 314 crashed: Cat 5 and struck off strength.
XE 315	26.10.54	6.5.55	Ex G-AMWM. On loan to Bristol Aircraft Company for RAF crew training 18.8.54 - 2.9.54. To FEAF 6.9.54. Ditched in the river Pahang at Kuala Krau after failure of tail rotor clutch - caused by grease contamination. Cat 4(R) 4.5.55 but re-assessed Cat 5(C) and struck off. The crew, Wg Cdr W R Williams and Sqn Ldr T W G Godfrey, were rescued by boat.
XE 316	26.10.54	9.2.55	Ex G-AMWN. Approaching to land at Fort Selim on 30.1.55 Flt Lt J Badeni was unable to maintain control when XE 316 was caught by a severe downdraught and turbulence. The helicopter struck the ground heavily and rolled on to its port side. Assessed Cat 4(R) 30.1.55, but re-assessed Cat 5(S) 9.2.55.
XE 318	12.1.55	1.10.55	After landing at Fort Langkap on 10.6.55 and having been escorted by the crewman clear of the main rotors, M Plt D D Green's passenger, Dr S K Roy, walked into the tail rotor and was killed. Although Flt Lt W F J Stevens took over control from Sqn Ldr L L Harland when XE 318 began to roll to port on take off from the Sungei Besi training area on 13.9.55, he was unable to prevent the helicopter from rolling over on to its side before full power could be applied. Cat 4(R) but re-assessed Cat 5(C) 1.10.55.
XE 319	18.4.55	21.2.59	On 23.9.57, shortly after take off from No 2 F I B, M Plt C Stubbs experienced torque limiting clutch failure and made an immediate forced landing in a very restricted, built-up area. The tail rotor blades struck the edge of a monsoon drain, the tips broke off and damaged a main rotor blade: Cat 2(C). On 12.12.58 Flt Lt P R P Osborne made a successful forced landing following a series of loud banging noises coming from the engine. Subsequent examination revealed white metal in the engine oil filter. Cat 5(C) and struck off following blade break-up at low level in the KL local training area on 21.2.59. Both pilots killed: Flt Lt A G Mitchell (instructor who had joined 194 Sqn in Jan 59) and Flt Lt T Hillman (u/t who had joined on 18.2.59). Mr Chin Thong Kong, a civilian student in the area at the time of the accident, was injured.

APPENDIX

Sycamores HR Mk 14 Operated by 194 and 110 Squadrons

Serial No	Taken on Strength	Struck off Strength	Notes
XE 321	31.3.55	6.9.56	Whilst taking off from Ipoh, Flt Lt T Carbis experienced main torque limiting clutch failure and made an immediate landing on a sports field. The nose wheel dug into the soft ground bringing the helicopter to a sudden stop. The main rotors struck the ground and XE 321 was wrecked: assessed Cat 5(S) and struck off.
XE 322	30.3.55	(27.4.61)	To Seletar for storage and modification 21.7.59. On 30.7.60, whilst being air tested at Seletar prior to being delivered to 110 Sqn, Fl Lt J A Hughes experienced a momentary engine cut - although it picked up again when the collective lever was lowered. No cause could be found but the magneto and fuel control unit were changed. To 110 Sqn 5.9.60. **Post Emergency:** forced landing in river at VP 579699 after failing to gain height on take-off on 20.3.61. Pilot: Flt Lt A T Shaw. Cat 5(P) but re-assessed and struck off 27.4.61.
XF 266	14.5.55	(30.6.67)	On 27.8.55, whilst the pilot, Flt Lt F P Russell, was shutting down, an Air Movements officer opened the doors from the outside. As a result one of the doors was struck by a main rotor blade: Cat 2. To Seletar 21.7.59; to RAF Kuala Lumpur as spares back-up for XJ 918 on 25.10.59; to Seletar 8.3.60; to 110 Sqn 22.8.60. **Post Emergency:** on 21.12.60, whilst approaching to land at an LZ near Fort Kemar, Sqn Ldr C A E Simons experienced a sudden loss of power but made a successful forced landing on the top of a nearby ridge. The power loss had been caused by a large internal oil leak to all cylinders. To 389 MU 21.10.64; to 110 Sqn 15.10.65; Cat 5(C) and struck off 30.6.67.
XF 267	28.4.55	1.5.59	In storage at Seletar 11.7.57; returned to 194 Sqn 15.5.58. After leaving a clearing on 21.5.58 Sqn Ldr F Barnes experienced difficulty in maintaining control of XF 267. Having landed safely at 2 FIB, Ipoh, inspection revealed that the split pins were missing from six bolts on each of two main rotor blades. Cat 5(P) 27.4.59 following rotor blade break-up in mid-air. Re-assessed Cat 5(S) and struck off 1.5.59. Wreckage landed in Maxwell Road area of KL. Crew, Flt Lt P de B Daly (Flt Cdr), Flt Lt I W D Dray (u/t and who had also joined 194 Sqn on 18.2.59) and passenger, Sqn Ldr J E Scott (Stn Accts Off RAF KL), killed.
XG 508	25.7.60	(30.6.67)	Served only with 110 Sqn in Malaya. **Post Emergency:** on 30.9.60 Flt Lt D J Eldridge experienced a momentary engine cut when applying power in mid flight. Engine picked up again and a normal landing was made at RAAF Butterworth. To 398 MU 20.10.65; returned to 110 Sqn 23.2.66; Cat 5(C) and struck off 30.6.67.
XG 510	5.10.55	22.2.56	Cat 4(R) 5.2.56 after toppling over on the mat at Paddy's Ladang when a wheel jammed in the bamboo mat. The pilot, Flt Sgt A Nesbitt, and passenger, Tpr Wren, both injured. Re-assessed as Cat 5(C) and struck off 22.2.56.

© Helicopter Operations (Malaya Emergency) Association.   Page 7   All rights reserved   November 2001

THE FIRST HELICOPTER BOYS

Sycamores HR Mk 14 Operated by 194 and 110 Squadrons

Serial No	Taken on Strength	Struck off Strength	Notes
XG 519	3.1.56	(24.1.64)	On 6.6.56 Flt Sgt L J Baker experienced a severe downdraught whilst making an approach to a clearing 4,500 ft asl at Tringkap (VE 306617) and lost height rapidly. Attempting to escape by flying down a valley he struck some telegraph wires. Despite applying full power as he attempted to reach a road, Flt Sgt Baker touched down on a slope and the main and tail rotor blades broke off after striking trees and bushes. Cat 5(P) 6.6.56 but re-assessed by MU as Cat 4(R) 9.6.56 and eventually repaired. Returned to 194 Sqn 21.8.57; at Seletar for storage and modification 15.7.59; to 110 Sqn 20.7.60. **Post Emergency:** 24.1.64: crashed and burnt out 8 miles south of Fort Kemar; Cat 5. Struck off Feb.64.
XG 522	15.6.56	(5.4.61)	After a flight on 11.3.57 Flt Lt W H W Spencer reported a strong smell of petrol in XG 522. On inspection the fuel line was found to be fractured between the fuel pressure transmitter and the indicator. During an air test on 30.5.58 both engine and rotor rpm ran wild. Finding that closing the throttle had no effect, Flt Lt W H W Spencer shut down the engine and made a successful engine-off landing on a stretch of road. Subsequent inspection showed that the throttle linkage had become disconnected. To Seletar for storage and modification 17.7.59; to 110 Sqn 25.7.60. **Post Emergency:** Cat 5(P) 4.4.61after port wheel struck a retaining log at the edge of the mat whilst making a 180 degree hover turn before take-off from a clearing at VE 394686. Re-assessed Cat 5(C) and struck off 5.4.61. Pilot, Flt Lt D J Eldridge, and Cpl B G Dalziel 2NZ Regt, uninjured: slight injuries to Pte W R F Campbell 2NZ Regt. XG 522 is now a tourist attraction on the Belum Forest Reserve Trail.
XG 538	6.8.56	(28.9.60)	After take-off from 2 FIB, Ipoh on 13.5.58 Sgt C Tinkler heard the engine note change to a higher pitch and experienced a loss of power. After turning through 180 degrees to avoid near-by houses he made a forced landing. XG 538 rolled forward some 15-20 yards with the brakes on and stopped just short of a 3-4 foot deep monsoon ditch. As the two passengers were about to open the doors, the earth gave way and the helicopter slid to the left. The slowly turning rotor blades were destroyed when they hit the bank of the ditch. Classified Cat 3 and repaired by 13.5.58. To Seletar for storage and modification 10.7.59; to 110 Sqn 28.4.60. **Post Emergency:** Cat 4(P) 14.9.60 after rolling over on take-off from Na Plang, Thailand. Re-assessed Cat 5(S) and struck off 28.9.60. Pilot: Flt Lt J D Bradley. A young boy was injured by a fragment of rotor blade but made a full recovery after being flown to hospital by Flt Lt H H J Browning who, following initial reports of the accident, had been despatched from Butterworth with what proved to be a somewhat inadequate spare tail rotor blade! The boy was later flown back to his home by 110 Sqn and presented with a fishing rod - probably a safer pastime than watching 110 Sqn helicopters attempting to take-off.

APPENDIX

Sycamores HR Mk 14 Operated by 194 and 110 Squadrons

Serial No	Taken on Strength	Struck off Strength	Notes
XG 543	23.7.56	27.9.58	En route for a casevac mission on 10.4.57, Flt Sgt J Ward experienced a failure of the rotor tachometer and made a precautionary landing at Kluang using engine rpm indications only. The failure was caused by the flexible drive having sheared. To Seletar for storage 11.7.57; returned to 194 Sqn 12.8.57. On 20.8.57 XG 543 was returned to Seletar for repair having sustained cat 3(R) damage (no other details) and returned to 194 Sqn on 4.3.58. On 23.9.58, whilst making a vertical landing in a clearing 12 nm north east of Fort Kemar, the tail rotor struck a felled tree trunk and the helicopter crashed. The pilot, Flt Lt J A Hughes, suffered bruised ribs. XG 543 was assessed Cat 5 on 23.9.58 and struck off 27.9.58.
XG 549	15.12.56	20.5.58	On 28.3.57 Flt Lt P A Clarke was shutting down at 2 F I B, Ipoh when Lac G G Brown approached the helicopter and attempted to close a partly open window. In doing so he was struck a glancing blow to the back of the head by one of the main rotor blades and received slight injuries. Squadron records seem concerned only that XG 549 was undamaged. On 11.5.57 Sqn Ldr J R Dowling was giving Plt Off J F McCorkle dual instruction in engine-off landings. After his student had flared high, leading to a rapid final descent, Sqn Ldr Dowling was unable to take over control before Plt Off McCorkle moved the cyclic stick back, causing the tail skid to break on hitting the ground, smashing the tail rotor and damaging the tail cone: Cat 3(R). Returned to 194 Sqn 12.6.57. On 16.4.58 XG 549 suffered loss of power on approach to Fort Langkap whilst on a photographic/communications flight for a Board of Inquiry investigating a Pioneer crash. The pilot, Sqn Ldr F Barnes, and two passengers were uninjured. Initially Cat 4(R) but re-assessed Cat 5(C) and struck off 20.5.58.
XJ 381	14.8.56	16.8.57	On 6.5.57 Gp Capt P E Warcup was practising auto-rotations at KL. Failing to recover from the last approach resulted in the tail skid being bent, the tips broken off the tail rotor blades and slight fuselage skin damage. On 7.8.57 Plt Off J F McCorkle was diverting from an LZ in the Cameron Highlands due to bad weather when his tachometer failed. Deciding to land as soon as possible, he was making an approach to an LZ at Sungei Menlock, 10 miles east of Tanah Rata, when, just short of the landing platform, the helicopter sank rapidly. Despite corrective action, XJ 381 struck the ground with only the nose wheel on the platform. The main rotor blades hit the ground and broke up: Cat 5(P) 7.8.57; re-assessed Cat 5(S) and struck off 16.8.57. The passengers, Lt Cdr Parker, Malay Home Guard, and Major Price, 4 Bn Malay Regt, were uninjured.

THE FIRST HELICOPTER BOYS

Sycamores HR Mk 14 Operated by 194 and 110 Squadrons

Serial No	Taken on Strength	Struck off Strength	Notes
XJ 382	14.8.56	(19.12.62)	On 10.4.57 Flt Lt L J Wittin-Hayden experienced partial power failure whilst climbing out after take-off from Ipoh. After making a successful forced landing the cause of the failure was found to be inconsistent tappet clearance on No. 6 cylinder. To Seletar for storage and modification 10.7.59; to 110 Sqn 21.3.60. **Post Emergency:** written off in attempted forced landing following a fire warning on 9.7.62. Assessed Cat 5(S) on 9.7.62 but not struck off charge until 19.12.62.
XJ 918	10.6.60	(8.6.65)	Served only with 110 Sqn in Malaya although it was at Kuala Lumpur for trials in October 1959 (see also XF 266). **Post Emergency:** to 389 MU 20.5.65; returned to UK 8.6.65.
XL 821	28.4.60	(30.6.67)	Served only with 110 Sqn in Malaya. **Post Emergency:** Cat 5(C) and struck off 30.6.67.
XL 822	12.9.58	(21.5.63)	Cat 3 (R) 8.11.55 but re-assessed as Cat 2(R) 29.11.58 after it was involved in an accident on 8.11.58 when it made a forced landing in the Sungei Telum valley, 2,700' asl, whilst en route to Ipoh. The crewman, Cpl B L Thorpe, died as a result of injuries received whilst evacuating the helicopter. The pilot, M Plt A S Clarke, and the passenger - a medevac - were uninjured. XL 822 was repaired on site and returned to 194 Sqn. To Seletar for storage 2.7.59. On 17.6.60 Flt Lt J D Bradley was carrying out an air test at Seletar prior to XL 822 being returned to 110 Sqn when he experienced a sudden loss of power. Although at low altitude he was able to cushion the landing without causing further damage. On investigation No.2 cylinder exhaust tappet was found to be loose. To 110 Sqn on 5.8.60. **Post Emergency:** To 110 Sqn on 5.8.60. Suffered a partial engine failure near Long Murarao, Sarawak on 6.5.63 whilst taking part in a search for Belvedere XG 473. After a skilful approach and landing into a clearing the helicopter rolled over after striking a tree stump. Confirmed Cat 5(S) 21.5.63 and struck off charge. Pilot: M Plt E Leyden.
XL 825	29.8.58	(19.12.62)	To Seletar for storage 2.7.59; to 110 Sqn 18.7.60. **Post Emergency:** crashed at the Malakoff Estate on 28.9.62 killing the pilot, Fg Off J W Martin. Assessed Cat 5(S) but, like XJ 382, not struck off until 19.12.62.

Sources:
RAF Museum, Hendon: AM Form 78 (aircraft movement cards) and AM Form 1180 (accident summaries).

Public Record Office, Kew: Forms 540 and 541 - Operational Record Books.

Revised: 4.11.01.

APPENDIX

WS-55 Whirlwinds HAR Mk 4 Operated by 155 and 110 Squadrons

A number of RN Mk 1 Whirlwinds were used for a few months by 155 Sqn but these have not been included amongst the RAF HAR Mk 4 Whirlwinds listed below. Of the twenty-five Whirlwinds HAR Mk 4 operated by 155 and/or 110 Sqns eighteen had been returned to the UK by the time that the Emergency had ended. Seven were written off in major accidents - and several of those that made it back to the UK had also been involved in accidents but had been repaired and brought back into service again. Many of the survivors of the Emergency were converted to turbine-engined Mk 10 Whirlwinds and some of these returned to the Far East to fly missions with 110 Sqn during the Confrontation with Indonesia: remaining in service with 110 and/or 103 Sqns until FEAF was disbanded. Because of the Whirlwind's longevity 'Struck off Strength' dates refer to the date individual aircraft were taken off the establishments of either 155 or 110 Sqn before the Emergency ended - all of 110 Sqn's Whirlwind 4s had been replaced by Sycamores by then - but only just.

Serial No.	Taken on Strength	Struck off Strength	Notes
XD 163	28.10.54	31.5.58	From 155 Sqn to Seletar for storage 6.12.57: 20 MU 4.5.58; Westlands 23.7.58. **Post Emergency:** After serving with 275 Sqn (24.4.59), as a Mk 4, and 228 Sqn (28.10.59), first as a Mk 4 and later, after modification at Westlands, a Mk 2, XD 163 was sent again to Westlands for modification as a Mk 10. on 29.11.62. To the SAR Flt, AFME 16.6.65 and CFS on 13.12.65. To Rotorcraft Museum (now the International Helicopter Museum, Weston-super-Mare) 20.3.80.
XD 165	10.12.54	9.9.58	Cat 4(R) 9.9.58 - no other details; to Maintenance Base (MB) in reserve 23.9.58; in storage 15.12.58; to UK 31.1.59; Westlands 15.5.59. **Post Emergency:** to 225, 202 Sqns and 18 Gp SAR Wing as a Mk 10. To Halton 2.2.81.
XD 182	18.6.55	13.5.60	From 110 Sqn to Seletar for storage 13.5.60; Westlands 8.9.60. **Post Emergency:** to Odiham 8.1.79 for crash/fire practice.
XD 183	29.10.54	6.1.58	On 6.4.55, having rejoined the circuit at KL on completion of a training sortie, Flt Lt H W Gumbrell was approaching dispersal when the engine cut. Despite the pilot's attempts to cushion the landing XD 183 struck the ground heavily, smashing the tail rotor and damaging the stabilisers and tail rotor gear box: Cat 3(R). To Seletar Cat 3(R) 26.4.55; returned to 155 Sqn 3.9.55. To Seletar for repair, Cat 3(R) 18.10.57 - no other details - and in storage 6.1.58; to Westlands 7.8.58. **Post Emergency:** to 110 Sqn - and later 103 Sqn - as a Mk 10 on 19.6.63. Following forced landing after engine failure at Changi on 22.6.70, struck off (scrap) 10.12.70.
XD 184	11.11.54	18.1.59	To Seletar Cat 3(R) 3.11.55 - no further details. Returned to 155 Sqn 28.11.55; to Seletar for storage 18.1.59; to UK 1.5.59; to 228 Sqn 17.12.59. **Post Emergency:** to Westlands for conversion to a Mk 10 13.11.62.

© Helicopter Operations (Malaya Emergency) Association. All rights reserved November 2001

THE FIRST HELICOPTER BOYS

WS-55 Whirlwinds HAR Mk 4 Operated by 155 and 110 Squadrons

Serial No.	Taken on Strength	Struck off Strength	Notes
XD 185	19.11.54	24.2.58	To Seletar for fuel system modifications 9.3 to 14.4.55 & 27.5 to 23.6.55. Returned to 155 Sqn 23.6.55. After some seven minutes flying time positioning from KL for a troop lift on 3.1.57, Flt Sgt J Walentowicz heard a loud bang, immediately experienced loss of power and was told over the radio that smoke was coming from the engine. After making a successful emergency landing on Selangor golf course the crankcase was found to be holed between No 3 & 4 cylinders and there was no compression on No 6: Cat 2. On 14.1.57, shortly after carrying out an LZ recce at VK 154887 Flt Lt D A Youngs was returning to base when he experienced engine surge and loss of power. He returned to the LZ, which was on the top of a hill 3,900 ft amsl, and carried out a successful forced landing. Cause: defective magnetos. Whilst climbing at 4,700 ft near Fort Selim on 31.1.58, black smoke was seen streaming from the exhaust. When the engine cut the pilot, Flt Sgt W H McEachern, turned towards a landing area in an attempt to make an engine off landing. When it became apparent that he could not make his chosen spot the pilot was forced to land in a river bed. The main rotor blades struck the river banks and extensive damage was caused to the helicopter which, due to the location of the crash site, was deemed irrecoverable. Cat 5(C) and struck off strength 24.2.58. Both pilot and crewman, Cpl Tech C Upfield, were uninjured.
XD 186	1.11.54	10.4.57	Cat 3(R) 10.1.56 - no further details; returned to 155 Sqn 9.4.56; to Seletar 25.5.56; in storage 10.4.57; to UK 3.7.59. Whilst at Seletar XD 186 was sometimes flown by the C-in-C, Air Marshal the Earl of Bandon, with the MU test pilot, Fg Off D L Mitchell, as his instructor/safety pilot. At 16.40 hrs on 11.9.58 difficulty was experienced in re-starting the engine. Leaving the C-in-C at the controls, Fg Off Mitchell got out of the helicopter to make a manual engagement of the starter motor. At the second attempt the engine roared into life, there was a snatch-engagement of the main rotors and a retreating blade struck the tail cone, severing it completely. Guess who got the blame ...? 3.7.59: to UK and Westlands.
XD 187	30.10.54	5.4.57	On 22.3.56, whilst in a gentle climb shortly after take-off, XD 187 went into a gradual descent which could not be checked even though the pilot, Flt Lt D A Youngs, applied full power. With rpm decreasing, a forced landing was made in a stream at VE 564704. No defect was found, the accident being attributed to a downdraught: 3(R). Repaired and returned to 155 Sqn 4.4.56. Whilst engaged in a crop spraying sortie on 2.4.57 XD 187 ran out of fuel and crashed at VP 772547 (Johore grid): Cat 4(R) but re-assessed Cat 5(C) on 5.4.57. The pilot, Flt Lt T L Thompson, was uninjured, the crewman, Cpl J Orr, was slightly injured (cut hand and bruising).

APPENDIX

WS-55 Whirlwinds HAR Mk 4 Operated by 155 and 110 Squadrons

Serial No.	Taken on Strength	Struck off Strength	Notes
XD 188	29.10.54	14.12.56	Caught fire after dropping down through trees short of the landing pad at an LZ 8 nm east of Tanah Rata on 14.12.56: Cat 5(S). The pilot, Flt Lt K Alderson, and troops on board escaped with superficial injuries.
XJ 407	8.3.55	13.1.59	To Seletar 13.1.59; returned to UK 28.1.59; to 22 Sqn 21.9.59. **Post Emergency:** to Westlands for conversion to a Mk 10 24.9.62; to 110 Sqn 14.10.63; to 103 Sqn 25.2.65. Sold to Mr N Kalt, San Antonio, Texas 27.4.82.
XJ 408	8.3.55	26.8.55	Flt Sgt D G Ponsford, returning from an air test, experienced an hydraulic failure shortly before landing back at the squadron dispersal at KL on 26.8.55 and was unable to retain control. The helicopter landed heavily and rolled on to its side: Cat 5(S). Jnr Tech C T R Coles, ground crew, was seriously injured.
XJ 409	31.3.55	28.4.57	Fg Off S Evans and Flt Lt F G Rayner-Sharpe experienced a tail rotor drive shaft failure during a training sortie in the Sungei Besi training area on 11.9.56: Cat 3(R). To Seletar on 18.9.56; in storage 28.4.57; at 20 MU 15.5.58; Westlands 4.9.58. **Post Emergency:** sold 20.12.71 and now at RAF Llanbedr Museum of Memorabilia just south of Harlech, Gwynedd.
XJ 410	27.3.55	31.7.60	At Seletar for mods 23.6.55; returned to 155 Sqn 14.7.55; Cat 3(R) 1.9.55 - no further details. During a continuation training detail on 21.2.57 Flt Lt D A Youngs experienced reversion to manual control at about 100 ft shortly after take-off, followed, at about 300 ft, by the rpm indicator falling to zero. After going into autorotation and making a distress call the pilot realised that the lack of rpm was an instrument failure and went on to make a safe landing on the emergency strip at KL. Causes of the incidents were a clogged hydraulic filter and fracture of the tachometer drive shaft. Whilst cruising at 3,500 ft on 28.8.57, Flt Lt F Braybrook noticed the engine surge and, shortly afterwards, the engine and rotor rpm needles splitting. A successful forced landing was made at Maintin padang, 8 miles north west of Seremban. Cause: clutch slip due to oil on the clutch shoes. On 1.10.58 Flt Lt Reynolds landed in a clearing to find it occupied by two CTs who fled, leaving two packs behind, when four Malay Regt soldiers disembarked and gave pursuit. To Seletar from 110 Sqn on 31.7.60 after planned return had been delayed to allow participation in recovery of RAAF Sabre pilot. **Post Emergency:** as a Mk 10 with 22 Sqn XJ 410 hit high tension cables across River Torridge, near Bideford, whilst on SAR mission on 21.9.65.
XJ 411	13.7.59	26.7.60	Service with 110 Sqn only in Malaya; returned to Seletar (for UK) 26.7.60. **Post Emergency:** returned to 110 Sqn as a Mk 10 on 1.6.63.

THE FIRST HELICOPTER BOYS

WS-55 Whirlwinds HAR Mk 4 Operated by 155 and 110 Squadrons

Serial No.	Taken on Strength	Struck off Strength	Notes
XJ 412	20.5.55	27.11.58	Returning from a trooplift on 21.1.57 at an altitude of 600 ft, Flt Lt D A Youngs experienced loss of engine power but was able to make a safe landing at KL. Cause: defective magneto. During straight and level flight at 800 ft on 4.3.57 Flt Sgt J Dougan heard a loud bang from the engine followed by loss of power and more continuous banging noises. After making a successful forced landing on an overgrown tin tailing four and a half miles south east of Rawang, the cause was found to be a fractured cylinder head (No 2). During practice autorotations at the Serdang training area on 18.11.58 by Flt Lt R'C Hooper and Flt Lt J Severn, the helicopter sank very close to the ground before recovery action was effective. Noticing a strong smell of petrol afterwards, the helicopter was flown a short distance forward and landed. A large hole was found in the underside of the fuselage and petrol was running out of the rear port fuel tank. The damage had been caused by the helicopter striking a tree stump during its descent: assessed Cat 3(R) 19.11.58; to Seletar for repair and storage 27.11.58; to UK 31.1.59. **Post Emergency:** made its return to FEAF as a Mk 10 and was struck off strength from 230 Sqn on 6.11.66 after a successful forced landing, following a tail rotor failure, on Tinker's Hill, Sarawak by Fg Off P Shaw. The site was so remote that XJ 412 had to be abandoned.
XJ 413	20.5.55	20.9.57	Taking off from a clearing 8 miles north east of Rengam on 21.6.55, Flt Lt H W Gumbrell turned the helicopter some 20 feet above the ground. The tail rotor struck trees at the edge of the clearing and the helicopter crashed: Cat 3(R). The pilot and three soldiers on board were uninjured. To Seletar for repair 24.6.55; returned to 155 Sqn 12.7.55. Approaching Gua Musang airstrip (VE9707 downwind on 16.9.55 Sgt D W Sissons began to lose rotor rpm (Rrpm), put the nose down in an attempt to increase forward speed and regain Rrpm but struck a mound with the starboard nosewheel - the aircraft came to rest on rough ground, tilted on to its starboard side: Cat 4(R). To Seletar for repair 21.9.55; returned to 155 Sqn 9.3.56. On 9.1.57 Flt Lt T L Thompson had a dead cut when checking the engine after re-starting at Tanah Rata: suspected coil failure. Three days later (12.1.57) Flt Lt J J Hubicka had a dead cut on the No 2 magneto when re-engaging the rotors at Rambutan tin mine, 5 miles north east of Ipoh. On 20.9.57 XJ 413 crashed 5 miles north-north east of the Slim River padang killing all three crew members: Cpl P A S Cosens, Flt Lt E W Draper and Cpl R Simpson.

APPENDIX

WS-55 Whirlwinds HAR Mk 4 Operated by 155 and 110 Squadrons

Serial No.	Taken on Strength	Struck off Strength	Notes
XJ 414	29.4.55	8.7.60	Whilst on a cross country training flight on 15.2.57 Flt Sgt J Dougan experienced severe vibration through the rudder pedals followed by an apparent loss of power. A successful precautionary landing was made at Port Swettenham. Although suspect transmission units were changed, no defect was actually found. From 110 Sqn to Seletar for return to UK 28 July 60. **Post Emergency:** as a Mk 10 with 202 Sqn, XJ 414 broke up in mid-air and crashed into the sea off Great Yarmouth on 22.6.67.
XJ 426	14.5.55	21.6.60	During straight and level flight in the Sungei Patani area on 17.5.57 Flt Lt W F. Burke noticed a gradual loss of power - necessitating high boost to maintain speed and height. Full power was needed to prevent the helicopter sinking heavily to the ground during landing and, after a check had been made, the pilot found that he was unable to take off even when using full power. The cause of the incident was found to be a fractured tappet adjusting screw which prevented No 6 cylinder exhaust valve from opening. From 110 Sqn to Seletar for return to UK 21.6.60. **Post Emergency:** served with 22 Sqn as Mk 10, ditched off Lundy Island on 22.8.71 and struck off 23.8.71.
XJ 427	6.5.55	13.5.57	After experiencing engine surge during a trooplift from Ipoh on 1.1.57 Flt Lt J J Hubicka, despite having checked the magnetos and carried out a hover check in the clearing, again experienced engine surging - this time accompanied by banging noises - shortly after leaving the clearing. Deciding to make a forced landing at Rambutan tin mine, 5 miles north east of Ipoh, he went into autorotation at 800 ft; at 200 ft the engine cut. During the landing the tail cone was damaged: Cat 4 (R). Subsequently, both magnetos were found to be below acceptable standards. 22.1.57 to Seletar for repair: 13.3.57 in storage at Seletar. On 16.4.57 XJ 427 was prepared for an air test at Seletar. After Fg Off S Evans engaged the main rotor and applied more power the helicopter began to vibrate so severely that it broke up: one main rotor blade having become detached. Cpl R F Martin was killed after being struck by the rotor blade. Cpl Tech G W Carr, J Tech Dicken, J Tech P E J Sturgeon, Cpl G Wells and the passenger, Sqn Ldr E Darley, were injured but Fg Off Evans escaped unhurt. The cause of the accident was failure to correctly lock and secure one of the main rotor blades when they were spread on 15.4.57 prior to air test. Cat 5(S) and written off 13.5.57.

THE FIRST HELICOPTER BOYS

WS-55 Whirlwinds HAR Mk 4 Operated by 155 and 110 Squadrons

Serial No.	Taken on Strength	Struck off Strength	Notes
XJ 428	8.11.55	6.3.58	Five minutes after taking off from Kluang on 28.11.55 and at a height of 500 ft agl, the cockpit and cabin filled with smoke. The pilot, Flt Lt L Scorer, made an autorotative landing on rough ground which resulted in the rotor blades striking the tail cone and causing severe damage: Cat 4(R). The bulkhead fire was found to have been caused by an electrical short circuit after a terminal bolt head had sheared. To Seletar for repair; in storage at Seletar 7.6.55; to 155 Sqn 1.10.56. Whilst closing down at Bidor airstrip on 14.9.57 Flt Sgt W H McEachern heard a loud tearing and grinding noise from the main gear box. Subsequent examination found that the ring gear bolts were loose and one bolt nut had come off. The cause was not established. Whilst landing at an LZ on top of a 1700 ft amsl ridge in the Fort Brooke area on 6.3.58 XJ 428 began to sink when some 10 yards short and ten feet above the platform. The pilot, Flt Lt D W Helps, was unable to correct the situation and the helicopter struck the edge of the platform and rolled over: Cat 3(R). The pilot and three other occupants were uninjured. To Seletar for repair 10.3.58; in storage at Seletar 24.6.58; to UK 1.10.58; to FEAF 30.6.59; to 110 Sqn 15.10.59; to UK 2.7.60. **Post Emergency:** to 22 and 228 Sqns as Mk 10.
XJ 431	15.10.55	8.8.58	Flt Lt F G Rayner-Sharpe had noticed that the rudder pedal appeared stiff whilst hovering during trooplifting operations on 1.1.57. Returning to KL on 2.1.57 he carried out a hover check before returning to dispersal: the controls were satisfactory. After arriving at the landing point the controls stiffened once more. After the helicopter had been landed with some difficulty and the engine stopped, the rudder pedals jammed completely. Cause: excessive brinelling of the bearings in the tail rotor hub assembly. Cat 4(R) 1.8.58 following forced landing in tidal swamp north of Port Dickson. After XJ 431 had been submerged in the sea at high tide, re-classified Cat 5(S) 8.8.58. The pilot, Flt Lt T A Bennett, crewman, Sac B Swallow, and two passengers were unhurt.

APPENDIX

WS-55 Whirlwinds HAR Mk 4 Operated by 155 and 110 Squadrons

Serial No.	Taken on Strength	Struck off Strength	Notes
XJ 437	5.10.55	16.8.58	Precautionary landing carried out at Kulai by Flt Lt W F Burke and Sgt D W Sissins on 10.1.57 after Sgt Sissins noticed a leak from the hydraulic fluid reservoir. Cause: hydraulic charging valve failure. On 16.1.57 Flt Lt J J Hubicka noticed stiffness of the rudder during trooplifting operations at Ulu Remis padang. On return to KL the rudder jammed whilst in the hover prior to landing. The pilot required the crewman's assistance to break the lock and land safely. Cause: excessive brinelling of the roller bearing in the tail rotor hub assembly. Returning from a trooplift operation on 7.3.57 Flt Lt F H Hicks and Flt Lt R S Cooper carried out a precautionary landing at Bentong airstrip when the oil pressure dropped to 45 psi and the oil temperature by ten degrees. Cause: intermittent failure possibly caused by dirty connections. Whilst M Plt F J Showell was practising engine-off landings with Flt Sgt J M M Walker at KL on 4.8.58 the tail boom was struck by the main rotors just after landing: Cat 3(R) but re-assessed Cat 4(R) 5.8.58. A contributory cause of the accident was considered to be the fact that M Plt Showell had made 33 engine off landings already that day: consequently the maximum allowed was reduced to 20. To Seletar for repair 16.8.58; in storage 20.12.58; to UK 31.5.59.
XJ 723	6.2.58	13.5.60	Although delivered to Singapore in January 1956 XJ 723 was kept in storage until issued to 155 Sqn on 6.2.58. However, in storage or not, on 14.1.57 Fg Off S Evans was en-route from Tanglin to Kluang whilst making a 'VIP transflight'. At 700 ft agl and six minutes before his ETA a loud bang was heard. Since there were no indications of any fault the pilot continued to Kluang and landed safely. On inspection it was discovered that there had been a fracture of the clutch assembly cooling fan spinner at the flange attachment to the back plate. Disintegration of the spinner caused damage to the front bulkhead and controls. On 9.5.58 Flt Lt R S Cooper experienced a hydraulic failure and reversion to manual control whilst flying at 2000 ft agl. Deciding to land at Kampar padang (VJ 9738) he landed down wind, the only possible approach - and rudely interrupted a football match the crewman, Sac A J Tamblyn, reports. Breaking hard to avoid trees after a heavy landing, the helicopter pitched nose down causing the rotor to flap back and strike the tail cone: Cat 3(R). The hydraulic failure was the result of hydraulic fluid being lost because an incorrect blanking plug had been fitted. To Seletar for repair 13.5.58; returned to 155 Sqn 27.5.58; from 110 Sqn to Seletar and UK 13.5.60. **Post Emergency:** converted to a Mk 10 and now at Montrose Air Station Museum.

THE FIRST HELICOPTER BOYS

WS-55 Whirlwinds HAR Mk 4 Operated by 155 and 110 Squadrons

Serial No.	Taken on Strength	Struck off Strength	Notes
XJ 724	29.11.56	18.8.58	Returning to base after a trooplift mission on 25.6.57, the pilot, Flt Lt W F Burke, heard a change in engine note followed by a light bang. A few seconds later a loud bang was heard accompanied by rough running and severe vibration. The engine cut at 50 ft during the descent and Flt Lt Burke made a successful engine-off landing at Bidor airstrip. The engine failure was caused by a fractured valve stem leading to failure of No 2 cylinder: Cat 2. 3(R) 18.8.58; in storage at Seletar 10.10.58 - no further details; to UK 27.1.59; to Khormaksar 5.8.59.
XJ 761	19.1.57	13.11.57	On 20.2.57 Flt Sgt W H McEachern was flying at 500 ft en route for the jungle training LZ. Increasing power to climb above a ridge, he heard a loud bang and then the engine cut and the tachometer needles split. The engine picked up again but cut a second time when the collective lever was lowered. The pilot was able to return to base and land safely. The failure had been caused by earthing of the switch lead of No 2 magneto due to chafing. At 800 ft, ten minutes out of KL whilst positioning for a trooplift mission on 30.7.57, Sgt D W Sissons heard a loud bang from the engine followed by engine surge and loss of power. He made a successful forced landing on a football field 5 miles north-north east of KL. Investigation showed that No 7 cylinder head had fractured in the vicinity of the exhaust rocker box and the tail rotor drive had sheared at touchdown, possibly due to shock loading following the engine failure: Cat 2. Cat 3(R) 13.11.57, at Seletar for repair - no further details - and storage 21.11.57; to UK 6.1.58. **Post Emergency:** still as an HAR Mk 4, served with 228 Sqn and ditched off Great Yarmouth on 27.7.60.

Sources:
RAF Museum, Hendon: AM Form 78 (aircraft movement cards) and AM Form 1180 (accident summaries).

Public Record Office, Kew: Forms 540 and 541 - Operational Record Books.

Revised   5.11.01.

APPENDIX

Index

Serial No.   Page No

Westland Dragonfly HC Mks 2 & 4 Operated by the Casualty Evacuation Flight and No 194 Squadron 1
    WF 308 1
    WF 311 1
    WF 315 1
    VZ 960 2
    WZ 749 2
    WT 845 2
    WT 846 2
    WX 953 3
    XB 251 3
    XB 252 3
    XB 253 3
    XB 254 3
    XB 255 4
    XB 256 4
Sycamores HR Mk 14 Operated by 194 and 110 Squadrons 5
    XE 310 5
    XE 311 5
    XE 312 5
    XE 313 6
    XE 314 6
    XE 315 6
    XE 316 6
    XE 318 6
    XE 319 6
    XE 321 7
    XE 322 7
    XF 266 7
    XF 267 7
    XG 508 7
    XG 510 7
    XG 519 8
    XG 522 8
    XG 538 8
    XG 543 9
    XG 549 9
    XJ 381 9
    XJ 382 10
    XJ 918 10
    XL 821 10
    XL 822 10
    XL 825 10
WS-55 Whirlwinds HAR Mk 4 Operated by 155 and 110 Squadrons 11
    XD 163 11
    XD 165 11
    XD 182 11
    XD 183 11
    XD 184 11
    XD 185 12
    XD 186 12
    XD 187 12
    XD 188 13
    XJ 407 13
    XJ 408 13
    XJ 409 13
    XJ 410 13
    XJ 411 13

THE FIRST HELICOPTER BOYS

Index

XJ 412	14
XJ 413	14
XJ 414	15
XJ 426	15
XJ 427	15
XJ 428	16
XJ 431	16
XJ 437	17
XJ 723	17
XJ 724	18
XJ 761	18

Notes

1. Although in 1943 No. 529 Squadron was formed from the Trials Unit, 1449 Flight, it was still basically conducting trials with various marks of the Cierva Rota autogyro, and from 1945 the Sikorsky R4B Hoverfly. The squadron also had various fixed wing aircraft types on strength. It was disbanded in October 1945.
2. on retirement, Wing Commander MBE DFC AFC, who worked for the Air Historical Branch; he was also instrumental in the planning and execution of positioning the spire on Coventry Cathedral.
3. When delivered, the Dragonfly was fitted with two steel, external stretcher panniers, one either side, though in the tropical climate of Malaya their value was discovered to be nil! With both panniers fitted the aircraft could not even carry one casualty (never mind a nursing attendant or crewman) and flying with just one pannier fitted introduced unsurmountable control problems. So scrub the steel panniers; the solution was to design one in the field, which is exactly what happened. From plans drawn up locally by the RAF, a Chinese basket maker in Changi village was able to produce a lightweight, useable wicker basket that would fit inside the Dragonfly fuselage. These 'Moses baskets', as they became known, were very much lighter, and much more practical.

Index

230 Squadron back in Borneo, 276–80
848 NAS, 11–12, 19, 172–4

Aircraft Allocated to Squadrons, 286–312
Ashley, Corporal Bob, 101–104

Blackwell, Lieutenant Tony, 195–6
Blade Tracking, 24–7
Bowman, Sergeant Bob, 96–100
Breese, Lieutenant Commander DFC, 85–93, 174
Bristol Sycamore, 38–9
Browning, Flight Lieutenant Tom, 182–4, 217–26
Bucks Free Press report, 179–80
Burdet, Private Frank, 71–4

Casualty Evacuation Summary Jul-Sep 52, 200–202
Clarke, Master Pilot 'Nobby', 84–5
Cox, Master Pilot Gordon 'Wacker', 162–8
Cromer, Police Lieutenant John, 196–9
Crop Spraying Operations, 48–9

Dace, Corporal Peter 'Lofty', 111–12

Derbyshire, St John 'Titch', 194–5
Don't Get Helicopped!, 7–8
Dowling, Flight Lieutenant John R., 4, 19, 38, 97, 121–2, 138

Escape From Coastal, 280–3

Far East Casualty Evacuation Flight, 9, 11, 14, 19, 38, 180
Follows, Roy, 239–42
Fort Betau, 223
Fort Betis, 223
Fort Brooke, 215, 239–42
Fort Chabai, 215, 243–56
Fort Dixon, 215
Fort Islander, 215
Fort Kemar (Hardcastle), 215, 226–38
Fort Langkap, 217
Fort Legap, 217
Fort Selim, 220
Fort Shean, 221
Fort Sinderut, 222
Fort Tapong, 222
Fort Telanok, 222
Francis, Flight Lieutenant George, 146–7
Freeborn, Flight Lieutenant Tony, 193–4

INDEX

Gray, Flight Lieutenant Paul, 27
Ground to Air Signals, 203

Harland DFC, Wing Commander Leslie, 140–1

Jacques, Flight Lieutenant Brian 'Jacko', 58–60
Jungle Forts & Airstrips, 212–58
Jungle Rescue, 204, 208

Knight, Lieutenant Commander G.C.J., 144

Leaflets & Loud-hailing, 49–50

Mail to Balmoral, 3
Malaya Emergency, 6, 259–68
Malayan Races Liberation Army, 6
McConnell, Sergeant Ken, 123–6
McCorkle, Flight Lieutenant Jim, 28, 57, 75–80, 82–4, 148–54

NAS Sembawang, 12, 38, 136, 144

Parachuting Cats, 257–8
Pardoe, Keith, 117–19
Payne, Corporal Technician Alan, 109–11
Peet, Flight Lieutenant Terry, 169–71
Penning, Squadron Leader Ron, 74
Puddy, Squadron Leader George, 143–4

RAAF Butterworth, 83, 103–104, 111–12, 137, 243, 273, 275
RAF Changi, 10–11, 14, 17, 33, 58–9, 86, 96–7 99–100, 102–104, 135, 158–9, 180, 193, 205–206, 281

RAF Kuala Lumpur, 9–10, 19, 39, 46, 57, 82, 144, 155, 204, 243
RAF Seletar, 6, 9–10, 101, 107, 112, 117, 127–8, 155, 174, 190–1, 273–4, 276–7
Raven, Junior Technician Len, 104–106

Scorer, Flight Lieutenant Leslie, 154–62
Sikorsky, Igor, 1, 21
Sikorsky Hoverfly, 2–5
Sikorsky YR-4B, 14–17, 19
Sinden, Derek, 192–3
Stevens, Flight Lieutenant Bill, 56, 112
Suthers, Commander Sydney Hal, 12, 145–6

Taylor, Corporal David, 107–109, 136–9, 243–56
Turner AFC, Squadron Leader Cyril R., vii, 52–6, 62–70

US Air Commandos, 14–17

Walentowicz, Flight Lieutenant Jan, 141–2
Walker, Master Pilot John 'Taff', 107, 190–2
Ward DFM, Sergeant Joe, 60–3, 70
Westland Dragonfly, 6, 9–12, 17, 22, 24, 34, 36
Westland Whirlwind, 12–14, 22, 39–44,
Williams OBE, Wing Commander S., 119–22
Wombell, Dennis, 226–38
Woodward, Rear Admiral Rob, 172–3

315